William Blake: The Poems

ANALYSING TEXTS

General Editor: Nicholas Marsh

Published

Chaucer: The Canterbury Tales *Gail Ashton*

Webster: The Tragedies *Kate Aughterson*

John Keats: *John Blades*

Shakespeare: The Comedies *R. P. Draper*

Charlotte Brontë: The Novels *Mike Edwards*

E. M. Forster: The Novels *Mike Edwards*

Shakespeare: The Tragedies *Nicholas Marsh*

Jane Austen: The Novels *Nicholas Marsh*

Emily Brontë: Wuthering Heights *Nicholas Marsh*

Virginia Woolf: The Novels *Nicholas Marsh*

D. H. Lawrence: The Novels *Nicholas Marsh*

William Blake: The Poems *Nicholas Marsh*

John Donne: The Poems *Joe Nutt*

Thomas Hardy: The Novels *Norman Page*

Marlowe: The Plays *Stevie Simkin*

Analysing Texts
Series Standing Order ISBN 0–333–73260–X
(outside North America only)

You can receive future titles in this series as they are published by placing a standing order. Please contact your bookseller or, in the case of difficulty, write to us at the address below with your name and address, the title of the series and the ISBN quoted above.

Customer Services Department, Macmillan Distribution Ltd
Houndmills, Basingstoke, Hampshire RG21 6XS, England

William Blake: The Poems

NICHOLAS MARSH

palgrave

First published 2001 by
PALGRAVE
Houndmills, Basingstoke, Hampshire RG21 6XS and
175 Fifth Avenue, New York, N.Y. 10010
Companies and representatives throughout the world

PALGRAVE is the new global academic imprint of
St. Martin's Press LLC Scholarly and Reference Division and
Palgrave Publishers Ltd (formerly Macmillan Press Ltd).

ISBN 0–333–91466–X hardback
ISBN 0–333–91467–8 paperback

This book is printed on paper suitable for recycling and
made from fully managed and sustained forest sources.

A catalogue record for this book is available
from the British Library.

Library of Congress Cataloging-in-Publication Data
Marsh, Nicholas.
    William Blake : the poems / Nicholas Marsh.
        p. cm. – (Analysing texts)
    Includes bibliographical references and index.
    ISBN 0-333-91466-X — ISBN 0-333-91467-8 (pbk.)
        1. Blake, William, 1757–1827—Criticism and interpretation.
    I. Title. II. Analysing texts (Palgrave (Firm))

PR4147 .M37 2001
821'.7–dc21   2001019444

10 9 8 7 6 5 4 3
10 09 08 07 06 05 04 03

Printed in China

For Jethro, a whole book

Contents

General Editor's Preface

This series is dedicated to one clear belief: that we can all enjoy, understand and analyse literature for ourselves, provided we know how to do it. How can we build on close understanding of a short passage, and develop our insight into the whole work? What features do we expect to find in a text? Why do we study style in so much detail? In demystifying the study of literature, these are only some of the questions the *Analysing Texts* series addresses and answers.

The books in this series will not do all the work for you, but will provide you with the tools, and show you how to use them. Here, you will find samples of close, detailed analysis, with an explanation of the analytical techniques utilised. At the end of each chapter there are useful suggestions for further work you can do to practise, develop and hone the skills demonstrated and build confidence in your own analytical ability.

An author's individuality shows in the way they write: every work they produce bears the hallmark of that writer's personal 'style'. In the main part of each book we concentrate therefore on analysing the particular flavour and concerns of one author's work, and explain the features of their writing in connection with major themes. In Part 2 there are chapters about the author's life and work, assessing their contribution to developments in literature; and a sample of critics' views are summarised and discussed in comparison with each other. Some suggestions for further reading provide a bridge towards further critical research.

Analysing Texts is designed to stimulate and encourage your critical and analytic faculty, to develop your personal insight into the author's work and individual style, and to provide you with the skills and techniques to enjoy at first hand the excitement of discovering the richness of the text.

Nicholas Marsh

A Note on Editions

Two editions of Blake's poetry are referred to frequently in this book. The first is *The Complete Writings of William Blake*, ed. Geoffrey Keynes, London, Oxford University Press, 1966. Page-references to this edition are given in brackets as the page-number[s] preceded by the letter K, thus: (K 222–3). The second edition frequently referred to is Sir Geoffrey Keynes's facsimile edition of *Songs of Innocence and Experience*, London, Rupert Hart-Davis, 1967. When referring to this edition, the plate-number is given in brackets, preceded by K2, thus: (K2, 33).

Head-notes and other notes from another edition of Blake's poems, are occasionally mentioned; some other critics quoted in Chapter 6 use this text. It is *The Poems of William Blake*, ed. W. H. Stevenson, text by David V. Erdman, Longman, London, 1971, sometimes referred to as 'Erdman and Stevenson', or 'E & S'.

The author and publishers are grateful to the Syndics of Fitzwilliam Museum, Cambridge, for permission to reproduce the six plates from *Songs of Innocence and Experience* which appear on pp. 31–41.

PART 1

ANALYSING
WILLIAM BLAKE'S POETRY

Introduction

The Scope of this Volume

The aim of this book is to introduce the reader to Blake's thought, by way of the *Songs of Innocence and Experience*, and at the same time equip the reader to approach Blake's symbolic Prophetic Books with confidence.

The Prophetic Books have a reputation as 'difficult' texts. Intricate symbolic interpretations too often overwhelm any enjoyment of the poetry and drama in which they abound. The new reader feels bewildered by the scholarship of professional critics, who often make Blake's symbols seem more 'difficult' than they need to be. This book demonstrates that a sound grasp of Blake's ideas can be carried from the *Songs*, and confidently applied to the prophecies. The second, third and fourth chapters of Part 1 will show how to do just that: conclusions deduced from analysing the *Songs* are carried forward and applied to sample passages from *The Marriage of Heaven and Hell*; *Europe, A Prophecy*; *The First Book of Urizen*; *The Book of Thel*, and finally we consider some short extracts from *Milton, A Poem*, one of the three long prophetic works which stand like giants towards the end of the Blake canon.

Analysing Metre

We will make use of metrical analysis or 'scansion' when analysing the *Songs of Innocence and Experience*. Many courses no longer teach this, so a short explanation will help, before we start. First, I would point out that 'metrical analysis' is a useful tool, a convenient way of labelling patterns and units of rhythm, and no more. Critics often argue that 'scansion' was wrongly imported from classical poetry written in Greek and Latin, because English is a different language where sounds and emphases do not behave as a Roman thinks they should. This introduction explains the technical terms we will use; but we must remember to be flexible, and use common sense, when applying classical scansion to English.

Metrical analysis relies on recognising that language is a string of syllables (complete sounds), some of which we say with more 'weight', 'emphasis' or 'stress' than others. So, in any phrase there are 'stressed' syllables and 'unstressed' syllables. Look at the first line of one of Blake's most famous poems:

Tyger **tyger burning bright**

I have emboldened the stressed syllables. There is no real argument: everybody will naturally 'stress' these same syllables. To prove this, try to say the line aloud, stressing the wrong syllables, and you will hear something like this:

T**igerr** t**igerr** ben**ing**bret

It hardly sounds like English, and a listener would not understand what you are saying. You can try this with everyday phrases – it is surprisingly difficult to talk in reversed stress, and it sounds like gobbledegook.

Now look back at the correct 'stress' pattern of Blake's 'The Tyger'. The first rhythmic unit in the line is made up of one stressed syllable followed by one unstressed syllable: '**tyger**'. Each unit of rhythm is called a **foot**. This kind of unit, which goes stressed-unstressed, is called a **trochee** or **trochaic foot**. You can remember what a **trochaic foot** sounds like by memorising the word '**dum**dy'.

We have not quite finished with the first line of 'The Tyger'. There are three complete **trochaic feet** in the line, then there is one stressed syllable on its own: 'bright'. This is quite common, because

English poetic lines tend to end on a stressed syllable; it has the effect of adding an involuntary pause at the end of the line – we unconsciously wait the split-second it would take to say the expected but missing unstressed syllable before reading the next line. The point is that the end of the line is **irregular**. We hardly ever find pure, regular metre in an English poem. The language, and poets, constantly adjust, deny or change the over-rigid pattern. So we must be ready to be flexible when deciding what kind of 'metre' a poem has, and make a reasonable judgment. We will often have to settle for finding the 'predominant' metre, despite frequent irregularities like the missing syllable at the end of our line from 'The Tyger'.

This line introduced us to **trochaic feet**. There are three other metres. An **iambic foot** goes unstressed-stressed, and you can remember it by memorising the word 'de-**dum**'. Blake's 'The Divine Image' begins in a regular **iambic metre**:

> To **Mer** / cy **Pi** / ty **Peace** / and **Love**,
> All **pray** / in **their** / distress:

An **anapaestic foot** goes unstressed-unstressed-stressed, and you can remember its sound by memorising the word 'diddy-**dum**'. Blake's 'Nurse's Song' begins in **anapaests**:

> When the **voi** / ces of **chil** / dren are **heard** / on the **green**

The fourth and last kind of 'foot' is a **dactyllic foot**. This goes stressed-unstressed-unstressed, so it is a back-to-front anapaest. You can memorise the sound of a **dactyl** by memorising the word: '**dum**-diddy'. This is a rare metre: there are no full dactyllic lines in the *Songs of Innocence and Experience* although Blake sometimes uses a dactyllic foot or two and we will refer to them. Here is an example of dactyls, three lines from Alfred, Lord Tennyson's 'The Charge of the Light Brigade':

> **Cannon** to / **right** of them,
> **Cannon** to / **left** of them,
> **Cannon** in / **front** of them

Notice that these different 'metres' have different characters. Tennyson's **dactyls** are ideal for hinting at the rhythm of galloping horses. **Anapaests** give a lilt, and generally sound bouncy and light. **Iambs** are steady, and **iambic** is the most common and most flexible metre in English – it can be made to express almost any mood. **Trochees** tend to beat on the ear, with a heavy and immediate thump in the first sound (Blake's 'The Tyger' is full of the imagery of hammer, anvil and forge, which is further evoked by the heavy beat of the metre).

This is the technical information needed to follow the metrical analyses found in the next four chapters. It only remains to remember that 'scansion' is a useful tool, a convenient way of labelling units of rhythm: it is not a 'thing' in its own right. So, why is it interesting?

I have mentioned the different 'characters' or 'moods' that different metres can evoke; but there are many other ways that metrical analysis can help us to understand how or why a particular effect is created, or can point us to the crucial part of the poem where the poet breaks his pattern. For these reasons, metrical analysis can be a very enlightening 'tool'.

Blake's Engraved Plates

Blake wrote his poems and drew the designs that frame them onto rectangular copper 'plates'; he then used acid to corrode the unmarked portion of the copper surface. Finally, he inked this engraved 'plate' and used it to print his poem and its design onto paper. Usually, he then coloured the print by hand. He was passionate about combining words and vision into a single work; and he printed and coloured by hand, with small variations, because he wanted every print to be a different, unique, hand-produced work of art.

This fact has consequences for the way we study Blake's poems. When we merely read them, and address the poems as literature, we are engaged in a partial, even distorted response to the 'whole work' Blake created. On the other hand, it is inevitable that Blake's poetry will be studied in an exclusively literary way; there is not enough space in a book like this one to discuss both the poetry and its attendant graphic art together.

I have decided on a compromise. In Chapter 1, there are descriptions of the design for each poem analysed, and interpretation of the designs is discussed. Six of the designs discussed in Chapter 1 are reproduced on pages 31, 32, 34, 36, 39 and 41. After Chapter 1, however, the designs are only occasionally mentioned and this book concentrates on the poetry. Readers are urged to obtain, or find in a library, an illustrated copy of the *Songs of Innocence and Experience* to use while studying Blake. Seeing the 'whole work' in which text and graphic art interweave and interact is a great advantage. It will enrich your pleasure and appreciation of the works themselves, and it is the honest way to read Blake – the way he meant us to see his poetry.

1

Innocence and Experience

'Introduction' (*Songs of Innocence*)

When you first take up the challenge of studying his writings, William Blake seems to be a special case. He claimed to have visions, he was an eccentric (some people will tell you he was mad), and he did not publish his poems in the ordinary way by having them printed. Instead, he engraved them on metal plates using acid to eat away the designs, and each page is a sinuous, living swirl of shapes, with branches, snakes and other emblems often growing between the lines of poetry. When they had been printed, Blake, or his wife, coloured the plates carefully by hand. The finished works were sold to patrons and friends, in small numbers. You may feel that Blake was an oddity, and will be difficult to understand.

If you then turn to the critics, you are likely to find them indulging a rage for symbolic interpretation that can increase your confusion. If we plunge into the longer Prophetic Books, *Milton*, *Vala or the Four Zoas*, and *Jerusalem*, we are likely to lose our way quickly: Blake invented so many deities and symbolic characters that it is difficult to acquire a sense of what they all signify. Also, even in Blake's own day, few readers would have been erudite enough to recognise all of the mythological and theological references, coinages and puns in which his work abounds.

However, we refuse to succumb to all the 'expert' pressure, and pseudo-biographic prejudice, that surrounds Blake's reputation. We believe that we can read the poems as poems. We must not bring any preconceptions to this work; on the contrary, we are convinced that a detailed, analytical study of the poems will reveal their significance.

We start, then, by looking in detail at the first two poems from *Songs of Innocence*. We should notice, however, that the title of the collection already provides us with an aim: to find out what Blake meant by the word 'Innocence'. Here is the first poem, 'Introduction':

'Introduction'

Piping down the valleys wild
Piping songs of pleasant glee
On a cloud I saw a shild.
And he laughing said to me.

Pipe a song about a Lamb:
So I piped with merry chear,
Piper, pipe that song again –
So I piped, he wept to hear.

Drop thy pipe they happy pipe
Sing thy songs of happy chear,
So I sung the same again
While he wept with joy to hear.

Piper sit thee down and write
In a book that all may read –
So he vanish'd from my sight,
And I pluck'd a hollow reed.

And I made a rural pen,
And I stain'd the water clear,
And I wrote my happy songs,
Every child may joy to hear.

(K2, 4)

This clear song is not at all difficult: the story it tells is obvious on a first reading, and it has the short lines, easy rhymes, regular metre and simple vocabulary of a nursery rhyme or children's song. Nonetheless, we will analyse the poem in detail.

The story is clear. A 'piper' meets a child who first asks for 'a song about a Lamb', then encourages him to pipe, then sing, and finally write down his happy songs that 'Every child may joy to hear'. This is a simple story, but it is helpful to look at its stages or sections more closely. The music begins as non-specific 'songs of pleasant glee'. The child then specifies a subject: the music will be 'about a Lamb'. Next, he urges the Piper to 'Drop thy pipe' and sing instead, so we assume that the music 'about a Lamb' is no longer just a melody: it has words which fit the music and express the Piper's meaning. Finally, the song becomes only words, which are not the Piper's spontaneous singing any more: they are written down 'In a book that all may read'. Notice that the child made the Piper pipe the same song twice (stanza 2), and when he sang it was 'the same again', so the song itself has been performed three times, becoming more and more fixed, less and less spontaneous, as it develops from a purely musical expression of pleasure ('Piping songs of pleasant glee') and turns into a permanent written record ('In a book that all may read'). Blake emphasises that the final written song is unchanging, and universal, by his repetition of this idea. It is a book that may be read by 'all'; and the songs will be heard by 'Every child'.

What is Blake's subject? For the time being, we can only speculate. We notice that the pure music of a moment's pleasure changes into written lyrics. There is something about change in this poem, then. Perhaps Blake is writing about poetic creation, explaining his own natural inspiration in 'the valleys wild', and how he fashions and transforms this into poems for the joy of all children? So far, we have a well-defined understanding of the story and its structure; but our ideas about the poem's overall intention are only guesswork. Now we can turn our attention to the style, hoping that details of diction, or rhythm, may give us further clues to the meaning.

We have already commented that 'Introduction' has an apparent simplicity of style reminiscent of a nursery rhyme. There is liberal use of repetition (*piper / pipe / piping / piped; happy; chear; sing / song / songs / sung; child; joy* are all parts of a strong pattern of repetition in the poem); the vocabulary is simple, using common words of one or two syllables only. The metre is regularly trochaic, each line ending on the stress so that a 'ghost' unstressed beat emphasises the end of the line. So, the first line goes 'Pi ping / down the / valleys / wild' and we wait for a further syllable to complete the fourth foot of the line. As we read, this has the almost-unconscious effect of separating each line of the poem from the next. Only once does Blake punctuate in the middle of a line: the comma after 'piped' in line 8 stands out, and emphasises that this line includes both sides of the poem's action: 'I piped' and 'he wept'.

However, Blake manages some very subtle effects within what appears to be a simple and regular form. It comes as a surprise, for example, that the rhyme-scheme is not regular. The first stanza is ABAB, but this is not repeated in stanzas two, three and five. In these stanzas the second and fourth lines rhyme, but not the first and third. However, Blake has created a sound-link between these stanzas because lines 6, 8, 10, 12, 18 and 20 all rhyme – indeed there are only three rhyme-words in total (*hear* comes three times and *chear* twice); and the third lines of stanzas two and three end in 'again'. So, the manipulation of rhyme is much more complex than we notice at first, and contributes to the sense of a build-up of repetitive events that runs throughout the poem as the piper performs his song again and again.

Blake achieves a curious effect with the metre, also. It occurs because the second syllables in twelve lines of this poem are pronouns, either 'I', 'he' or 'thy'. We do not throw a pronoun away as we read: we naturally give it greater stress than, say, a falling participle ending (such as the '-ing' on the end of 'piping' which is the second syllable in line 1, or the article 'a', second syllable in line 5). Arguably, we invest a slight extra effort in these pronouns so that the first three syllables for twelve of the lines are of almost equal value. This emphasises the transaction between the child and the piper: the child's commands ('Drop thy pipe'), the piper's efforts ('So I piped') and the child's response ('While he wept') are all conveyed with a heavier, fuller beat than the metre alone would create. The parallelism of lines 16–19, all beginning 'And I', builds this effect further, so that the absence of this extra effort in the final line gives a feeling of relief and release, enhancing the flow of the final achievement: 'Every child may joy to hear'.

We have not learned a great deal more about Blake's meaning

from our analysis of rhyme and metre; but we have begun to appreciate what a consummate and subtly-crafted poem this is. With regard to diction, we have noted the intensive use of repetition but should also notice the 'odd-words-out' which help Blake achieve an effect similar to that he achieves in rhythm. We noted that *because* so many lines begin with three heavy syllables, this *enhances* the contrast of the flowing final line. Similarly with diction: *because* repetition is so widespread, the poem's diction seems even more limited to a narrow choice of words. This *enhances* the contrasting effect of those few words which display some difference: 'vanish'd' (line 15), 'pluck'd' (line 16) and 'stain'd' (line 18) stand out for this reason. They seem sudden actions, and are more violent than the continuous verbs elsewhere in the poem such as 'piping', 'laughing' and 'wept'. In addition, 'vanish'd' is slightly disturbing: the child has been the audience, repeatedly demanding the piper's song and delighting in the performance, so the suddenness of 'vanish'd' is an unexpected shock to the reader; and 'stain'd' carries overtones of dirt and corruption, the disturbing suggestion that the piper here interferes with water, spoiling nature's purity or innocence.

What is the overall 'meaning' of this poem, then? The title, calling it the 'Introduction' to a collection of nineteen poems, provokes us to interpret the 'piper' as representing the poet. However, our thinking should be careful and precise: this means that the 'piper' is the poet who writes *Songs of Innocence*, but is not necessarily Blake himself. Blake stands behind, having created both this 'piper' – the poet of *Innocence* – and the 'Bard' we meet later, the poet of *Experience*.

Other elements of the poem also provoke us to interpret. The child and the capitalised 'Lamb' are both references to Christ, particularly evoking ideas of gentleness, humility, love and innocence associated with Him. Meanwhile, the setting in 'valleys wild', 'rural' and with 'water clear' also brings to mind ideas of an unspoilt and therefore uncorrupted nature. In this poem, then, the qualities of the world of 'Innocence' are plainly evoked. Innocence is natural, unspoilt, and filled with gentleness and love.

The emotions expressed harmonise with this picture of an 'Innocent' world. 'Pleasant glee' and 'merry chear' give rise to 'laughing'. As the emotion grows, however, we find that the child 'wept with joy'. This is a curious conjunction of extremes. On one level, we can imagine a happiness so intense and poignant that it makes the child weep with joy. On the other hand, opposite extremes meet in this phrase. It appeals to us as a paradoxical truth – that opposite states of emotion tend towards each other. Paradox is a surprisingly sophisticated, unresolvable kind of idea to find in a simple, 'Innocent' world.

Finally, as we have already noticed, the setting loses some of its 'innocence' before the poem ends. The 'water clear' has been 'stain'd'; the piper has used natural materials to manufacture a 'pen', and a 'book' now exists which permanently records what began as the natural expression of present happiness. The pen is 'rural' – a word which supposes the existence of its antithesis, 'urban', and which refers to an agricultural landscape, not 'valleys wild'. So, in this short and simple poem we have already travelled a long way. We have moved from 'wild' nature to a still gentle and comforting, but nonetheless tamed and exploited nature, in 'rural'; and we have moved from the expression of momentary happiness in melody, to remembered happiness recorded in words in a 'book'. The crucial uncertainty in this poem is expressed by Blake's indefinite word 'may' in the final line. We are provoked to ask: how far is the world of 'Innocence' already an artificial ideal, an attempt to prolong inno-cence and protect it from change, by writing 'joy' into a book? We should also notice that 'wild' and 'rural' are not the same thing: 'wild' encompasses all of nature, including its powerful, sometimes frightening energy; 'rural', on the other hand, suggests a tamed nature.

For the moment we have met only the first poem. This presents a repetitively-reinforced impression of an 'innocent' world of nature, with christlike overtones. At the same time, we have noted that there are several elements within the poem which imply their antithesis: this 'innocent' world has an opposite, or 'contrary' world, which is still outside the poem; but which exists just as surely as 'urban' exists when the poet mentions 'rural'.

'The Shepherd'

The second poem is 'The Shepherd':

> How sweet is the Shepherd's sweet lot,
> From the morn to the evening he strays:
> He shall follow his sheep all the day
> And his tongue shall be filled with praise.
>
> For he hears the lambs innocent call.
> And he hears the ewes tender reply.
> He is watchful while they are in peace,
> For they know when their Shepherd is nigh.
>
> (K2, 5)

This poem also appears simple. It tells of a Shepherd who cares for his flock, and the poem only includes positive language about the relationship between shepherd and sheep. He follows his sheep 'all the day'; he 'hears' everything and is 'watchful'. The flock is 'innocent', 'tender' and 'in peace'. The Shepherd's presence gives them this 'peace', while their innocence affects him by giving him a 'sweet' life, and filling his tongue with 'praise'. The dependent and caring inter-relationship of shepherd and sheep seems idyllic, then.

There are two places in this poem where some slight uncertainty is left hanging, however. First, in line 4 we are told that the Shepherd's 'tongue' is 'filled with praise', but we are not told whether he praises the sheep, or God. As in 'Introduction', Christian symbols are called to mind by this poem: the Shepherd himself, with his watchful and loving role, can be seen as symbolic of God; and no higher or divine power is mentioned in the poem. So, we are left uncertain whether the Shepherd praises himself, his 'sweet' lot in life, or the innocence and tenderness of his flock. Secondly, the final two lines are linked by the logical conjunction 'For', which proposes a conditional relationship between the flock's 'peace' and the Shepherd being present. As with the word 'rural' in 'Introduction', this statement implies that a time may come when the Shepherd is not there and the flock will consequently not be at peace. Similarly, 'day' implies 'night', and we notice that the Shepherd's watchful care is only specified as lasting 'all the day'. By implication, the flock may be deserted and terrified at night. At our present stage in reading *Songs of Innocence*, the implication of a contrary, disturbing world outside these poems is little more than an unspoken hint. Predominantly, the poem presents an idyllic picture. However, as we become more used to Blake's recurrent references to mornings, days and evenings in this collection, the implication that there is a dark and frightening future night, just outside 'Innocence' and threatening its peace, gains power and presence – even while the world of 'Innocence' itself remains an idyll.

'The Shepherd' is written in regular anapaests, a metre which gives it a more bouncy and tripping rhythm than 'Introduction'. The style is again very simple, with no punctuation-breaks within the lines, rhyme between the second and fourth lines of each stanza, and the only word of more than two syllables is 'innocent' (l. 5). This carefree and uncomplicated style enhances the simple and positive picture presented. We can say that the simple writing suits a simple, positive subject; but Blake's metre in this poem is so regular that, together with the redundant repetition of 'sweet' in line 1, it creates a slight exaggeration of simplicity. We cannot say that this 'exaggeration' is noticeable enough to be a parody: it does not mock or undermine the innocent world depicted. However, it does have the effect of defining the world of 'Innocence'. It is as if the style says: *'Here is the world of Innocence. Lovely, isn't it? But it is exactly **this** limited'.*

What have we learned about 'Innocence' from these two poems? First, there is a mood of happiness which feels 'glee'; there is laughter and weeping for joy, and a gentle, caring love. Secondly, there is a sense of fragility which is produced by the style in two ways: language and metre are simple and limited, and this makes us aware that the poem itself is vulnerable to any incursion of more violent or complicated writing (remember how the word 'stain'd' strikes a slight discord in 'Introduction'); and some of the words belong, in our minds, in antithetical pairs (for example, 'day' and 'night'; 'rural' and 'urban'). Blake reminds us of the existence and threat of the contrary, by excluding it from his 'Innocence' poem (for example, the Shepherd is there 'all day'; why not at night as well?).

Thirdly, we notice that 'Innocence' is a world with a purpose: it is *for* children and sheep. In 'Introduction', the Piper writes songs that 'Every child may joy to hear'; and in 'The Shepherd', the aim is for the sheep to be 'in peace'. On the other hand, we have met two adults – the Piper and the Shepherd – and their role in relation to 'Innocence' is ambivalent. The poet would enjoy living the 'sweet' life of a Shepherd, but by implication does not do so, while the Shepherd only watches during the day. The Piper changes and tames nature, putting it to use in a 'rural' setting; and his spontaneous songs become fixed, written in a book.

This is already an understandable combination of hints: many emotions relating to childhood, such as fear, protectiveness, carefree laughter, and hints of the unknown beyond what is already known, have already been touched. We can suggest that change is a central, crucial concept in this complex of emotions. These poems are already building a range of relationships, between the world of 'Innocence' on the one hand, and natural, inevitable change on the other.

'Introduction' (*Songs of Experience*)

We now turn to *Songs of Experience*. We will use the same approach, looking closely at the first two poems of the collection, hoping to reach a preliminary insight into Blake's concept of 'Experience'. As in *Innocence*, the first poem is called 'Introduction':

> Hear the voice of the Bard!
> Who Present, Past, & Future sees
> Whose ears have heard,
> The Holy Word,
> That walk'd among the ancient trees.
>
> Calling the lapsed Soul
> And weeping in the evening dew:
> That might controll
> The starry pole:
> And fallen fallen light renew!

O Earth O Earth return!
Arise from out the dewy grass;
Night is worn,
And the morn
Rises from the slumberous mass.

Turn away no more:
Why wilt thou turn away
The starry floor
The watry shore
Is giv'n thee till the break of day.

(K2, 30)

We will begin by examining the metre and rhyme. This poem looks regular and simple on the page, but the visual impression is misleading. The metre is much more varied, and less regular, than we found in the *Songs of Innocence*. The opening line has three heavy stresses: '**Hear** the **voice** of the **Bard**!' and does not conform to any set metre. We can say that it is almost iambic, but the first foot has been reversed: but that is as much as we know, so we have to wait for the second line before the dominant iambic metre of the poem becomes recognisable. The first line of the second stanza is also irregular, and is different again: '**Calling** the **lapsed Soul**'. Other irregularities are the openings of lines 15, 16 and 17 ('**Rises**' and '**Turn away**' both stress the first syllable; '**Why wilt thou**' stresses the first three).

Blake adds to the destabilising effect of metrical irregularity by varying the length of lines. In 'Introduction' and 'The Shepherd' from *Innocence*, all lines have the same number of stresses. Here, by contrast, the pattern of stresses in each stanza is 3, 4, 2, 2, 4. Rhyme has also developed into something more complex than we found in *Innocence*: here, Blake uses an ABAAB rhyming pattern in each stanza; but the new elements are half-rhymes (Bard / heard; return / worn; grass / mass), with the use of single and two-syllable words as rhymes (Soul / controll; dew / renew). This more sophisticated rhyming reduces the chiming sing-song effect of rhyme, and introduces us to more complicated relationships between sounds.

The overall effect of this poem is very different from that we have met in *Innocence*. Reading it keeps us alert: we take time to recognise the underlying patterns, we meet surprises and changes, and Blake does not allow us to settle down. In *Innocence*, by contrast, the form conspired to lull us, reassuring us that we could predict the poem. Only slight variations were allowed into the poems from *Innocence*, none of them strong enough to overturn the regular, predictable whole.

The overall effect of metre and rhyme here, then, is to involve and destabilise the reader. Now we can turn to the meaning: why does Blake write in such a markedly different manner? The poem begins with a forceful imprecation to the reader: we are commanded to 'Hear', and the opening line – as previously remarked – is rather lumpy and ugly in sound and rhythm. The rest of the first two stanzas are subordinated to this command, grammatically connected by relative ('the Bard / Who . . .'), participle ('Calling'), and finally pronoun ('That'). The sentence appears to be structured, with each part related to the command. However, the more we strain to make sense of what Blake is saying, the more elusive it becomes. Two voices and acts of listening are described in the first stanza: first, the 'voice of the Bard' of line 1, and secondly, the 'Holy Word' heard by the Bard. These two voices create two ambiguities. First, we cannot know whether 'Calling' in line 6 refers to the Bard 'calling', so we should listen, or alternatively refers to the voice of God ('Holy Word') 'calling', which the Bard heard in the past. Secondly, we cannot know whether the voice 'That might controll / The starry pole' is the Bard's voice, or the 'Holy Word'.

At this stage we are building up a sense of the poem as a whole, so we will set these ambiguities aside for later discussion. All we know for sure is that the poem shouts at us rather brashly in the first line, and immediately follows this with a confusion of meanings. The third and fourth stanzas are not ambiguous, however. There can be no doubt that everything from 'O Earth O Earth return!' until 'Is giv'n thee till the break of day' should be enclosed in quotation marks. This is the actual 'voice of the Bard' which we are supposed to hear.

What is the message of the last two stanzas? The voice urges 'Earth' to 'return' and 'arise', and orders her to 'Turn away no more'.

This command is surrounded by phrases which fix the time of the poem as just before dawn ('Night is worn', 'the morn / Rises', 'till the break of day'). Here again, however, oddness and ambiguity in Blake's meaning become increasingly apparent the closer we look. For example, we are told that the morning rises from a 'slumberous mass' which could be either night itself, or the 'dewy grass' in line 12. Also, the two phrases 'starry floor' and 'watry shore' are hard to unravel. We would accept a starry roof or vault, but 'floor' surprises us; and does 'watry shore' simply mean the shore of the sea, or does it mean a limit or 'shore' of water? Finally, the Bard's tone of voice seems ambivalent. The third stanza appears optimistic, while the tone of 'Why wilt thou turn away' recognises that Earth may not respond to the Bard's call, but cannot understand Earth's reason.

Having acknowledged that 'Introduction' contains ambiguities, we should nonetheless focus on what we can interpret, and build an understanding of Blake's intentions from there. Our first job is to define the Bard himself. We are told that he sees 'Present, Past, & Future'. The Bard's knowledge of the past is demonstrated because he heard the 'Holy Word'. This is a reference to Chapter 3 of Genesis. Immediately after Adam and Eve ate fruit from the Tree of Knowledge, and became aware of their nakedness, they 'heard the voice of the Lord God walking in the garden in the cool of the day'.[1] So, Blake's 'ancient trees' stand in the Garden of Eden, and the odd expression of a word which 'walk'd' echoes the ellipsis of the Bible.

The Bard's knowledge of the future is suggested by his references to a coming dawn, particularly 'Night is worn, / And the morn / Rises', and the final words 'till the break of day'. His knowledge of the present is shown in his definition of the current situation: it is night, but soon it will be morning. The world is ruled by a 'starry pole' and everything – Earth, the weeping 'Holy Word', and the reader – is in a 'fallen fallen' state.

The Bard, then, contrasts with the carefree Piper of *Songs of Innocence*, who is only aware of the present moment's sensation as he pipes 'songs of pleasant glee'. The Bard is much more aware of time

---

[1] Genesis Chapter 3, verse 8. Future references to the Bible will be given in brackets in the text thus: (Genesis 3, 8), and are from the Authorized (King James) Version.

and change, even to the extent that he has a prophetic vision of a
new dawn and Earth's awakening. However, it would be a mistake to
conclude that the Bard is Blake himself. We have noticed that his
prophetic tone is ambivalent, and his question 'Why wilt thou turn
away' casts doubt on the eventual outcome: this Bard is struggling
against a recalcitrant will which prevents Earth from waking, and he
is far from sure that the coming morning will rejuvenate the world.
This Bard has a broad vision including prophetic insight; but he
cannot enjoy the present moment as the Piper of *Innocence* can.
Indeed, he doubts whether such innocent pleasure can exist.

This is an important distinction. The Bard is the poet of *Songs of
Experience*. He is not Blake himself, but the Piper's 'contrary'. As
such, his insight sees a world which excludes the world of *Innocence*,
just as surely as the world of *Innocence* is limited by excluding
Experience. The Bard's hesitant references to an imminent 'morn'
therefore balance the darker world we found implied but outside the
poems from *Innocence*. He is caught inside the limited world of
'Experience' just as surely as the Piper is restricted from further
knowledge by his 'Innocence'.

What more can we learn about the world of *Experience* from this
poem? We have noticed that some of the phrases, such as 'starry
floor' and 'watry shore' are difficult to confine within a clear
meaning. On the other hand, these images cry out for interpretation. We can try approaching the remaining elements of the poem
from a more impressionistic standpoint. If we look at the language,
and attempt to describe its effect, this may help us to understand
better.

In 'Introduction' there are a number of words which contribute to
a negative feeling: 'ancient', 'lapsed', 'weeping', and the repetition of
'fallen fallen'; 'worn' and 'slumberous mass'. This language evokes an
atmosphere of weariness and sadness, as if after a long-sustained
effort. A hard and unwelcome effort is also evoked by other words
and phrases: 'Calling' and 'might controll' lead to the begging tone
of 'O Earth O Earth return! / Arise . . .', and as we have noted, there
is some fatalism in the Bard's querulous imprecations: 'Turn away no
more: / Why wilt thou turn away'.

Next, there are the two images of a 'starry' pole and floor, and the 'watry shore'. When in contrast to the 'morn', the word 'starry' suggests coldness, distance and darkness. The words it is coupled with (pole, floor) both suggest fixed limits and are also, emotionally, rather cold words. 'Pole' is ambivalent: it suggests both the final waste point at the end of the world, and a measuring-pole or a 'rod' of authority such as that held by judges or kings. 'Watry' again evokes coldness, and possibly hints at chaos, since water has traditionally been an emblem of chaos in our culture. Like 'floor' and 'pole', a 'shore' is an edge or limit. As we study more of Blake's poems, we will be able to put forward firmer interpretations of these images. For the time being, we can already conclude that the world of *Experience* is a cold, sad, despairing place bounded by strict limits and – seemingly – lacking the energy to escape from them. The poem records a plaintive call, something like *'You **could** escape, **please** escape: why **won't** you try?'* in conflict with a despairing sense that, if any renewal is achieved, it will be after a weary struggle, and against the odds.

Now that we have allowed ourselves to respond to the poem's effect, we can look back at the Bard. 'Introduction' tells us that this singer differs from the Piper of *Innocence* because his 'ears have heard / The Holy Word'. We traced this reference to Genesis Chapter 3. The 'Holy Word', then, was God's judgment on Adam and Eve for their sin and disobedience; and the punishment he pronounced on them:

> Unto the woman he said, I will greatly multiply thy sorrow and thy conception; in sorrow thou shalt bring forth children . . . And unto Adam he said, . . . cursed is the ground for thy sake; in sorrow shalt thou eat of it all the days of thy life; Thorns also and thistles shall it bring forth to thee; and thou shalt eat the herb of the field; In the sweat of thy face shalt thou eat bread, till thou return unto the ground; for out of it wast thou taken: for dust thou art, and unto dust shalt thou return.
>
> (Genesis 3, 16–19)

When we put this 'Holy Word' into the context of the poem, God's voice seems to add to the negativity of the whole. His words are curses, depriving Adam and Eve of their innocence and sentencing the human race to mortality in 'sorrow', pain and 'sweat'. God's final words giving 'dust' as the origin and end of human life evoke a cycle of pointlessness.

This Bard, then, has heard the unforgiving, punishing words of God. In the negative context of this poem, Blake conveys a clear feeling of antipathy towards Jehovah's judgment. Astonishingly for its time, 'Introduction' to *Experience* seems to call for the expulsion to be undone, and it implies two ideas which would have shocked the religious establishment. First, the poem highlights God's punishment of Adam and Eve, rather than their sin – as if the Fall was caused by the 'Holy Word' and its pitiless intransigence. Secondly, the Bard speaks as if 'Earth' could throw off God's punishment (the 'floor', 'pole' and 'shore') by her own efforts, if she only had the will to do so. This, as I have remarked, is an extraordinary and subversive suggestion. Blake tells us that all the sufferings of mortality are only a temporary dream, that we can throw them off and nullify Jehovah's curse, if we have the will.

'Earth's Answer'

The second poem in *Songs of Experience* is 'Earth's Answer':

> Earth rais'd up her head,
> From the darkness dread & drear,
> Her light fled:
> Stony dread!
> And her locks cover'd with grey despair.
>
> Prison'd on watry shore
> Starry Jealousy does keep my den
> Cold and hoar
> Weeping o'er
> I hear the Father of the ancient men
>
> Selfish father of men
> Cruel jealous selfish fear
> Can delight

Chain'd in night
The virgins of youth and morning bear.

Does spring hide its joy
When buds and blossoms grow?
Does the sower?
Sow by night?
Or the plowman in darkness plow?

Break this heavy chain,
That does freeze my bones around
Selfish! Vain!
Eternal bane!
That free Love with bondage bound.

(K2, 31)

'Earth's Answer' can be read straightforwardly as a reply to the Bard's call. We quickly realise that the answer it gives is to pass the buck: Earth feels cruelly imprisoned, expresses her misery powerfully, but in the final stanza she puts the question back to the Bard. She cannot arise, but calls on him to 'Break this heavy chain' for her. Having summarised the general sense of the poem, we can begin analysis by looking at rhythm and rhyme.

This poem takes the lumpy and irregular rhythm of *Songs of Experience* further. Metrically, it is an unpredictable mixture of trochaic (see '**Earth** rais'd **up** her **head**' and '**That** free **Love** with **bond**age **bound**') and iambic (see 'When **buds** and **bloss**oms **grow**'), and in many lines we find extra unstressed syllables which briefly add an unexpected anapaestic lilt (see, for example, 'From the **dark**ness' in line 2, or '**virg**ins of **youth**' in line 15) or wearily extend the line (see '**Fath**er of the **an**cient' in line 10). The overall effect is of constantly changing rhythms which are driven by powerful emotive emphasis, the poet's and Earth's natural need for self-expression, rather than by any pattern. Even the paired, rhymed short lines (the third and fourth of each stanza) are often metrically opposed:

Her **light fled:**
Stony **dread!**

The changing rhythms of the poem also give a flexible pace which alters with mood. So, for example, the double stress ('**locks cover'd**') and open endings ('**grey despair**') of line 5 slow the pace, suiting the negative mood expressed.

As in the previous poem, there is wide variation in line-length. The number of 'beats' per line follows the same pattern in each stanza: 3, 4, 2, 2, 4.[2] However, the pattern of rhymes established in the first two stanzas (ABAAB) is changed in stanzas 3 (ABCCB, where A rhymes with the final line of stanza 2) and 4 (ABCDB). These two stanzas express Earth's condemnation of Jehovah as 'Selfish', and her outraged rhetorical questions about nature, and the speaker's violent hostility may explain why she breaks through the rhyming pattern, refusing to be restricted by the poem's form. Certainly, our analysis of metre and rhyme has revealed a boiling tension between content and form in this poem. It is as if the ideas are unhappy at being imprisoned in the form, and constantly batter against their frame, threatening to break it.

Imagery intensifies the sense of cold and darkness already apparent from 'Introduction'. The landscape of Earth's imprisonment, however, has become more barren, harder; suggestions of colour have been drained away from it. 'Darkness', 'grey', 'starry', 'hoar' and 'night' all contribute to the monochrome scene. Other elements in the poem further emphasise white, black and grey: 'Stony', 'Chain'd', 'chain' and 'freeze' are all colourless. The sad green of 'dewy grass' and 'ancient trees' we met in the previous poem have disappeared: Earth does not sense any softness or movement of water. Metal, stone and ice are her surroundings.

When we analysed 'Introduction', we commented that 'starry' suggests coldness and distance. In this poem, the impression is reinforced when 'starry' describes 'Jealousy' which, in the next stanza, is further defined as a 'Cruel jealous selfish fear'. The limits ('pole', 'shore' and 'floor') we noted have also become stronger and more clearly expressed in the form of a narrow imprisonment ('Prison'd' in a 'den' and 'Chain'd'). These cruel elements which cause Earth to despair are

---

[2] It can be argued that line 10 has 5 beats, if 'of' is stressed.

now openly identified with the God of Genesis: the God who pun-ished Adam and Eve. Earth is outspoken, saying that the 'Father of the ancient men' is 'Selfish'. He is cruel, jealous, selfish and afraid and his curse is an 'Eternal bane' which binds 'free Love' in 'bondage'.

This poem, then, makes a more direct and hostile attack on the God who punished mankind. Again, however, we should consider the question of voice. The first stanza of this poem is spoken by the poet of *Experience* (who is neither the Bard nor Earth). The tone is sympathetic, telling us that the poet feels Earth's 'dread'; but the restriction he describes is a covering of 'grey despair', not any literal chains or prison. It is important to make the distinction between what the poet sees, and what Earth herself perceives; and we should remember the difference as it will help us a great deal when we come to unravelling – in particular – *The Marriage of Heaven and Hell*. In this case, we can conclude that the prison and chains described by Earth may be illusory. She is prevented from rising by her own despair, not any concrete object.

The tendency of abstract and emotional states to be coupled with concrete images, so that they seem to have a material existence, is characteristic of Blake. Here, for example, Earth's 'dread' is described as 'Stony'. This technique, of accreting concrete metaphors to abstract terms, gives great force to the ideas in Blake's poetry. However, we must keep in mind that the poet himself is on top of this process: he sees how solid fear can become in a frightened mind (such as Earth, here); but he never concedes that fear actually *is* a concrete object. As a result, the poem contains two radically dif-ferent perceptions of reality. Earth is convinced that she cannot rise, because of the chains she sees and feels freezing around her bones, and the prison she perceives around her. The poet, on the other hand, sees a character suffering in agony, who could arise without hindrance if she could only see that she could, i.e., if only she were not in despair. In the poem 'London', later in the *Songs of Experience*, this process of solidifying abstract restrictions is encapsulated in Blake's phrase, 'the mind-forg'd manacles'. In 'Earth's Answer' we can distinguish objective and subjective perceptions because the poet's view is given in stanza 1, and Earth's in the remaining four stanzas. The difference between these two voices is vital.

Earth's series of four rhetorical questions deserves close attention. She begins by asking whether 'delight' can bring forth 'youth and morning' while she is 'chain'd in night'. The implied answer is no, and this is part of her answer to the Bard's call: *I cannot arise because I am chained.* She is *not* literally chained, however, so this question is not valid and the argument becomes an impasse, along the lines of: '*You're not chained*', '*Yes I am*', '*No you are not*', and so on.

We could also take 'bear' in its other sense of 'endure'. This gives a different implication to Earth's question: that she could not bear (endure) to see the hopeful 'virgins of youth and morning'. It is as if she would *prefer* to suffer and complain. Hope would be frightening because it would threaten to change the status quo.

Earth's second question is more complex. She asks:

> Does spring hide its joy
> When buds and blossoms grow?

This seems to reverse the order. Her first question implied that she could not create in darkness. This time, procreation seems to be occurring anyway, naturally ('When buds and blossoms grow') and the question centres on whether the new growth remains hidden (in 'night', we presume) or displays itself in a joyful form, which must mean in bright daylight. We sympathise with the feeling behind Earth's question: it is horrifying to contemplate the beauty and energy of nature unnaturally hiding itself away. However, our minds are forced to return to her conviction that she is 'delight / Chain'd in night'. If it is unnatural for nature to hide its joy, then she is guilty of doing exactly that. If the inevitable cycle of procreation, here represented by spring, is proceeding anyway and putting forth buds and blossoms in the natural way, then Earth is somehow distorting and hiding the process. The night she thinks 'eternal' is 'worn', and her fearful perceptions are only delaying her own rebirth. The growth of buds and blossoms is a further hint that the 'night' she sees is a creation of her own darkened brain.

Earth's third and fourth questions, about 'sower' and 'plowman', return to her first point: that she cannot initiate a new age by rising up, because it is still night. The second question has invalidated these, however. What she proposes is an unresolvable paradox, what in the present day we might call a 'Catch-22'. She will not arise while she still fears that it is night. The 'buds and blossoms' of new life, 'joy' and 'delight' will not show themselves, and cannot grow, until she arises. One cannot happen without the other. The other cannot happen without the one. QED. In the meantime, her rhetorical questions all provoke the opposite answer to the one she implies. As long as her imprisonment continues and she fails to arise, spring *does* hide its joy, and buds and blossoms grow unnaturally in darkness; sowers and plowmen *do* sow and plow, also in darkness. The Bard calls for her to break out of this destructive cycle; and she calls on the Bard to break it for her. How can this deadlock end?

What is responsible for this hopeless state of affairs? This poem provides us with two figures who bear a part: the punishing God of Genesis, and Earth herself. One quality is emphasised in relation to both: fear. God is filled with 'jealous . . . fear'; Earth feels 'Stony dread' and is covered with 'grey despair'. We can suggest, then, that fear is an important target of Blake's criticism. Fear leads to the vicious self-righteousness of God's unnatural, punishing laws. The poem shows how these laws bind 'free Love', 'delight' and 'joy', and force nature to hide in darkness. Fear of this punishment acts equally powerfully on nature itself, however; and Earth contributes to the deadlocked status quo by refusing to abandon her 'dread'.

The above discussion of 'Earth's Answer' has inevitably been abstract. The figures we meet in these first two poems of *Experience* – the Bard, Earth, and the 'Father of the ancient men', are all allegorical in kind. That is, they are personifications of the concepts they represent, and make no pretensions to being 'realistic' people. We have therefore discussed Earth as representing nature, both human and plant life in its seasonal cycles of growth and regeneration. The Bard represents a form of prophecy – a kind of insight into history, the present and the future. God, in these poems, is exclusively associated with the punishment of sexual sin. He represents the law, which oppresses nature by forbidding natural behaviour.

These poems tend to deal in abstracts, then: many of the nouns are abstracts, too, such as fear, dread, jealousy, delight, joy, love.

What is Blake writing about? Is he simply playing with concepts, or do these poems relate to our experience of everyday life?

The first part of an answer to this question has already been given. We have commented on the sympathy and emotional power with which these figures are invested. The horror and hatred with which Earth speaks of the 'Father', for example, creates a powerful and convincing relationship between them; and the way in which Earth's metaphors give concrete existence to her imprisonment and fear, moves us. Also, we have analysed the Bard's urgent, yet fatalistic tone of voice, building a naturalistic character to his feelings. Nonetheless, we may still wonder what is so important about the situation these figures find themselves in?

Much of the answer to this will gradually come to us as we study more of the *Songs of Innocence and Experience*. We will find that individual poems elaborate real-life situations, showing us how the 'two contrary states' emblematically presented in these opening poems are lived out by actual people, from children playing on a green, to chimney sweepers plying their trade in Blake's London, beadles and pauper children, nurses, soldiers, priests and others. However, it will be helpful to stop and think at this early stage. The poems are passionately written, and an effort to connect with Blake's passion, to understand how his ideas relate to ordinary life-experience, will be both rewarding and enlightening.

We have also met elements of fear in the *Songs of Innocence*. In 'The Shepherd', fear of the night, and of the Shepherd's absence, is implied by the emphasis on how 'watchful' he is, and the flock's 'peace'. We are beginning to see a pattern emerging, because the worlds of Innocence and Experience are both presented to us in the form of limited, subjective perceptions. *Innocence* is a beautiful, warm and affectionate world; but it is limited because its inhabitants fear dangers from the outside, and the terrors of a night which must come. The world of *Experience* expresses critical insights which are more penetrating than we find in *Innocence*. So far we have noticed that the punishing God of Genesis is castigated for cruelty and selfishness, and we will find the society and institutions of Blake's time critically analysed, exposed and condemned in such poems as 'Holy Thursday', 'The Garden of Love', 'London' and 'The Chimney

Sweeper'. Yet the subjective perception of *Experience* is also limited by fear. This time, fear centres on the sufferings and punishments which follow any attempt to be free and natural. We can suggest the conclusion, then, that in Blake's view fear itself is an enemy. It does not matter whether it is fear of experience (in *Innocence*) or fear of freedom, which could be expressed as fear of innocence (in *Experience*): it is always fear which prevents the human spirit from achieving wholeness, and keeps us thralled within a restricted, distorted perception of reality.

Innocence and *Experience*, then, are related to each other in a complex but symmetrical way. We may look at the setting of morning and daytime in *Innocence*, and that of night in *Experience*, to deduce that the second state is a later, older 'state of the human soul'. However, we can already see that it would be wrong to think of *Experience* as any wiser than *Innocence*. It is a later state, but its inhabitants are just as restricted by fear and delusion as are those of *Innocence*. Since each of these states is disabled by its fear of the other, we can suggest that *Innocence* and *Experience* are in need of each other. It appears that the route towards wholeness and a 'true' vision lies through combination of the two, not rejection of either of them.

The Designs

William Blake was an engraver by trade. The *Songs of Innocence and Experience* were 'published' by being engraved, printed in Blake's workshop, and finally coloured by hand. Each poem, then, is integrated within a design which Blake intended as a part of the whole artistic work. Blake's designs complement the poems they present. In some cases the design carries an independent but related meaning, enlarging on the poem's significance; in other cases the design functions more in the manner of an illustration to the poem. However, even in these simpler cases, the design often clarifies, or adds to, the words of the poem. We will study the designs for the four poems we have analysed in this chapter, both as a brief introduction to the interpretation of Blake's visual images, and as a reminder of the way Blake wished his work to be appreciated.

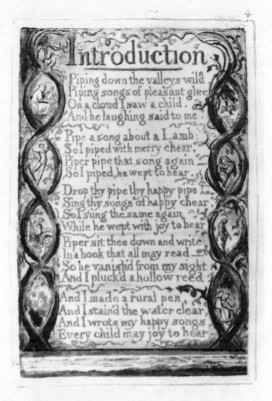

Figure One: The 'Introduction' to *Songs of Innocence*. Reproduced by permission of the Syndics of the Fitzwilliam Museum, Cambridge.

The 'Introduction' to *Innocence* is set within a marginal design consisting of two trees, each having two trunks which twine up beside the poem. Small vines grow up each tree, and branches of these grow partly across between each stanza. They grow across and almost join at the top of the page. The two trees with double trunks twining are derived from medieval illuminated manuscripts and stained-glass windows depicting the Tree of Jesse. The ground at the base of the page seems very regular and flat, and the trees rise without visible roots: some commentators see a sill, or even Jesse's coffin here. However, most copies show a narrow contained stream on this ground, flowing across the bottom of the page.

Each twining of the trunks is used as the frame for a different tiny design. These are of figures variously male, female and child, clothed or naked, with birds or in some cases indistinct objects near them (one of these is seen variously as a printing-press or a bed). One frame (top right) is of a bird flying upwards. We cannot be sure what these tiny figures are doing, but some are certainly concerned with writing (or printing), while one depicts a woman sowing and another a woman and child in a domestic scene. Also, some are expressions of freedom of spirit, such as the bird flying upwards, and the clear naked figure with spread arms which is the second design on the left.

The poem 'Introduction' has been illustrated in the frontispiece to *Songs of Innocence*: there we see the Piper looking up at a floating

Figure Two: The frontispiece to *Songs of Innocence*. Reproduced by permission of the Syndics of the Fitzwilliam Museum, Cambridge.

child, with a feeding flock in the background. The design we are studying, then, is a second visual presentation, not an illustration. We remember that the poem's story is ambiguous: on the surface it appears cheerful, and the Piper's songs are such that 'every child may joy to hear'; yet at the same time nature becomes 'stained' and tamed, and the exuberance of 'glee' changes into a permanent written record. The variety of figures and designs up and down each side of the page certainly echo this ambiguity. Some are agricultural (the woman sowing) and domestic, suggesting a settled life, and the exploitation of nature. On the other hand, the bird and the naked figure are more free and energetic images. Similarly, some of the figures seem upright or expansive: the naked child, for example, spreads his arms and is walking. Others, in contrast, are bowed or huddled in attitudes which suggest submission, preoccupation or fear: attitudes which visually enclose these figures, and present them as unaware of what is beyond or outside their downcast view. Clearly, the sad ambivalence of the poem is reflected in these designs. It is a pity that we cannot be sure exactly what each one is, and so we cannot analyse how they link together in sequence.

Interpreters of Blake's designs point out features which represent the limitations of *Innocence*. An example of this is the stream across the bottom of the page: it is narrow, and contained within straight banks, and this is interpreted as a sign that *Innocence* is fertilised by a limited and narrow source. The vines' failure to join across the top of the design may also be significant, as well as the trees without roots, whose growth seems insecure.

The design around 'The Shepherd' is more of an illustration: the poem occupies a limited space at the top, and the rest of the page is a picture of the shepherd and his flock, with a tree to the right and a bird rising on the left. In the background are woods, a distant hill and a burst of light in the sky. Some smaller birds in the distance, and two lark-like birds on a branch, confirm that it is dawn and we are looking east.

Even in this illustration, however, Blake has used his design to indicate a clear meaning. Compare the figure of the Piper from the frontispiece to that of the Shepherd on the next page. The Piper looks up, the Shepherd looks down. The Piper is naked, the

Figure Three: 'The Shepherd' from *Songs of Innocence*. Reproduced by permission of the Syndics of the Fitzwilliam Museum, Cambridge.

Shepherd is clothed in a tunic-like garment. The Piper carries his
pipe, emblem of music and his songs of 'glee'; the Shepherd carries
his crook and his shepherd's wallet hanging by his right side. The significance of these developments is that 'the piper's role is prophetic,
the shepherd's protective'.[3] Blake visually underlines the transition
from unspoilt natural energy to a more settled, agricultural rural life.
At the same time there is a hint of a 'fall', a loss of innocence, as this
figure is clothed. As you study Blake's designs in *Songs of Innocence
and Experience*, you notice that clothing and nakedness are indicative. Many of the figures in *Songs of Experience* wear dresses and

[3] Erdman, David V., *The Illuminated Blake*, London, Oxford University Press, 1975, p. 46.

robes which completely obscure the shape of their bodies. Here, the
departure from unspoilt nature is slight: we can see the outlines of
the Shepherd's body clearly through his clinging and short garment.

The sheep graze peacefully. Ram and ewe graze together next to
the Shepherd's leg. Two of the sheep have raised heads, however.
One calls to the Shepherd, and the other looks out of the picture.
This seems to suggest both a desire for reassurance, for the
Shepherd's care, and some alert fear of what may lie beyond the con-
fines of this peaceful scene to threaten its safety in the future.

It is a lovely design: the flock huddles as a single, warm and
woolly unit; the Shepherd's pose is willowy and relaxed leaning on
his crook, and both the tree and a blossoming plant twining up the
trunk echo the figure's pose. However, we should not ignore the
energy of the splendid bird of paradise, of the dawn whose rays are
strongly lined to burst into the sky, and of a wind which appears to
be blowing powerfully, making the tree's foliage bend towards the
dawn and leaving the ends of branches somewhat ragged. It is reasonable to read this picture as an emblem of rural peace encircled by
wild natural energies, and the signs of development we have noted,
from natural to cultivated life, support such an ambivalent reading.

The frontispiece to *Songs of Experience* on page 36 should be considered next, as it is a direct development from the figures of Piper,
child and Shepherd from *Innocence*. Several changes have taken
place, and these indicate something of the 'contrary' collection of
poems readers are about to meet.

The child which flew free, with expansive arms, in *Innocence*, now
sits upon the Piper / Shepherd's head and is held there gripped by
both hands. The child now has wings and (in some copies) a halo: it
has become a cherub. Both child and man now look directly at us
with serious but otherwise unreadable expressions. The man is
dressed much as he was in 'The Shepherd', but he now has no pipe,
crook or wallet and is clearly walking away from his flock and
entering a darker foreground, with his right foot taking a pace
forward, towards us. A tree is on the right of the design again, but
this time it has a thick, older trunk which seems scarred by striations
(one commentator suggests lightning) and has ivy growing upon it
with dark and sharp leaves. In place of the verdant woods, there is a

Figure Four: The frontispiece to *Songs of Experience*. Reproduced by permission of the Syndics of the Fitzwilliam Museum, Cambridge.

single young tree (in some copies apparently two trees with crossed trunks) in the background, as well as hills and a sky with a yellow, possibly evening light above the horizon.

The significance of some of these changes is obvious, but several features of this picture are still a matter for conjecture and argument between the commentators. We will record the obvious points first.

The child reappears transformed into a holy cherub. This change, whatever it means, is parallel to the man's development from naked Piper to a serious, clothed Shepherd who is abandoning his protective role. The man is making a determined move forward, away from the world of *Innocence*, and the absence of crook and wallet shows that he will no longer protect innocence. The tree indicates violence and suffering, and the evergreen ivy seems to suggest endurance through a hard winter, in contrast to the blossoming and therefore seasonal plant that twined the tree in 'The Shepherd'. The picture as a whole suggests both courage and determination, danger and endurance, while the world of innocence in the background is barer, and the flock continues grazing rather obliviously. To me, there is a mood of loss and decline in the background, in contrast to the man's determined foreground stride.

Uncertainty in the interpretation of this design centres on the cherub, and the fact that the figure advances with his right foot. Commentators agree that Blake distinguished symbolically between right and left, and some[4] read the two sides as spiritual (right) and material (left). However, most take a more flexible view: Blake seems to advance the right side of a figure to indicate a positive movement, perhaps a movement towards change and development – whether in a spiritual or material context – and he advances the left side to indicate a negative movement or attitude, perhaps when forces of oppression or stagnant conservatism are dominant. In this case, the firm stride leading with the right foot indicates a positive movement. This is in keeping with the general idea we will find conveyed by poems in this collection, and other prophecies (notably *The Book of Thel*, which is discussed in Chapter 4): that it is positive and necessary to leave the world of innocence behind. Trying to maintain innocence beyond its natural time leads to ignorance and idiocy; and the world of experience, however fearful it seems, must be entered.

The child's cherubic wings and halo, and his position on the man's head, have spawned some ingenious interpretations. Keynes[5] sees a reference to Ezekiel 28. 14 where the King of Tyre is likened to 'the anointed cherub that covereth', as he has been 'perfect' from the day he was 'created' until 'iniquity' was found in him due to his great riches. Ezekiel continues:

---

[4] For example one of the earliest and most influential interpreters of Blake's designs, Joseph Wicksteed, whose *Blake's Vision of the Book of Job* appeared in 1910.
[5] *Songs of Innocence and Experience, with an Introduction and Commentary by Sir Geoffrey Keynes*, London and Paris, Rupert Hart-Davis, 1967.

By the multitude of thy merchandise they have filled the midst of
thee with violence, and thou hast sinned: therefore I will cast thee as
profane out of the mountain of God: and I will destroy thee, O covering cherub . . .

The story of the King of Tyre is clearly related to Blake's parable of
passing from Innocence to Experience: the King's original virtue is
corrupted and destroyed by material riches and the temptations
associated with Experience. In Blake's other writings there are references to the 'covering cherub', which represents what Blake called
the 'Selfhood', that selfish and greedy aspect of a person that
becomes hard and cruel with time.

Keynes's interpretation is persuasive, but as with the 'spiritual'
right foot, it is likely that Blake uses symbolism in a looser, less
directly allegorical way than Keynes proposes. If we look again at the
child's figure, we are left with more questions than answers. The
child has definitely become holy – an object of worship rather than
the free and natural spirit it was in *Innocence*; and this implies a negative move towards religion, and submission to oppressive, fixed
doctrine. On the other hand the child is young and naked, and so
contrasts with the many white-haired, white-bearded and robed old
men who visually represent religious oppression in *Songs of
Experience*. Is the man holding the child as a protection for himself,
or carrying the child towards experience?

It seems sensible to accept the reference to the 'covering cherub' in
general terms. This picture includes the dangers which come with
Experience, and the 'covering cherub' is an emblem of material
riches, greed, and the corruption they may bring. Its transformation
into a cherub with wings and halo also reminds us of religious laws,
which delude and oppress. We have already met the beginnings of
this theme in our analysis of the poems 'Introduction' and 'Earth's
Answer', where a tyrannical God makes his appearance, terrifying
Earth into submission, and punishing 'free Love' with 'bondage'.

Later in this study we will find that Blake was opposed to any
doctrine which divided the body (wicked) from the soul (good):
instead, he favours the idea of a whole person, body and soul
together and inseparable. In this case, then, the cherub may be

viewed as a warning of the dangers of Experience. As winged and haloed figure, it warns of the dangers of false spirituality; as 'covering cherub' it warns of the dangers of materialism.

So, the design as a whole can be summarised as a complex challenge to the reader. We are not spared the doubts, fears and risks which accompany the move from sweet Innocence to harsh Experience; yet the figure's courage and purpose, as he steps resolutely forward, are clear. At the same time, both man and child look directly at us, as if challenging us to join them on their frightening but resolute journey into the darker, more violent world we are about to meet in this collection of poems.

Figure Five: The 'Introduction' to *Songs of Experience*. Reproduced by permission of the Syndics of the Fitzwilliam Musuem, Cambridge.

The design for the 'Introduction' to *Experience* is a simpler affair. The poem appears engraved upon a large multiple cloud which occupies most of the plate, and is bordered by a deep indigo starry sky. A naked figure, probably female, reclines upon a scroll-like couch upon a smaller cloud at the bottom of the page, head turned to her right in profile and with her back to us. Commentators differ about her identity: she is either Earth, lying on her couch and resisting the Bard's call to her to 'return!'. Or she is the Bard himself who 'Present, Past & Future sees'. I incline to the first interpretation as the figure appears female. Looking back to our analysis of this poem and 'Earth's Answer', we concluded that Earth's perception of chains, a 'den' and imprisonment was false, produced by her fear. Therefore Blake's 'true' picture of her, upon a cloud in comfort and able to survey the sky and stars, as well as able to turn toward us if she will only realise that she can, expresses a truth implied but not put into words, in the poem. So, this design acts as an expansion of the poem's significance, and confirms the theme of Earth's delusions we developed in our analysis.

'Reading' the design, it is apparent from the constellations shown around the border, and from the slight yellowness glowing on Earth's cloud (and around her head in some copies), that it is early Winter and near 'break of day' as it says in the poem. The figure is looking West. This again underlines that Earth could turn, and look out of the plate, Eastward, towards a rising sun.

Finally, let us look at the design for 'Earth's Answer'. This again is one of Blake's simpler designs; yet again, the visual plate extends the meaning of the poem. The illustration consists of stems leading up the left and branching across between stanzas and over the top of the poem, to leaves and tendrils hanging down on the right. At the bottom a serpent crosses from left to right, its mouth open and forked tongue extended. A vine grows from the words 'father of' in stanza 2, leading to a bunch of dark purple grapes.

The serpent is a common symbol in Blake, and often represents the selfish lust male sexuality becomes when suppressed and frustrated by Holy Law. The grapes may be a natural fruit, a sign of natural regeneration with Spring and Summer, and the fruits of sexual love. They are out of reach, and the serpent – and Earth in

Figure Six: 'Earth's Answer' from *Songs of Experience*. Reproduced by permission of the Syndics of the Fitzwilliam Musuem, Cambridge.

the poem – are prevented from enjoying them by the 'selfish father of men': religious laws with their denial of natural energies. In this case, then, the serpent contributes to the significance of the poem. In the poem Earth, a female, laments her lack of fulfilment and that 'free Love' is 'with bondage bound'. If we see the serpent as perverted male lust, the design adds a masculine dimension to the denial of sexual love. So, this design can be seen as prefiguring the powerful poem about destructive sexuality, 'The Sick Rose', later in *Songs of Experience*.

Conclusions

We began this chapter with the aim of learning about *Innocence* and *Experience*, and Blake's teasing phrase 'the two contrary states of the human soul'. It will be helpful to summarise our progress before moving on to look at the natural world in Chapter 2.

When we first face *Innocence* and *Experience*, and try to grasp these two concepts, it is tempting to run to certain stock responses. There are a number of antithetical pairs of ideas which are common in our culture and background, and we are tempted to apply these to Blake's poems first. They include such paired ideas as ignorance and knowledge, illusion and disillusion, nature and society, optimism and pessimism, and good and evil. In this chapter, we have found that none of these conventional dualities fits what Blake has in mind. A short discussion will show how misleading they can be.

Optimism and pessimism. There is certainly something more positive in *Innocence*, and something negative in *Experience*. For example, the anticipation of pleasure in the Piper's songs which 'every child may joy to hear', and the security of the sheep who 'know that their Shepherd is nigh', point to trust in the future, in *Innocence*, which could be called optimism; while Earth's despair and her belief that she is unable to rise might be called pessimism. On the other hand, the limitations we discerned in *Innocence*, with its exclusion of change and its vague awareness of the coming night, are not optimistic; and Earth in the world of Experience does not expect the worst, like a conventional pessimist. Rather, she fears hope itself, while at the same time she knows that 'buds and blossoms grow'. When we bring into consideration **ignorance and knowledge** and **illusion and disillusion**, we find ourselves even more at a distance from what Blake portrays. Ignorance is not the right word to describe what we see in *Innocence*, where the child undergoes the extremes of emotion when he weeps 'with joy' to hear the Piper's songs, and the sheep are sensibly at peace because they 'know that their Shepherd is nigh'. Knowledge is even less accurate to describe the state of *Experience*. Earth will not 'arise' and is blindly covered with 'grey despair', while the Bard castigates her ignorance, asserting, contrary to her denial, that 'Night is worn, / And the morn / Rises'.

Clearly, the outlook of *Experience* is at least as ignorant as that of *Innocence*. In fact, both disillusion and our conventional assumption that 'experience' brings knowledge are portrayed as destructive illusions in the poems we have studied.

Blake re-orders our concepts in these opening poems, then. Many of the facile assumptions we make about gaining knowledge and experience, and growing up, simply do not fit his vision, and we are sent back to the poems to rethink our understanding of the 'contrary states' he has taken as his theme.

Our stock concept of a dichotomy between **nature** and **society** suffers a similar fate. Readers of these songs must never forget what happens in the 'Introduction' to *Songs of Innocence*: there is a clear distinction between the 'valleys wild' and 'songs of merry glee' at the start of the poem, and the 'rural' pen and 'stained' water near its end. A long pastoral tradition provokes us to associate sheep, meadows, woods and shepherds with nature; and pastoral contrasts with the world of courts, palaces and sophistication as well as cities and industries. Many of Blake's poems feed this assumption by contrasting rural and urban settings. However, it would be wrong to confuse Blake's pastoral with nature itself. Nature is 'wild' and its emotion belongs to the present moment only, like the Piper's 'merry glee' expressed through his songs. The pastoral world of Shepherd and sheep is in contrast to this, supervised, protected and tamed.

The more we think about *Innocence* and *Experience*, the more we are struck by the similarities between these two states rather than their differences. Both of the worlds Blake presents are societies: supervision and authority exist in both of them, in the persons of the Shepherd (*Innocence*), and the 'jealous selfish father of men' (*Experience*). Both worlds also have a population – the flock of sheep in *Innocence* and Earth herself in *Experience*. In our analyses we have found that the relationship between authority and the individual is fraught and ambiguous in both worlds, and both depend to some extent on fear, which supports dependence and illusion.

At this point we can return to some plain commonsense: are there really two separate, symmetrically opposed worlds around us? Of course not – we share only the one world in which we live. This is a timely reminder, as it points firmly towards the insight that Blake's two 'contrary states' are not different worlds at all, but only different perceptions of the same world. Somewhere there is an objective reality, but truth can only be perceived through a 'state of the soul', and different or contrary 'states of the soul' can only see different truths.

Applying this insight to the figure of authority, we can suggest that the gentle caring Shepherd of Innocence and the cruel punishing tyrant of Experience are one and the same: the difference between them is entirely a matter of how they are perceived. The Innocent are grateful for what they see as benevolent loving care. They willingly obey their shepherd's commands because they believe that he has their well-being at heart. The Experienced believe that their tyrant enslaves and imprisons them, that his laws are cruel and selfish, and that his power deprives them of freedom and happiness.

The idea that the two contrary states of Innocence and Experience are only different perceptions of the same world focuses our attention on the differing visions of Piper and Bard. These two figures, and the relationship between their two visions of the world, are complex and difficult to define. For the present time, we can only begin to interpret their roles by noticing – as with the contrary states themselves – that they have elements in common. Both Piper and Bard share the perceptions of the 'state' in which they exist. The Piper clearly shares feelings of 'glee' and 'joy' with the innocent world surrounding him, finds the Shepherd's life 'sweet' and full of 'praise' while the flock is innocent and tender. Similarly, the Bard shares *Experience*'s perception: he hears the 'Holy Word', feels the power of the 'starry pole' and recognises the need to renew 'fallen fallen light'. We should also notice, however, that both Piper and Bard are capable of a wider vision than the limits of either *Innocence* or *Experience* would allow. The Piper begins by expressing the wild pleasure of untamed nature in music, so his imagination is capable of a freedom unknown to the protected world of *Innocence*. The Bard sees 'Present, Past, & Future', and his imagination is capable of a more prophetic range than that of Earth, who lives within the state of *Experience*. The Bard can see that 'morn / Rises from the slumberous mass'. He is aware of a coming 'break of day' while Earth herself sees only a continuing night.

The functions of the two poetic figures differ, however. The Piper composes and then writes songs which will give 'joy' to children living in the protected world of *Innocence*; the Bard calls impatiently for Earth to throw off her chains and arise. Which poetic role is appropriate depends on which version of 'truth' is perceived. If the world is protected by a benevolent Shepherd, then the poet celebrates with songs of 'joy'. If, on the other hand, the world is cruelly imprisoned and mercilessly punished by a selfish, jealous God, then the poet must become an agent of rebellion with a vision of freedom and a call to Earth to rise and throw off her chains. The poet's role, then, is either to celebrate joy, or as a revolutionary prophet, depending what the 'truth' is that is perceived in such different ways. The effect is to focus our attention on the crucial question: what is the 'truth'? In this chapter, we have found limitation and distortion in both perceptions – *Innocence* and *Experience* – and we already guess that truth and its perception will be a complex theme in Blake's poetry.

At the same time, we have begun to appreciate that the symbolic figures in Blake's poetry need to be understood as symbols rather than as people. They do not act conventionally as characters in a story. The kindly Shepherd, seen through different eyes, can turn into a vicious old tyrant, and vice versa; the carefree Piper can turn into the prophetic Bard. As we continue to study, and meet more of the symbolic figures of Blake's imagination, it will be important to remember that they represent states and perceptions, not permanent deities, but attitudes, beliefs and desires which can change into each other with a change of mood or viewpoint, with bewildering speed.

Methods of Analysis

In this chapter we have used a standard approach to the analysis of poetry. Our attention focused on the following:

1. The general sense, circumstances or 'story' in the poem. In the *Songs of Innocence and Experience* this is often clear on a first reading; but some poems present less of an obvious 'story',

demanding some interpretation even at first. It is worthwhile to think about the whole poem as soon as you have read it. Try to formulate simple statements about it, which give a general idea of what it is about. For example, looking at 'The Shepherd' in *Innocence*, we quickly came to the conclusion that 'The dependent and caring inter-relationship of shepherd and sheep seems idyllic'.

2. The metre of the poem. Analysing patterns of rhythm, we have concentrated on:

   [i] describing the predominant metre or metres, and the overall effect on the poem.

   [ii] noticing where the metre is irregular, then relating this to the meaning. We seek to explain why Blake altered the poem's pattern at that point.

3. Diction. We have looked at the 'diction' of poems as a way of adding to our understanding of the way Blake uses sound and language. This has included thinking about the length and kind of sound a word makes, and the tone or 'attitude' of the language, as well as simpler effects such as alliteration. We have approached 'diction' flexibly, then, ready to notice anything about the language used; so, for example, we noticed the *absence* of the word 'urban' from the poem 'Introduction' in *Innocence*.

4. Imagery, both of actual objects which are part of the narrative, and in figurative references which add a figurative idea to the experiential pattern of the poem. In the *Songs of Innocence and Experience* we have found that many elements of the poems prompt us to interpret them – they are natural, literal things like the Piper's valleys 'wild' and his 'rural' pen made out of a hollow reed, but we are provoked to add significant meaning to them because of the context (so we contrasted 'wild' with 'rural' and thought of the development of a society) or because they are common symbols which carry overtones of extra meaning in themselves (such as the 'buds and blossoms' and 'heavy chain' Earth refers to in 'Earth's Answer').

5. In particular, we have paid interpretative attention to landscape or setting, animals, and the roles of emblematic figures such as Piper, Bard / Prophet, Shepherd and so on. The roles and quali-

ties of various figures in Blake's poetry will deepen and fill out as we continue to study, developing into the complex emblematic figures we will meet in the Prophetic Books, and we will further investigate the role of setting and animals in the next chapter. This amounts to observing *the way in which the poem is written* very closely, and involves an open-minded, detailed scrutiny. As you become more practised and experienced, your approach to a poem will become less dependent upon looking at 'compartments' such as 'diction' or 'metre' in turn, and will become faster and smoother. You will naturally appreciate how and what each element contributes to the whole, and that they are ultimately inseparable from the poem itself. Also, it is important to remain receptive to anything you notice in what you read: whatever you *notice* about the writing is of interest, because it must be *noticeable*, i.e. a feature of the style. Describe the feature and its effect as accurately as you can.

6. The designs. We have looked at the designs of Blake's plates. We found that:

[i] the designs often reflect and support interpretation of the poem, and sometimes add to that interpretation.

[ii] Blake will sometimes add a contrasting image to the design which highlights an element which appears as an implication of the poem, so that the design brings out and complements the 'subtext' of the writing rather than its more overt primary meaning.

Suggested Work

At this stage it will be helpful to carry on with the investigation we have begun in this chapter, building up further understanding of Blake's concepts *Innocence* and *Experience*. Follow the same method we have used on the opening poems of each collection, but choose a 'group' of poems to look at in detail.

In *Songs of Innocence*, look at 'The Ecchoing Green' and 'Nurse's Song'. In the first of these poems the subtle modulations of metre, rhyme, diction and subject-matter imply a more disturbing picture than the explicit calm of the surface 'story', which is typically restrained within the world of *Innocence*, would suggest. Look at the designs (this poem extends over two plates and has three distinct pictures); consider in particular the incompatible dual activities of white-haired, protective age and grape-eating youth on the second plate and the progress of the children from naked to clothed in all three pictures, as well as the kind of clothing they wear.

A detailed study of this poem will add to your appreciation of the subtle undercurrents, what we can call the 'implications' or 'subtext' Blake creates within the apparently restricted world of *Innocence*. This contributes to the impression that, within the simple apparent form of these poems, other shapes, processes and forms are living and developing unseen. Turning from this to 'Nurse's Song' we find a dramatisation of the conflict between anxious adults and playing children, as the end of the day draws near. In this poem, the theme of fear is further developed and there are some subtle, ominous touches which will refine your responsiveness to sounds and rhythms. For example, attempt to describe the effect of the final word.

In *Songs of Experience*, a 'contrary' poem to 'The Ecchoing Green' and 'Nurse's Song' is 'NURSES Song'. Here, the speaker is a nurse caring for children who play on a green. The time is the same as at the end of 'The Ecchoing Green' and the 'Nurse's Song' of *Innocence*. This is a short poem, so you will be able to make a close and very detailed comparison between its treatment of the adult's perspective, and the view of adults ('old folk' and 'mothers' as well as the nurse) in the poems from *Innocence*. You may also find it rewarding to consider how Blake renders the same metre differently in all three poems.

Making a detailed study of these poems will also develop your sense of the inter-relatedness of 'groups' of poems within these two collections. In the next chapter we will be studying a group of poems about lost and found children, for example. We will look at four of them in detail, but there are a further two in *Experience* that we will not have the space to analyse. The three poems suggested for study here are all about adults watching children play, but they are not the whole group (which might include 'The Garden of Love' as well), while the motif of childhood play spreads into a much more socially-concerned 'pair' of poems such as the two entitled 'The Chimney Sweeper'; and these can arguably belong in a 'group' with the two poems – one in each collection – called 'Holy Thursday'.

2

Nature in *Innocence* and *Experience*

Nature in the *Songs* is more complicated than a simple contrast between country and town, as we noticed in Chapter 1. In particular, we noticed that wild nature disappears halfway through the first poem in *Songs of Innocence*. This means that the world or outlook of Innocence is not 'wild' at all: it is a limited rural part of nature in which vulnerable creatures such as children and lambs are kept safe and at peace. We also moved beyond the idea that Innocence and Experience represent a story of before and after, and suggested that they are contrary perceptions of the same world. We therefore begin this chapter, an exploration of the nature theme in the *Songs*, with the understanding that Blake is exploring an ambiguous reality, different perceptions of truth. Looking at nature will lead us toward Blake's concern with 'vision', or ways of seeing, both in the *Songs* and elsewhere.

We also know that Blake's poems provoke us to interpret, and that our interpretations often work on different levels at the same time. So, for example, Earth in the poem 'Earth's Answer' exemplifies a difficulty on both personal and social levels. The poem explores a psychological problem, where the character is depressed and her vision of reality is distorted by fear. At the same time, the poem makes a social comment: a whole population is terrified into submission; people are unable to challenge the status quo or assert their right to freedom, because a tyrannical, authoritarian law is all they know or can imagine.

This chapter's discussion of the nature theme is complicated by the two factors discussed above. First, we must allow for the fact that perceptions are constantly shifting in these poems. So we will be asking: how is nature perceived here? And, what truth about nature lies behind this perception? Secondly, we will examine the relationship between mankind and nature that Blake presents; but we must remain aware that this relationship is developed in both personal and social contexts, at the same time, in the poems. We begin with a close examination of the poem 'Night' from *Songs of Innocence*.

'Night'

The sun descending in the west,
The evening star does shine,
The birds are silent in their nest,
And I must seek for mine,
The moon like a flower,
In heavens high bower;
With silent delight,
Sits and smiles on the night.

Farewell green fields and happy groves,
Where flocks have took delight;
Where lambs have nibbled, silent moves
The feet of angels bright;
Unseen they pour blessing,
And joy without ceasing,
On each bud and blossom,
And each sleeping bosom.

They look in every thoughtless nest,
Where birds are coverd warm;
They visit caves of every beast,
To keep them all from harm:
If they see any weeping,
That should have been sleeping
They pour sleep on their head
And sit down by their bed.

When wolves and tygers howl for prey
They pitying stand and weep;
Seeking to drive their thirst away,
And keep them from the sheep,
But if they rush dreadful;
The angels most heedful,
Receive each mild spirit,
New worlds to inherit.

And there the lions ruddy eyes,
Shall flow with tears of gold:
And pitying the tender cries,
And walking round the fold:
Saying: wrath by his meekness
And by his health, sickness,
Is driven away,
From our immortal day.

And now beside thee bleating lamb,
I can lie down and sleep;
Or think on him who bore thy name,
Grase after thee and weep.
For wash'd in lifes river,
My bright mane for ever,
Shall shine like the gold,
As I guard o'er the fold.

(K2, 20–21)

Begin by looking at the metre. We notice very few irregularities in this poem, apart from grace syllables added or omitted in a way which does not interrupt the metrical flow (for example the dactyllic lines can begin with one or two unstressed syllables, as in 'With **silent** de**light**' and 'sits and **smiles** on the **night**'; while the same lines can end on stressed syllables, such as '**night**' and 'de**light**', or end on a falling cadence into an unstressed syllable, as in a '**flower**' and '**bower**', in the first stanza). These are variations rather than irregularities, and the poem as a whole flows steadily and rhythmically from beginning to end. This steadiness emphasises the few real irregularities there are. In line 23, the stress is extended over two syllables as the angels '**pour sleep**' on the heads of restless and fearful creatures. This lengthens and slows the line, conveying the soothing effect of sleep. In line 27, the first foot of the line is reversed in '**seeking**', and this surprise emphasis seems to highlight the angels' effort to drive away the cause of the beasts' cruelty, their 'thirst'. Line 40 is irregular, being iambic in a dactyllic quatrain. This brings a more regular beat, and therefore a sense of inevitability, to '**our im**mor**tal day**'. Finally, in line 46, the words '**bright mane**' extend the stress in the same way as happened with 'pour sleep'. On this occasion, however, the effect seems invigorating rather than relaxing, due to the sense and perhaps also the tight and pure vowels of the two words.

The irregularities we have noticed all have slight effects, however. They are further evidence that Blake was a master of metrical variation, but they do not have nearly as powerful an influence on the reader as the harmony Blake achieves by alternating iambic and dactyllic quatrains throughout the poem. Somehow, both the heavier beat of iambs and the delicate lilt of dactyls are highlighted by being set off against each other. It is difficult to describe the aesthetic satisfaction this provides. For the moment we can remark that the alternation of heavier and lighter rhythms is particularly suitable to a poem where the world of innocence, a pastoral idyll of 'green fields and happy groves', confronts darkness, violence and death.

As with most of the poems in *Songs of Innocence*, the story of this poem is easy to follow, even if we are surprised by the roles ascribed to angels and lions. In the first stanza evening turns into night, and this event immediately reminds us that Innocence is associated with morning and day; that the protective Shepherd is there 'all day' and 'to the evening'. Therefore, the approach of evening is an anxious and ambiguous time in the *Songs of Innocence*. The sense of day ending, and the need to seek shelter and rest at night, is strong in the first four lines. The birds 'silent' and the descending sun set the mood for the poet of *Innocence* to admit that he, too, needs to find a 'nest' in which he can shelter. By implication, his voice will also cease at the end of the day. A new movement begins, however, with moonrise. The simple simile 'like a flower' brings a complex effect: the moon normally drains colour, yet 'flower' associates with vivid colours. The benevolent happiness of the night is present in 'delight' and 'smiles', and the idea of 'nest', a place of peace and safety, is echoed as the moon sits in 'heavens high *bower*' (my italics).

The second stanza opens by saying goodbye to the world of *Innocence*: the pastoral landscape where 'flocks have took delight'. All seems set for the coming of a night of 'experience', and the arrival of danger, as time and life move on. Again, however, the second part of the stanza introduces an unexpectedly positive vision of the night. Just as the moon 'smiles' in stanza 1, so angels enter stanza 2, pouring 'blessing, / And joy without ceasing' onto the delicate and vulnerable, 'each bud and blossom'.

Stanza 3 follows the angels on their rounds. Nests are 'thoughtless' in the senses that they are both without worry, and ignorant of danger. The angels appear warm and caring; but we should notice that Blake is characteristically accurate about what they do. They 'look in' the birds' nests, 'visit' the beasts; and their only effective action is against fear and sorrow – represented by those 'weeping' – because the angels can soothe these emotions and induce sleep. The angels do all this 'To keep them all from harm'; but their actions are limited to watching, and influencing the creatures' mood: they do not intervene in any actual event.

The fourth stanza goes into more detail of the angels' role: again, we find them static, and focusing their efforts on relieving mood and emotion. They 'pitying stand and weep', and their strategy for protecting sheep from ravening wolves and tygers is 'Seeking to drive their thirst away'. Their pity is given to the wild wolves and tygers, and the 'thirst' they try to destroy is the bloodlust of animals of prey. Throughout, the angels are 'most heedful' in their watching and caring role; so, when wild beasts follow the ordinary dictates of nature, and 'rush dreadful', killing lambs and sheep, the angels are on hand to receive the spirits of these slaughtered innocents and transport them into 'New worlds'. On the other hand, the angels do not prevent the slaughter which takes place.

The final two stanzas describe the 'New worlds' that follow death. The poem increasingly focuses on the lion, who begins this section crying 'tears of gold', and speaks the whole of the last stanza. Pity is the crucial word: the wild beast, previously pitied for his hunger by the angels, can now pity his prey and be transformed from predator into guardian 'As I guard o'er the fold'. To underline the Christian message, the lion says that 'wrath by his meekness' (that is, the meekness of Christ) is 'driven away'. The concept of Christ's 'meekness' has been exemplified by the angels, who did not intervene or act, but pitied the wild beast for his savage instincts. The transformation of the lion is emphasised by bright light and two similes, likening his tears and his mane to 'gold'. Supporting this brightening phase of the poem, the lion is 'wash'd', and night is left in the natural world, so that all exist in 'our immortal day'.

We should notice what Blake has done in this rhythmically beautiful poem. The world of *Innocence* has passed beyond its limits into the night, saying goodbye to its pastoral idyll on the way; then, night has been banished and we end the poem in the glory of a new, and eternal, day. On the other hand, 'night' has not been mitigated in any way. The innocents have been slaughtered, ravaged by beasts of prey made savage by their hunger. The passing away of youth, life and peace as the sun descends is inevitable; and death is inevitable, too, no matter how much pity the angels lavish on the whole process. At the same time, the poem's outlook remains uncompromisingly that of the poet of *Innocence*. The vision presented is of the power of the Lamb, with resurrection into a cleansed and loving afterlife; and this permeates the poem. Not only is this vision treated as a matter of fact (in contrast, say, to the social blackmail implicit in 'The Chimney Sweeper' of *Innocence*, and the hypocrisy apparent in 'The Chimney Sweeper' of *Experience*, where the establishment 'make up a heaven of our misery'); it also transforms the perception of night into a positive image presided over by a flower-like moon which 'smiles' in 'delight'. The whole poem, in fact, is a consistent expression of trust and faith that love can overpower all obstacles and turn all disasters to good:

> But if they rush dreadful;
> The angels most heedful,

This poem, then, presents a particular vision, a particular perception which is carried through to the imagined heaven where the lion says:

'now beside thee bleating lamb, / I can lie down and sleep'. Blake includes one reminder that 'Night' represents an 'Innocent' perception of death and the afterlife: the poet's own statement that he must now 'seek' his own nest where he can sleep. Within the pattern of the poem, this aligns him with the birds in their 'thoughtless' nests, and reminds us that the Piper and the Bard provide contrary visions of which this is only one. It is possible to interpret the Piper's remark about his need for a 'nest' further: we could say that the vision and belief expressed by the final stanzas *is* a nest for the Piper. It is a belief which enables him to sleep. It promises a final victory of love, after death. This faith soothes, and helps him to suffer and dismiss the dangers of the night.

'Night' is filled with references to biblical prophecies. In particular, there are echoes of Isaiah, and references to Revelation, the allegorical prophecy of the end of the world, which is the last book of the New Testament. 'Wash'd in life's river' refers to the river of life described at the start of Revelation 22:

> And he shewed me a pure river of water of life, clear as crystal, proceeding out of the throne of God and of the Lamb. In the midst of the street of it, and on either side of the river, was there the tree of life, which bare twelve manner of fruits, and yielded her fruit every month: and the leaves of the tree were for the healing of the nations . . . And there shall be no night there; and they need no candle, neither light of the sun; for the Lord God giveth them light: and they shall reign for ever and ever.
>
> (Revelation, 22, 1, 2 and 5)

This 'river of life' is a reiteration of a prophecy from Ezekiel 47; but for our purposes in understanding Blake's 'Night', it is the broader correspondences between the poem and Revelation that are enlightening. First, the 'immortal day' of the poem corresponds to the light of God which shines to light the 'new heaven' (Revelation 21, 1) inherited by the saved, just as Blake's 'mild spirit[s]' are gathered by the angels, 'New worlds to inherit'. In the poem, however, there is a difference, as light seems to shine from the lion's mane after it has been 'wash'd in lifes river', rather than from God – and it is the lion himself rather than God who will eternally 'guard o'er the fold'.

What has happened to the lion to transform him? He has changed from a savage beast of prey which obeys cruel natural laws, and will 'rush dreadful' to slaughter the innocent, into the guardian and giver of light – the role of God himself – in heaven. The poem hints symbolically at the transformation. The lion's eyes were 'ruddy', suggesting a bloodthirsty nature, but the colour changes when they 'flow with tears of gold' after the death of the innocent. From then onwards 'gold' is the lion's colour. Blake suggests that a changed vision is responsible, and the bold hint of this poem identifies the beast of prey with God. What happens in this poem, then, is that God sees the innocent through different eyes (through the 'tears of gold' of 'pitying') and at the same time we are brought to see God through different eyes. Blake suggests that, where once we feared God as a destroyer, the revelation of a new vision shows us the lion / God in a new aspect, as light and protector.

The mood of the lion in the final stanza is also a surprise. It is clear that he is relieved of a burden – the natural instinct to 'howl for prey' which is his 'thirst' in nature. He rejoices that 'now' he 'can' lie next to the lamb, without being driven to kill. The change is attributed to Christ, whose meekness has driven away wrath, and whose bloody sacrifice has inspired the lion's pity and regret ('think on him who bore thy name, / Grase after thee and weep'). That the 'river of life' is associated with the blood of the Lamb is also the case in Revelation. The daring implication of Blake's poem, however, is that Christ's blood not only redeems the world: it also redeems God himself. God, Blake implies, was in great need of redemption. He was a savage, bloodthirsty beast of 'wrath', seemingly incapable of the vision that could save Him.

The whole of this poem turns on a question of perceptions. There are several different 'visions' involved, and a list of those we have found is a helpful way to clear the mind:

1. The poet of *Innocence* (the Piper) reaches his limit as night falls. Notice that the Piper tells of the angels' care in the present tense, but of 'new worlds' in the future.
2. The lion's 'ruddy' eyes are blinded by bloodlust, and see only prey.

3. The lion's eyes washed by 'tears of gold' see with pity and grief ('weep').
4. The birds see nothing – they are 'thoughtless' in their nests.
5. The moon sees the night, and 'smiles' on it.

As a whole, 'Night' presents us with ambiguity, not answers. It is left up to us to choose our belief from the different perspectives available, or to accept them all. The poem presents a natural world, the 'here' of evening and night, where the innocent are heedless victims of savage predators. The angels of 'here' are utterly ineffectual, and when night comes there is widespread slaughter. We are left to choose whether to accept the Piper's 'innocent' vision of 'there', the future 'shall' of the final two stanzas, where night, death and wrath are conquered by love. Blake's bold link between these worlds – the lion – undermines both perceptions. Are natural eyes blinded by fear, unable to see the lion's 'truth'? Or is a loving lion the stuff of fantasy, a delusion created to reassure the fearful?

'Night' gives us no further direction to guide our beliefs: it simply presents us with the conundrum of faith in a complex form. However, we should also notice the strictness of Blake's creation, which keeps it within the limits of *Innocence*: the natural world, and death, are presented without mitigation, and the 'vision' of heaven is placed firmly in a future and other world by tense. We will meet other variants of this 'innocent' vision as we continue to study, each providing a new – and slightly different – window onto the conundrum. 'The Chimney Sweeper' in *Innocence*, for example, gives our response more direction than 'Night'; but as we will see in the next chapter, this makes the reader's dilemma different without making it any easier.

The poem we have studied from *Innocence*, then, treats death ambivalently: there is an uncompromising picture of nature, and no angel or saviour intervenes before the beasts of prey 'rush dreadful'. This is followed by a vision of redemption in another world, in an unspecified future, where gentleness, tears and love are triumphant.

'The Fly'

In *Experience*, death is the clear theme of 'The Fly':

> Little Fly
> Thy summers play,
> My thoughtless hand
> Has brush'd away.
>
> Am not I
> A fly like thee?
> Or art not thou
> A man like me?
>
> For I dance
> And drink & sing:
> Till some blind hand
> Shall brush my wing.
>
> If thought is life
> And strength & breath:
> And the want
> Of thought is death;
>
> Then am I
> A happy fly,
> If I live,
> Or if I die.

(K2, 40)

Metrically, this poem is very simple. It is written in four-syllable lines, two iambs per line, and some of the lines assume the first unstressed syllable, being reduced to three syllables (such as '**Am** not I', and '**Then** am I'). The short lines imitate the momentary dashes of a fly's flight, and the very smallness of the language (many of the words are only one, two or three letters long) calls to mind the little insect of the title. In addition, the movement of thought in the poem is in quick bursts, with sudden changes of direction, like the flight and life of a fly. For example, look at the reversals of thought

between 'A fly like thee' and 'A man like me'; and between 'If I live /
Or if I die'.

'The Fly' is not only a brilliant imitation of tiny zipping flight in
words and form, however. Some of the sudden movements of
thought are deaths: 'brush'd away', 'brush my wing', 'the want / Of
thought is death' and 'if I die' all represent the suddenness with
which life will end. So, in this small poem, there are four moments
of extinction. Each of these is held back to the final line of the
stanza, so each one has an added quickness and finality.

The theme of the poem is death. The poet kills a fly in the first
stanza, then develops symmetrical thoughts on the subject. First, he
compares himself to a fly (death will 'brush' him away as thought-
lessly as he did the fly); and to balance this, he compares the fly to
himself (the fly is an individual being, as precious as a man). This
reasoning is quite easy to follow, but in the fourth and fifth stanza
the poet sets up a chain of logic which – despite its simplicity of
expression – is far from easy.

Blake proposes that 'thought is life', and he then follows this idea
to its conclusion. First, if 'thought is life', then to balance that the
opposite is also true: thoughtlessness is 'death'. What follows? Blake
then inverts the proposition, as it were (i.e. 'life is thought' and
'death is without thought'). This gives him the basis for his assertion
'Then am I / A happy fly' because living and thinking is a happy
state, and if there is no thought in death, it is a mere vacuum, so
there is no reason for unhappiness in death either. This sounds satis-
fyingly logical and has a pleasingly symmetrical intellectual appeal.

The form of this poem reminds us of such *Songs of Innocence* as
'Infant Joy' or 'Spring', and the final stanza's 'Then am I / A happy
fly' may beguile us into thinking that this song really belongs with
the cheerfulness of the contrary collection. This is a deceptive
impression, however.

There are subtle indications that the truth is less simple than this
poem's speaker proposes. First, the word 'thought' is ironic because
the speaker himself, while still alive, has 'thoughtless' killed the fly.
So the statement 'the want / Of thought is death', with reference to
the start of the poem, has a secondary meaning: the want of thought
may *cause* a death, but not necessarily the death of the thoughtless!

Indeed, the word 'blind' in the third stanza must stand for thought-lessness, and in that context death itself is described as carelessly destructive. In the same event, the poet unashamedly admits to living without thought of death: 'For I dance / And drink & sing: / Till . . .'. So, the concept of thoughtlessness has several branches, each more morally dubious than the simple absence of mental activity that justifies the speaker's conclusion.

Secondly, we question the logical 'If . . . Then' structure of the final two stanzas, because the speaker's logic relies on inverting the proposition. We should all be familiar with the fallacies this can lead to, as statements have a habit of being true only one way around. Look, for example, at the two propositions (1) 'it is the sea, *therefore* it is wet', and (2) 'it is wet, *therefore* it is the sea'. The effect is that the apparently neat thought of the poem becomes increasingly spurious the more we think about it. The beautiful form of 'The Fly' is intentionally brittle, and its subtext reveals more questions than the speaker would like. This leads us to take a critical attitude towards the speaker, and ask:

What has the poem's speaker done? He has killed a harmless fly, cruelly and carelessly. Then, he has proved to himself that the fly, although dead, is happy. This is very convenient for the speaker: if we look at this poem's utterance psychologically, the speaker is a crass, happy killer, who rationalises to deny his guilt.

What has the speaker not done? He has not felt any remorse for killing the fly. His 'thought' – such as it is – is an exercise in dry logic, and its purpose seems to be to divert his mind away from moral responsibility. Is this kind of 'thought' the same as 'life'?

Finally, we begin to notice the chilling conclusion of the poem. It does not matter whether you are alive or dead. In either state you are 'happy', but this happiness consists of a merely stupid senselessness in life, where the character kills and dances and drinks and sings; and an actual senselessness in death. So, the claim 'happy' is hollow. What the poem's speaker actually proves is that there is equally no point in living or dying because both are equally stupid. It is in the chilling 'thoughtlessness' of such logic that we discern the limited and destructive viewpoint of *Experience*.

The outcome of Blake's use of a brittle, vulnerable viewpoint in

'The Fly' is not that we are impressed by futility in life and death. Instead, we are impressed by the poverty of the speaker's view, which renders his own life and death futile in his own eyes. Remember the obstinate despair of Earth, refusing to see that 'the morn / Rises from the slumberous mass', and refusing to turn towards the light despite the Bard's call. The speaker of 'The Fly' is another figure imprisoned by his own limited perceptions. Life is not futile, but he creates his own futility and maintains it with all his mental energy.

Another poem which develops a theme of the waste of life is 'The Angel':

'The Angel'

> I dreamt a Dream! what can it mean?
> And that I was a maiden Queen:
> Guarded by an Angel mild:
> Witless woe, was neer beguil'd!
>
> And I wept both night and day
> And he wip'd my tears away
> And I wept both day and night
> And hid from him my hearts delight
>
> So he took his wings and fled:
> Then the morn blush'd rosy red:
> I dried my tears & armd my fears,
> With ten thousand shields and spears.
>
> Soon my Angel came again:
> I was arm'd, he came in vain:
> For the time of youth was fled
> And grey hairs were on my head

(K2, 41)

Blake interchanges trochaic and iambic lines in this poem, but the effect is of an even and predictable rhythm, enhanced by the perfect rhyming couplets that we find throughout. There are two places where the metre is irregular, and in both cases Blake extends the stress over two syllables (spondee), creating extra weight, and slowing the poem. These two moments emphasise first, the defensive armaments of the speaker ('With **ten thou**sand . . .') and second, the heavy passage of time into old age ('And **grey hairs** were . . .').

What is the story of this poem? Unlike the two we have looked at in this chapter so far, this one presents a narrative that does not explain itself straight away. It seems that the speaker is (in a dream) a maiden queen tended by an angel. There is much weeping and fear, the angel goes away and comes back again, but the queen has grown old. As with the 'Introduction' to *Experience*, we sense significance on a first reading, but we have to look more closely to find out why the poem's events occur. In this situation, it is helpful to build a picture of the character: this will give us a psychological insight into the story.

The figure of the 'maiden Queen' follows a clear psychological progress in the poem. She begins by weeping 'night and day', and continues to weep 'day and night'. However, we know that her grief is a pretence as she tells us that she 'hid' her 'hearts delight'. When the angel leaves she stops weeping ('dried my tears'). At this point she feels vulnerable, and consequently she changes her approach to life. Now she is scared, so she 'armd' her fears with shields and spears. We noticed in Chapter 1 that fear is at the root of much evil in the *Songs*, and this poem is no exception. Clearly, the 'maiden Queen' becomes a hostile and defensive personality, hypocritically hard and protected within an insensitive shell. When the angel returns, the line 'I was arm'd, he came in vain' tells us clearly that her heart could not be touched, and she rejected the angel's advances. The poem finally tells us that she grew old in this futile rejection.

The maiden's story, then, is a tale of distorted emotions. Her constant weeping is an appeal for attention, and the angel responds by comforting her ('And he wip'd my tears away'). This is the attention she seeks, and she hides from him the secret satisfaction she gains by making him a slave to her emotional demands. Instead, she persists in weeping until, in the end, he 'fled'. This word implies more than the angel leaving: it suggests that he has to run away from her possessiveness, that he escapes.

In the second phase of her existence, the maiden distorts her emotions in a different way. This time, instead of appealing for attention, she becomes cold and hostile in order to defend the hidden fact that she has been hurt. In both phases, her dishonesty about herself has prevented her from forming a relationship. The sad futility of her life is conveyed at the end of the poem, when Blake underlines the reality of natural boundaries. The 'dream' of being a 'Queen', and having a guardian 'Angel' suddenly vanishes like the self-centred fantasy it was all along. A harsh natural reality underscores that she has wasted her natural life:

> For the time of youth was fled
> And grey hairs were on my head

Blake's targets in this poem are repression, denial, possessiveness, defensive fears, and all the distortions and unnatural lies they lead to. The sense of loss and waste in the final couplet suddenly shifts the viewpoint, and acts like a sudden painful realisation as the maiden wakes up from the false 'dream' in which she has lived, to face her old age.

Yet again, Blake focuses on false perceptions. As we build our understanding of nature as a theme in the *Songs*, we realise that nature is an uncompromising constant behind the shifting perspectives of each poem. So, danger and death are certainties in 'Night', despite the angels' pity; death is a certainty in 'The Fly', whether you are aware or 'thoughtless' in your life; time and old age are certainties in 'The Angel', whatever fantasy you sustain while wasting your life. Nature, then, is beginning to emerge as a dour and constant theme, and the various poems play upon the variety of visions and dreams through which people attempt to view, or distort, its reality.

'The Little Boy Lost' and 'The Little Boy Found'

Our next group of poems focuses on mysteries, dangers and the deceptive appearance of nature. They are the 'lost' and 'found' poems, and we begin by looking at the two from the *Songs of*

Innocence. We will take these two poems together as they clearly tell one story, the second being a sequel to the first:

'The Little Boy Lost'

Father, father, where are you going
O do not walk so fast.
Speak father, speak to your little boy
Or else I shall be lost,

The night was dark no father was there
The child was wet with dew.
The mire was deep, & the child did weep
And away the vapour flew.

'The Little Boy Found'

The little boy lost in the lonely fen,
Led by the wand'ring light,
Began to cry, but God ever nigh,
Appeard like his father in white.

He kissed the child & by the hand led
And to his mother brought,
Who in sorrow pale, thro' the lonely dale
Her little boy weeping sought.

(K2, 13 and 14)

The apparent simplicity of these poems, with their easy rhythm and clear rhyme, each poem a mere two quatrains, is an impression created by Blake from some quite complex alternations between iambic and dactyllic metres. The rapidity of two adjacent unstressed syllables in dactyllic parts of the poem (e.g. 'The **little** boy **lost** in the') gives an added effect to subsequent iambs. This works on the reader's expectations while reading: we expect two adjacent unstressed syllables in between each stress. To put this in audible terms: if we hear the rhythm as 'di-**dum**-diddy-**dum**-diddy . . . etc.', this sets up our expectation that we will find a 'diddy' after each 'dum'. When we don't find what we expect, we make an automatic adjustment: we add to the stress in order to make up for the missing syllable we were expecting. In this way, the stressed syllable in iambic feet is made to hang and ring out longer than it otherwise would. Blake uses this effect to give an extra, mournful resonance to some of the sounds and words in the poems. In particular, look at the second 'speak' in line 3 of 'The Little Boy Lost', which adds sound value, and therefore desperation, to the child's plaintive cry; in 'The Little Boy Found' look at the mournful ringing sound of '**lonely fen**', and the accent on the mother's distress and a bleak setting in line 7: 'Who in **sorrow pale**, thro' the **lonely dale**'.

The content of these poems is relatively straightforward. A little boy follows a 'vapour' – an illusion of his father, a will o' the wisp which leads him astray. The poem places the child outside the world of *Innocence*, categorically telling us that 'no father was there' and 'the night was dark', so he has entered the night of *Experience*; and that he was 'wet with dew', commonly a symbol of being stained by the materialism of *Experience*. In this poem, a false illusion of paternal care has misled the child, and leaves him in lonely misery. This is an uncompromising poem, telling a story of cruel deception by the 'vapour'; and there are no pitying angels here, as there are in 'Night', to soothe the child's distress.

The sense of a situation on the brink of disaster is intensified by the design above the poem. Two heavy trees are on the right; in the middle, a child, with his arms outstretched, runs towards the left of the plate where a lurid, star-shaped yellow light with a rather grotesque, sharp white lingua at its centre, represents the false 'vapour' or will o' the wisp rushing away off the plate. The whole design is set at a descending angle, so that the trees push the child, and the child is apparently about to topple over, running on a downward slope.

Blake chose to set the sequel as a separate poem, and in doing so he emphasises the altered perception. In the second poem, God appears and reunites the boy and his mother, so all is made right in the end. However, there are two elements in the second poem which cast doubt on the happy ending. First, Blake carefully inserts the simile that God appeared 'like his father in white'. We notice that there is still no actual father in the story, and the simile leaves an uncomfortable hint that God impersonates a father, so the child is still deluded. Secondly, the picture of the mother who 'in sorrow pale, thro' the lonely dale / Her little boy weeping sought' ends the poem on a note of fear, loss and grief which strikes a discordant note against the happy ending. There is a hint, here, of the pale fears of Lyca's parents in 'The Little Girl Found' of *Experience*. 'Pale' maternal fear is also hauntingly echoed in 'NURSE'S Song' in *Experience*:

> When the voices of children, are heard on the green
> And whisprings are in the dale:
> The days of my youth rise fresh in my mind,
> My face turns green and pale.

Through several poems, then, Blake uses sinister phrases such as 'sorrows pale' and 'whisprings are in the dale' to convey a fear of *Experience* and its dewy night. In many of the *Songs*, this fear leads all too quickly to over-protection and stagnation, or the oppressive laws which prevent children from passing naturally into a healthy, uninhibited maturity (see particularly 'The Garden of Love' and our discussion in Chapter 3). We will return to the issue of an artificially-prolonged Innocence later, when we discuss *The Book of Thel*.

The design of 'The Little Boy Found' contrasts with that for the first poem, being level and balanced. Two trees on the left and one on the right form an incomplete arch above two figures, both halo'd, walking towards the viewer. They are the child and the white-garbed 'God . . . like his father', leaving the forest hand-in-hand. The doubts we have noticed in the poem are hinted at in the design too, for the figure of 'God' is apparently female. Perhaps Blake hints that the deity in this poem's frightened vision, who soothes the child and returns him to *Innocence*, fulfils a maternal function. Certainly the design casts further doubt on God's 'impersonation' of the father and the truth of what the child sees.

For the moment it is enough to notice that Blake has again presented us with a choice of beliefs. In the first poem he explicitly describes a false illusion of God; while in the second, he describes something ambivalent, and nonsensical, a sort of 'true illusion' of

God. The mother finds her child, and he is returned into her fearful care. The boundary of *Innocence*, with its faith in supernatural care, is not quite crossed. At the same time, all is not right in *Innocence*'s deluded, frightened world.

In particular, we are left to choose our belief about nature: is the world a 'lonely fen' where 'the mire was deep' and 'no father was there' in a 'dark' night? Or, is the world cared for by 'God . . . like [a] father in white', who will soothe distress and re-unite families?

'The Little Girl Lost' and 'The Little Girl Found'

Our next two poems are 'The Little Girl Lost' and 'The Little Girl Found' in *Experience*. These poems were originally included in the *Songs of Innocence*, but were transferred to *Songs of Experience* in later copies. We place them in *Experience* partly because of the content (see the discussion below), and partly for convenience because our source text does.

'The Little Girl Lost'

In futurity
I prophetic see,
That the earth from sleep,
(Grave the sentence deep)

Shall arise and seek
For her maker meek:
And the desart wild
Become a garden mild.

*   *   *   *

In the southern clime,
Where the summers prime,
Never fades away;
Lovely Lyca lay.

Seven summers old
Lovely Lyca told,
She had wanderd long,
Hearing wild birds song.

Sweet sleep come to me
Underneath this tree;
Do father, mother weep, –
"Where can Lyca sleep".

Lost in desart wild
Is your little child.
How can Lyca sleep,
If her mother weep.

If her heart does ake,
Then let Lyca wake;
If my mother sleep,
Lyca shall not weep.

Frowning frowning night,
O'er this desart bright,
Let thy moon arise,
While I close my eyes.

Sleeping Lyca lay;
While the beasts of prey,
Come from caverns deep,
View'd the maid asleep

The kingly lion stood
And the virgin view'd,
Then he gambold round
O'er the hallowd ground:

Leopards, tygers play,
Round her as she lay;
While the lion old,
Bow'd his mane of gold,

And her bosom lick,
And upon her neck,
From his eyes of flame,
Ruby tears there came;

While the lioness
Loos'd her slender dress,
And naked they convey'd
To caves the sleeping maid.

'The Little Girl Found'

All the night in woe,
Lyca's parents go:
Over vallies deep,
While the desarts weep.

Tired and woe-begone,
Hoarse with making moan:
Arm in arm seven days,
They trac'd the desart ways.

Seven nights they sleep,
Among shadows deep:
And dream they see their child
Starv'd in desart wild.

Pale thro' pathless ways
The fancied image strays,
Famish'd, weeping, weak
With hollow piteous shriek

Rising from unrest,
The trembling woman prest,
With feet of weary woe;
She could no further go.

In his arms he bore,
Her arm'd with sorrow sore:
Till before their way,
A couching lion lay.

Turning back was vain,
Soon his heavy mane,
Bore them to the ground;
Then he stalk'd around.

Smelling to his prey,
But their fears allay,
When he licks their hands:
And silent by them stands.

They look upon his eyes
Fill'd with deep surprise:
And wondering behold,
A spirit arm'd in gold.

On his head a crown
On his shoulders down,
Flow'd his golden hair.
Gone was all their care.

Follow me he said,
Weep not for the maid:
In my palace deep,
Lyca lies asleep.

Then they followed,
Where the vision led:
And saw their sleeping child,
Among tygers wild.

To this day they dwell
In a lonely dell
Nor fear the wolvish howl,
Nor the lions growl.

(K2, 34–36)

These poems alternate iambic and trochaic lines without any great disturbance of the rhythm, and with only minor irregularities (one of the most noticeable is the line '**Arm** in **arm seven days**' in the second stanza of 'The Little Girl Found', where the extra stress on '**seven**' perhaps conveys the length of time the parents search). The regularity of three stresses in each short line, and Blake's facility in couching most of the lines as separate phrases, give these poems an aura of simplicity. We have noticed this apparent plainness of rhythm in several poems so far: it can be said that Blake's unforced control of simple metres gives an impression that the poems themselves are obvious. The metre seems to say to the reader: *'there is nothing complicated here, see for yourself'*.

The story is straightforward: Lyca, the 'little girl' of the poems, is not really lost. She simply does not have the fear of experience from which her parents suffer. Lyca trusts the benevolence of nature, does not suffer from inhibitions but follows her natural instincts, and comes to no harm. Her parents, on the other hand, 'dream they see their child / Starv'd in desart wild' and, in terror of nature itself (represented here by 'pathless ways' and the wild beasts) they follow this 'fancied image'. In the final part of each poem a lion plays the part of a different perception of nature, at once overpowering, apparently wild; and at the same time actually loving.

There is no doubt, also, about the conclusion to be drawn from these poems. Lyca's parents were wrong to be so frightened, and Lyca herself was wise to follow her instincts without fear. The parents have to learn – from their daughter – not to be so over-anxious. They learn that the terrors of nature which obsessed them are really a fantasy, a 'fancied image' created by their own fears. They learn to overcome these fears, and end the poems living happily with the wild beasts and their daughter. Blake's final couplet underlines their victory over false fears:

> Nor fear the wolvish howl,
> Nor the lions growl.

This is an appealing and time-honoured 'message': we can hear generation after generation of teenagers speaking through this poem, begging their parents to be more trusting and permissive, to allow their children to take more responsibility for themselves.

How do these poems add to the theme of nature in the *Songs*? Clearly, two opposed views of the natural world are in conflict here:

the parents' fears, and Lyca's own trusting instinct. Blake intensifies this conflict by juxtaposing the two perceptions, and this provides a crucial moment in each poem.

In 'The Little Girl Lost', stanzas 5 to 8 tell of the conflict between Lyca's trust and her parents' fears. From Lyca's viewpoint, 'Sweet sleep' is welcome and she has no cause for distress except consideration for her mother's feelings:

> If my mother sleep,
> Lyca shall not weep.

The other side of this conflict alternates with Lyca's view. The parents cannot imagine their daughter trusting to sleep, and say so three times ('"Where can Lyca sleep"', 'How can Lyca sleep', and 'Then let Lyca wake'). However, their concern for their daughter becomes progressively more self-centred until it is unmistakeably emotional blackmail. The first expression of the parents' idea is simple disbelief: as far as they can see, there is nowhere safe. The second time they worry, however, they connect Lyca's state with that of her mother: 'If her mother weep'. This introduces a moral prescription: Lyca *ought* to be worried; and we notice that this is justified by her mother's distress, not by any danger she faces. The third and final statement of the parents' view is in the form of a command: 'Then let Lyca wake'. Here, Blake shows us exactly how fear turns into tyranny. Notice that the parents' fear of nature has made them wholly unreasonable. They now command their daughter to be unhappy, simply because they are.

Stanza 8 resolves the conflict. The first line continues the parents' view, and Blake hints that this is exaggerated by doubling the adjective 'frowning'. In the second line, however, the adjective 'bright' is a surprise, and Lyca's forbidding surroundings begin to be transformed to make way for the positive perception dominating the rest of the poem. The final couplet of the stanza is Lyca's voice, accepting nature in its entirety, including the night her parents find so fearful:

> Let thy moon arise,
> While I close my eyes.

Lyca contradicts her parents, then. She decides to trust herself to nature, despite her mother's tears. Blake underlines the girl's opposition to her parents by using the same imperative form 'Let' as her parents used in the preceding stanza.

In the stanzas we have looked at, the two opposed perspectives on nature alternate five times, intensifying the pressure of emotional blackmail from the parents, and building up to a sense of relief when Lyca finally sleeps. We should also notice the effect of the word 'bright', which suddenly introduces light into the poem. There has been no colour or light up to this point, but 'gold', 'flame' and 'Ruby', which make the lion glow towards the end of the poem, echo the unexpected word 'bright': it stands between the parents' and Lyca's attitudes to nature, like a sudden illumination or revelation. This could be called the pivotal word of the poem.

In 'The Little Girl Found' the conflict between false parental fears and 'true' nature occurs in stanzas 6 to 10. We will follow the development of the parents' perspective from the moment when they find themselves facing a 'couching lion'. Notice that we begin this episode clearly from their frightened point of view: 'Turning back was vain'. However, Blake introduces an element of absurdity in the same stanza, as the parents believe that it is the 'heavy mane' of the lion that forces them to cower on the ground. Their fear dominates, and they are defeated by the threat they believe the lion to be, not by his strength or his teeth. To be specific, it is the lion's display of masculine energy – his mane – that overpowers the parents.

The lion continues to do what the parents expect. He walks around them and sniffs them, and this is described in their diction, 'he stalk'd around. / Smelling to his prey', as they expect to be eaten. In this poem, the moment of revelation when the lion licks their hands, does not change the perspective but enlarges the parents' viewpoint. As they experience this revelation they are 'Fill'd with deep surprise' and 'wondering'. The lion is transformed into 'A spirit arm'd in gold' wearing a crown, and with golden hair falling to his shoulders. Their sudden vision of the lion's true spirit comes when they 'look upon his eyes'. In both poems, then, the crucial moment arrives with an emphasis on sight and light.

We have no doubt that the 'spirit arm'd in gold' which is revealed to Lyca's parents is a vision of the truth; and this truth was previously hidden from them by their own fear. The remainder of the poem confirms that the 'kingly' lion is not a misleading fantasy: the family is reunited and lives in wild nature without fear at the end of the poem. We must therefore distinguish between two kinds of interpretative 'seeing' in this poem.

First, there is the parents' 'dream' of Lyca's death, which is a 'fancied image'. In this kind of 'seeing' the lion appears so threatening that the parents are defeated by his 'mane' and convinced that he will eat them. The second kind of interpretative 'seeing' is their vision of the lion as a 'spirit arm'd in gold'. Blake dignifies this with the word 'vision'. We know that it reveals a truth rather than deception, yet it is no more the literal truth than were the parents' fears: literally, it is still a lion and not a king that the parents follow. At the end of the poem, literal nature continues: they see their 'sleeping child, / Among tygers wild' and have no fear of 'the wolvish howl, / Nor the lions growl'.

So, the poem does not ask us to believe that the lion is not a lion. Instead, it asks us to believe that, if we see with our 'visionary' eyes, the lion is 'A spirit arm'd in gold'. This visionary way of seeing is a further and more penetrating perspective in Blake's poetry. New readers of the *Songs* can find it confusing, since we are introduced to so many false perspectives in the poems, and it can be difficult to distinguish the true imaginative 'vision' from among so many viewpoints. However, the visionary eye is vitally important in understanding Blake's ideas, so we will take a pause to say something about it before moving on with our analysis of the poems.

In a poem in a letter to Thomas Butts, Blake recounts a vision he claims to have experienced when living at Felpham:

> On the yellow sands sitting,
> The sun was emitting
> His glorious beams
> From heaven's high streams.
> Over sea, over land,
> My eyes did expand
> Into regions of air,
> Away from all care;

Into regions of fire,
Remote from desire;
The light of the morning
Heaven's mountains adorning,
In particles bright
The jewels of light
Distinct shone and clear –
Amazed and in fear
I each particle gazed,
Astonished, amazed:
For each was a man
Human-formed . . .

(K 804)

In this account Blake conveys a beautiful, bright morning which he views from the beach. However, he includes the phrase 'My eyes did expand' to describe how a moment of more significant 'seeing' opened up to him. It is important for us to remember two features of his 'vision', however. He focuses on motes in a sunbeam, and we must notice that Blake remains aware of what he is literally looking at: he is clear that 'I each particle gazed'. Blake himself then feels 'Astonished, amazed' – in the same way as Lyca's parents felt 'deep surprise' – as he discerns a visionary form within each 'particle': each one seems to be a human form. The first important feature of Blake's vision, then, is that he does not lose sight of the 'particles': he knows what they are throughout his experience.

Next, the particle / humans seem to speak to Blake, saying:

. . . Each grain of sand,
Every stone on the land,
Each rock and each hill,
Each fountain and rill,
Each herb and each tree,
Mountain, hill, earth and sea,
Cloud, meteor and star
Are men seen afar.

(K 804–5)

This speech is a philosophical statement. It is an assertion that all of nature is alive, and each tiniest part of nature is individually alive and conscious. Such a statement can be placed within a tradition of romantic thought alongside, for example, Wordsworth's suggestion that natural things express God's will, or Gerard Manley Hopkins's resurrection of St Thomas Aquinas's 'principle of individuation'. We do not wish to enter into philosophical intricacies here, however, to distinguish between Blake and pantheism, or to contrast his concept of individuality with that of Hopkins. The important point for us to remember is that Blake's 'vision' has a clear rational meaning. Whatever we think of 'visions', we will find that Blake's are never inconsistent or mad: they all tie-in to a single, integrated and thoughtfully-developed world-view.

It is crucial to remember the above two points. Blake was an eccentric in his own time, and his writings were both unconventional and shocking: he was socially and politically subversive. In the next chapter, we will see that his political views have been attacked by some of the establishment throughout the twentieth century, let alone in his own day. For example, substantially the same politics as Blake's was the target of Senator McCarthy's witch-hunts in 1950s America, and was the target of Mrs Thatcher's anti-union and anti-socialism rhetoric of the early 1980s in Britain.

Blake was also an outspoken man, and he had a lively sense of irony and fun: he loved to 'wind up' the simple-minded. In short, he enjoyed teasing people by acting strangely.[1] So, many people believe that Blake was mad. If we remember the above two points, however: that he never lost sight of literal reality and that his ideas are always justified and logically co-ordinated, we will not fall into the error of dismissing what Blake says, just because it is a 'vision' or because he was 'mad'.

Another poem in a further letter to Thomas Butts confirms the relevance and significance of Blake's concept of 'visionary' seeing. He initially points out that his vision differs from ordinary seeing:

---

[1] A good example of Blake's propensity for ironical jokes may be seen in his painting 'The Ghost of a Flea' (c. 1819, Tate Gallery, London), apparently done for the so-called 'disciples' whose admiration Blake enjoyed in his final years. Arguably, the design for 'The Tyger', discussed on p. 90, is another visual joke.

. . . before my way
A frowning Thistle implores my stay.
What to others a trifle appears
Fills me full of smiles or tears;
For double the vision my Eyes do see,
And a double vision is always with me.
With my inward Eye 'tis an old Man grey,
With my outward, a Thistle across my way.

(K 817)

Clearly, Blake remains literally sure that this is a thistle and at the same time, he sees a deeper significance in it, which is developed into an allegory of his own life, in the remainder of the poem. Apparently, the allegorical or metaphorical significance of the thistle is as 'an old man grey', and this is what Blake sees with his 'inward eye'. Later in the same poem, Blake points out that it would be nonsense to lose sight of natural reality: as you perceive further levels of 'vision', you do not discard your earlier insights. If you did, you would be guilty of the same narrow and limited outlook in 'vision' as you were trapped in when you could only perceive a simple, physical object. Blake hated the mere scientific measurement and classification of things, and insisted that his 'vision' had to be multiple, constantly expanding, and never 'single' like that of a mere natural scientist:

Now I a fourfold vision see,
And a fourfold vision is given to me;
'Tis fourfold in my supreme delight
And threefold in soft Beulah's night
And twofold Always. May God us keep
From Single vision & Newton's sleep!

(K 818)

We will not go into 'fourfold', 'threefold' and 'Beulah' here. The important point for us is the contempt Blake expresses for 'single vision'. This, in his view, reduces the world to mere physical rules. Blake therefore calls it 'Newton's sleep'.

The lion of 'The Little Girl Found', then, is both lion and 'spirit arm'd in gold'. Lyca's parents enter a higher plane of perception: they begin to see with what Blake calls 'double' vision. In this higher state they have a clearer understanding of nature than was possible in 'single vision', when their perception was restricted by fear. The wild and powerful creatures in nature are fine, bright and strong – like the lion. Lyca's parents now understand that these natural forces are not hostile: they are merely strong. The parents' response to natural energy is no longer fear, but wonder.

Blake's poem suggests a parallel, more specific message at the same time. Notice that the lioness 'loos'd' Lyca's 'slender dress' before conveying her 'naked' to their caves. This suggests that Lyca had to cast off the thin covering of her parents' upbringing. Symbolically, this removes the shame about her naked beauty, which she has already acquired from her parents. Notice also that it is the lion's masculine display – his mane – which overpowers the fearful parents. The poem thus hints at the need for sexual liberation, and suggests that the natural energy Lyca's parents fear is sexual energy. Blake's target here is sexual prudery, which gives rise to shame, disgust and fear. He asserts that natural sexuality is strong and wonderful. It can shine like the 'gold' that suffuses the final part of each of these poems.

We have not yet considered the opening stanzas of 'The Little Girl Lost', however. These place the story of Lyca clearly within the context of *Songs of Experience*, and specify the kind of vision the two poems represent. First, Lyca's story is set 'In futurity' and the Bard of *Experience* sees the story 'prophetic'. This is not the present time of *Experience*, then, but a time beyond that state. To underline this point, Blake places the story in terms of the 'Introduction' and 'Earth's Answer': for the present time of *Experience*, we remember, Earth is still dominated by fear, and refuses to 'return' or see the growing morning. She is imprisoned in despair. However, in 'The Little Girl Lost', the Bard of Experience asserts ('prophetic') that the earth will 'arise and seek / For her maker meek' and so throw off the 'grave . . . sentence deep' of her 'sleep'. The final couplet of this first section of the poem tells us of the transformation we are about to read:

> And the desart wild
> Become a garden mild.

These lines produce a disorienting effect we are becoming used to. Blake appears to assert that nature will change completely. Really, he suddenly exposes us to Earth's viewpoint. Nature itself may remain the same; but Blake wants us to understand that as long as Earth perceives a 'desart wild', that is her reality. So, from her point of view, a new reality ('a garden mild') suddenly appears. The suddenness of Blake's perceptual shift catches the reader unawares. It emphasises the complexity, and multiplicity, of vision.

The Lyca poems, then, are from a vision the Bard of Experience ('Who Present, Past, & Future sees') can see. Other inhabitants of *Experience* cannot see this vision, however, because it is a 'prophetic' vision of 'futurity'.

'The Lamb'

We can now turn to 'The Lamb' and 'The Tyger', a pair of contrary poems which go a long way to defining concepts of nature in *Innocence* and *Experience*. Here is 'The Lamb':

> Little Lamb who made thee
> Dost thou know who made thee
> Gave thee life & bid thee feed,
> By the stream & o'er the mead;
> Gave thee clothing of delight,
> Softest clothing wooly bright;
> Gave thee such a tender voice,
> Making all the vales rejoice:
> Little lamb who made thee
> Dost thou know who made thee
>
> Little lamb I'll tell thee,
> Little lamb I'll tell thee;
> He is called by thy name,
> For he calls himself a Lamb:
> He is meek & he is mild,
> He became a little child:
> I a child & thou a lamb,

We are called by his name.
Little Lamb God bless thee,
Little Lamb God bless thee.

(K2, 8)

This is a beautiful and simple poem, in which the repeated lines framing each stanza underline the plain development of the child's thought from his initial question, through his own answer, to the final blessing. The metre is trochaic, but we notice that the 'framing' lines all have an unstressed or 'feminine' ending (e.g. 'Little **Lamb** who **made** thee'), whereas the central lines of both stanzas, where the child's thought is elaborated, all end with stressed syllables (as in 'We are callèd by his **name**'). This gently distinguishes between the child's direct address, with its accent on the verbs 'made', 'tell' and 'bless', and his elaborating thoughts which are clearly separated from each other by the strong final sound. The impression created is of a series of clear and straightforward ideas framed in between the child calling out that he has something to say.

'The Lamb' is set firmly within *Innocence*. Its background is 'mead', 'stream' and 'vales', a gentle agricultural background echoed by the cottage or byre, and the secure oak tree, which can be seen behind child and sheep in the design. The child's idea makes a three-way unity of child, lamb and God, and the first stanza emphasises joy and comfort, mentioning 'Softest clothing wooly bright', and a 'tender voice' to make 'vales rejoice'. Line 5 deserves less controversy than it has attracted: 'clothing of delight' obviously conveys that the lamb exudes 'delight', and that his soft woolly clothing is 'delightful' as the next line explains. We can admire the economy with which Blake combines meanings, but there is no difficulty in the sense. What is absent from this poem is any shadow of sorrow, fear, evening or night. It is a poem entirely without danger, and entirely suiting the simplicity of the naked toddler we see in the design.

With regard to a theme of nature, however, the child's question is important. The simple question, 'Little Lamb who made thee' tells us what the child is attempting, and we realise that his question is the same as that of countless thinkers over the centuries. He looks at the world around him, and deduces a concept of God from what he sees. It is a clear thought process: 'I see this kind of nature, it was created by God, therefore God must be this kind of being'. The child sees a soft, woolly and happy lamb, well provided-for and refreshed by 'mead' and 'stream', and deduces that God is – to put it plainly – soft, woolly and meek. God, then, is just like 'me and my friend'.

The child's happiness and the joy of the whole countryside is delightful; and we have every reason to believe that Blake saw love and innocent happiness in the world around him. We are not seeking to take away from the pleasure of this lovely poem, then; but Blake's varieties of viewpoint in the *Songs* have taught us to recognise a limited world. Also, the child's approach to understanding God raises questions in our minds: Does nature express God? Can we decipher the deity by looking at the world around us? What if the child saw a world of drudgery and ugliness (like 'little Tom Dacre' in 'The Chimney Sweeper'): what sort of God could be deduced from that? Then, the time-honoured problem of evil comes to mind: good does not always triumph over evil, in nature. How can this be, if God is more powerful than Satan?

The point about the child's faith expressed in this poem is not that he is deluded, or that distant dangers are hinted at to undercut its validity. The point is that this beautiful, touching faith is dependent: it *depends on* the child continuing to see a gentle and joyous nature around him. His faith is good, but only good for the world within which, for the space of this poem, he exists.

'The Tyger'

The contrary poem in *Experience*, 'The Tyger', underlines our point by starting with same question the child of 'The Lamb' asks; but this time it is directed at a frightening beast:

> Tyger Tyger, burning bright,
> In the forests of the night;
> What immortal hand or eye,
> Could frame thy fearful symmetry?

In what distant deeps or skies,
Burnt the fire of thine eyes?
On what wings dare he aspire?
What the hand, dare sieze the fire?

And what shoulder, & what art,
Could twist the sinews of thy heart?
And when thy heart began to beat,
What dread hand? & what dread feet?

What the hammer? What the chain,
In what furnace was thy brain?
What the anvil? What dread grasp,
Dare its deadly terrors clasp?

When the stars threw down their spears
And water'd heaven with their tears:
Did he smile his work to see?
Did he who made the Lamb make thee?

Tyger Tyger burning bright,
In the forests of the night:
What immortal hand or eye,
Dare frame thy fearful symmetry?

(K2, 42)

Alongside the words for the hymn 'Jerusalem', this is possibly Blake's best-known poem. We have to overcome our instinctive knowledge of the first verse, and the sing-song '**symmetry**' with a long 'y' that we may have heard chanted since we were very young. Our task is to appreciate sound, rhythm and image, and to follow Blake's complex thought as closely as we can.

Metrically, 'The Tyger' is predominantly trochaic: the powerful drumbeat begun with '**Tyger Tyger**' keeps beating virtually throughout. The final stanza repeats the first, emphasising the heavy, steady beat. The only change between first and last stanzas is one word in the final line, the change from 'Could' to 'Dare'. This also alters the metre, so the gentler iambic line ('Could **frame** thy **fearful symmetry**') of stanza 1 is replaced by a heavy, hammering double stress, landing on two long vowels ('**Dare frame**') in the final stanza. This change reflects the fact that the terror and wonder of the poem's question itself has grown during the poem: the more the poet meditates on the tyger, the more impressive the Creator's power seems.

Stanza three is metrically different. The second and third lines of this stanza are iambic. The first and final lines, however, contrast with the extra speed and regularity of the middle lines. The first and last lines have, as near as we can scan them, three successive stresses in both halves of each line, thus: '**And what shoul**der, **& what art** . . . **What dread hand?** & **what dread feet?**' In the first of these lines, you may argue against the stresses on 'and', which depend on the way the poem is read; however, there are still two heavy spondee in the line. The final line of the stanza scans definitely: only '&' is not stressed, and every other sound is heavy. These two lines describe the extraordinary strength the tyger's creator must have. It is as if Blake has pushed twice as much weight and power into a unit of language as it ordinarily contains. The result is relentless: virtually every sound hits hard. In between, in two rhythmic iambic lines, the tyger's great heart begins to beat. Even here the placing of stresses accentuates the violent verb 'twist', and connects it in assonance with the stressed syllable of '**sin**ews'.

The third stanza, then, seems to perform the powerful feat of creation, and set the tyger's heart beating, by means of the poetry itself. Doubling and trebling of stresses creates further and similar effects elsewhere in 'The Tyger' as well. We have already remarked on '**Dare frame**' in the final line, but the repeated 'what' of the poet's question gives rise to several bunched stresses, which maintain this rhythmic evocation of the Creator's power. Look, for example, at '**In what dis**tant', '**On what wings**', '**In what furn**ace', '**What dread grasp**', and the long vowels adding to the effect in '**dare sieze**'.

'The Tyger' appears to face the problem of evil head-on. Blake continues the association between wild beasts and flame (or golden) colouring that we have found in the 'Lost' and 'Found' poems. Perhaps the 'burning' refers to the tyger's eyes, mentioned more specifically in the next stanza, but it could equally suggest that the whole beast glows with strength and energy. The question seems to attempt an understanding of the Creator in the same way as the child in 'The Lamb': deduce God from his creation, the tyger. 'Burning' implies wild energy, and 'fearful' sets the mood of the terrified questioner, so impressed by the tyger's power that he cannot imagine a being strong enough to be able to 'frame' the seemingly uncontainable beast.

Ambiguity begins in this first stanza, however. First, the question of perspective or viewpoint is present in 'In the forests of the night'. We know that the world of *Innocence* is one of meadows and 'vales'; and that forests and night are the setting of *Experience*. This line, then, tells us that the tyger appears to burn 'bright' when seen from within the dark forest of *Experience*. Secondly, 'frame' seems to have a dual effect. It expresses the enormous task of the Creator, but at the same time it suggests making a work of art: imaginative creation. Finally, 'symmetry' is a surprising word. It does not suit 'burning' wildness, or its adjacent word 'fearful', since fears and wildness are generally in antithesis to 'symmetry'. The word suggests perfect proportion: it is as if the tyger's beauty is so wonderful that it is frightening.

We have already met transformations of wild beasts marking sudden changes of perception. Is this tyger really dangerous, are his eyes really 'burning', or will he suddenly drop 'ruby tears' like the lion in 'The Little Girl Lost'? Is the dweller in 'the forests of the night' seeing the tyger as he is, or creating a dangerous beast out of his own fear and pessimism? In this suggestive poem, the possibility exists that the tyger's fearsomeness is a delusion; yet the speaker's awe and fear also remains present and convincing. The extraordinary courage needed to confront and create the tyger appears in 'dare' in the second (twice), fourth and final stanzas, yet two of these convey the Creator's mental courage – the power of his imagination to 'aspire' (how could God have enough faith in himself to believe that he could create the tyger?) and the range of his imagination to 'frame' the tyger. The idea of the Creator who 'dare sieze the fire' brings physical courage and intolerable pain to the reader's mind. At the same time, there is an abstract dimension to this image, for the 'fire' is that of the tyger's 'eyes', emblematic of the beast's own energy, vision and imagination. Physical and abstract concepts are again brought together in the 'grasp' that 'dare' clasp 'deadly terrors'.

The fear that permeates the poem passes seamlessly from the tyger itself to its Creator. We know that the beast is 'fearful', and this gives rise to fear of the Creator in 'What dread hand? & what dread feet?', 'What dread grasp, / Dare its deadly terrors clasp?'; finally, the tyger is again 'fearful'. Fear and courage, then, dominate the mood of the poem, and Blake's images pull together both physical and mental strength at the same time, attributing both forms of power to the tyger and his Creator.

Imagery enhances our impression of power and strength. Much of the making of the tyger is likened to heavy industrial work, particularly metalwork: 'fire', 'hammer', 'chain', 'furnace' and 'anvil' all contribute to this. We receive an impression of a smith's great strength, the extreme heat of the furnace, and the unforgiving hardness of metal. However, this strain of images also suggests a further association: with the industrial revolution and the enslavement of the population, servants of machines, prisoners of production and the profit-motive. The mention of 'chain' in particular gives us a hint of slavery and forced labour.[2]

On the other hand, there is another perspective present in 'The Tyger'. We remarked that 'symmetry' does not suit the prevailing mood of wildness and fear in the poem. 'Symmetry' is the first hint that there may be another vision in which the tyger does not terrify, but can be seen as a beautiful creation, and symmetrical or balanced. In stanza five, this alternative perspective is alluded to again. 'When the stars threw down their spears / And water'd heaven with their tears' introduces a contrasting mood even if we are not aware that it is a Biblical or Miltonic reference. The action of these two lines is of disarmament, and a softening of emotion which is portrayed as fertile when the stars 'water'd' heaven with tears. The lines also change the music of the poem. The heavy and dull 'd' sounds, and hissing closed 'asp' rhyme-words at the end of stanza four disappear, and these lines introduce a beautiful openness, a more lingering music, largely created by the long and open 'stars', 'threw' and 'spears', (with alliteration and modulated assonance between 'stars'

---

[2] Blake's revolutionary views on society, commerce and industry are discussed in Chapter 4.

and 'spears') followed by the aspirant 'heaven'. A different setting from the harshness of heavy industry has been introduced.

When did the 'stars thr[o]w down their spears'? This line makes two allusions, both relevant to the subject-matter of 'The Tyger'. Blake's adaptation of wording seems to include both. First, in the Book of Job in the Bible, God answers Job out of a whirlwind. Job has been brought to despair, questioned his faith and cursed his life. God's answer comes – like Blake's poem – in the form of a series of rhetorical questions which underline the difference between Job's human understanding and God's infinite knowledge. God starts by asking where Job was at the creation:

> Where wast thou when I laid the foundations of the earth . . .
> When the morning stars sang together,
> And all the sons of God shouted for joy?
>
> (Job 38, 4–7)

In Job, the stars 'sang' and 'shouted for joy'; yet the context of Blake's line is that the 'stars' are responding to God's act of creation – just as in Job. So, we can reasonably take Blake's line as an allusion in which the moment of creation destroys militance and defensive fears ('threw down their spears') and fills the stars with an emotion more complex than simple 'joy', as they refreshingly 'water' heaven with tears. Blake was interested in paradoxical extremes of emotion, as we will see in *The Marriage of Heaven and Hell*, where one of the Proverbs of Hell reads: 'Excess of sorrow laughs. Excess of joy weeps'. We also remember the redeeming 'ruby tears' of the lion in 'The Little Girl Lost', and the child who 'wept with joy' hearing the Piper's song. The weeping pleasure of the overwhelmed 'stars' should not surprise us.

When we identify an allusion to another text in a poem we are studying, it is often useful to read around the original lines, to gain a fuller idea of the relationship between one text and the other. In this case, the more we read of God's answer from the whirlwind in the Book of Job, the more we realise a similarity of theme between the Biblical text and Blake's 'The Tyger'. God's account of the creation, couched in relentless questions, is filled with violence and power, and the imagery associated with these qualities. So, asking whether Job gave strength to the horse, God asks 'Hast thou clothed his neck with thunder?' This and many other examples are reminiscent of Blake's characteristic imagery in which different qualities are surprisingly conjoined. In Job 41 God gives an extended description of Leviathan 'Who is made without fear', and many elements of the description express wonder at his power and the fear he inspires, reminding us of the prevalent mood of Blake's poem: the tyger is a latter-day Leviathan:

> He esteemeth iron as straw,
> And brass as rotten wood.
>
> (Job 41, 27)

The second context to which Blake's lines are thought to allude is the fall of the rebel angels described in Book VI of Milton's *Paradise Lost*:

> . . . they astonished all resistance lost,
> All courage; down their idle weapons dropt;
>
> (*Paradise Lost*, VI, 838–9)

The argument for this allusion is that the angels' rebellion makes their fall into hell, and the consequent creation of Earth as well as man's creation and fall, inevitable. That is, that this moment is the crucial exercise of God's power and prefigures the creation of all good and evil in nature, including the tyger. So, to smile at this demonstration of divine power, is to smile at the making of the tyger.

We can take our choice, or keep both of these referential contexts in mind as we consider Blake's poem. The first suggests infinite power greater than the thoughts of man, a power that is 'terrible' in the old sense, inspiring a terror filled with awe and joy – a paradoxical emotion that is profoundly creative (they 'water'd heaven with their tears'); the second suggests a destructive divine power, as well as reminding us of the paradox of evil: God's creation of, and mastery over, evil itself. In the view of many, including Blake, Milton struggled unsuccessfully with this paradox throughout *Paradise Lost*.[3]

---

[3] Blake wrote 'The reason Milton wrote in fetters when he wrote of Angels & God, and at liberty when of Devils & Hell, is because he was a true Poet and of the Devil's party without knowing it' (K 150).

We have digressed because this is a much-glossed couplet, and because it is a crucial moment. It alters perspectives within the poem. The open and softened tone continues in the final two lines of the stanza: 'smile' and 'see' extend the alliteration of 's', and a smooth clear diction is sustained by pure vowel sounds in 'smile', 'see', 'made', 'make' and 'thee'; while the open rhyme-words hang gently at the end of each line. The allusions – to the work of creation in the Book of Job and the defeat of the rebel angels in *Paradise Lost* – ambivalently conjure ideas of both creative and destructive power. They are followed by 'water'd', a natural image of fertile refreshment. It is at this point that Blake introduces both God's 'smile' and the lamb, in a rhetorical question whose tone is of wonder and astonishment.

The final stanza is a repeat of the first, with only one word changed: 'Dare' in place of 'Could'. Our attention is therefore drawn to this one word. What does the change signify? First, of course, it places emphasis on the courage of the Creator, and the intervening imagery of metalwork and furnaces justifies this development: the tyger is such a strong and fearsome beast that the stronger 'dare' is an appropriate question to ask of its creator. However, in the context of the penultimate stanza and its radical alternative perspective, the poem seems to ask a more trenchant question. Perhaps it is, again, a question of vision. The tyger appears frightening: it is strong and potentially destructive. From the perspective of *Experience*, it is 'burning' in contrast to the dark forests which are all the viewer can see. In a different vision, however, its creation is a triumph disarming and refreshing nature, an event to bring a smile. The suggestion here is that the tyger and the lamb, apparent opposites, belong together. They are both part of nature, a vast, wild and powerful, but innocent creation.

The form of 'The Tyger' tantalisingly supports this implication. Blake is strict in giving us a series of rhetorical questions, and we know the obvious part of the answers. So, when he asks who the Creator could be, we know that the answer is 'God'. When he asks whether the same Creator made tyger and lamb, we answer 'Yes'. The more challenging aspects of Blake's questions receive no answer, however. The implied questions are *Why create such a fearsome crea-*

ture? and *How could such power be controlled?* If we consider the problem of destruction, the 'problem of evil', further disturbing questions are provoked. Blake gives no answer to these, and rounds off his poem with a repetition of the initial question. We are therefore left with the tyger himself, and the alternative visions of his creation as an act of violence and strength, or a joyous moment of fertility.

The tyger remains an enigma. It remains stubbornly itself, and we should be careful to avoid 'reading into' the imagery. When we respond to violent ideas such as 'furnace', 'fire', 'hammer' and 'anvil', we respond to sheer power and strength, but we are given no information at all as to what use that strength will be put. It is important to remember that 'The Tyger' contains no evidence of malevolence or destructiveness. It is simply power, and the tyger remains stubbornly itself.

The two words 'Dare frame' in the final stanza, and the repeated oxymoron 'fearful symmetry', return us to the question of perception. How can we 'frame' this enigmatic creature, whose only sure attribute is unimaginable power? And how can we reconcile our natural reaction of fear with the concept of 'symmetry'? The poem thus issues a challenge to our imagination. We are challenged to open our visionary eyes, to partake of a 'double vision' in which we are aware of more than one perspective. The final line with its emphasised 'Dare' specifically challenges us to find the courage for this task.

The design adds to the enigmatic effect of the poem as a whole. A tyger stands beneath a bare tree which David V. Erdman sees as having a bogy face 'more absurd than frightening' above its third branch-arm and as 'helplessly collapsed' and 'feckless in its skinny arms'. The tyger's face appears differently in different copies; variously 'worried', 'smiling', 'supercilious', 'patient' and 'gentle'.[4] His eyes are round and quite comical, and in the Keynes facsimile edition, he seems about to explain, rather pedantically, why he has arrived late. The design, in fact, seems put there as a compensation,

---

[4] Erdman, David V., *The Illuminated Blake*, London 1975, Oxford University Press, p. 84.

a counterweight to the terrifying imagery of stanzas 2 to 4. It may cause us to 'smile', and will certainly not challenge our courage.

The final effect of the whole, then, is of an essay on the activity we are all engaged in throughout our lives: our constant effort to decode, interpret and master the world around us. At the same time, together with the contrary poem 'The Lamb', it is a gentle satire on the tools we bring to this mammoth task – our natural eyes and senses, our personal experience, and our pitiful reason which attempts to deduce the infinite from the finite.

Summary Discussion

We have looked at nine poems in our exploration of nature as a theme in the *Songs of Innocence and Experience*. We have discovered a great deal about Blake's poetry, and developed our insight into varieties of perception and the concept of 'vision'. The present conclusions, however, concern the theme of nature itself, and attempt to summarise what we have learned.

1. We have met various natural landscapes. First there is a gentle agricultural landscape of 'mead', 'stream' and 'vales', 'green fields and happy groves'. In the design for 'The Lamb', an agricultural building like a byre or a cottage stands in the background, and an oak tree adds security. There are birds, trees, 'bud and blossom', but no forests in this landscape. This is the landscape of the world of *Innocence*. Secondly, we have met a contrasting landscape of dark forest, the 'forests of the night' of 'The Tyger'. In this dark forest are wild beasts hungry for their prey. Two other landscapes seem to be alternative expressions of nature as perceived from *Experience*: there is the 'lonely fen' and 'lonely vale' where 'the mire was deep', which is soaked in dew; and there is the 'desart wild' with 'pathless ways' and 'valleys deep' through which Lyca's parents search for their lost daughter. The 'desart' is also the home of lions, tigers and wolves.
2. These landscapes are believable and natural: they are viable perceptions of nature in the *Songs*, and each kind of environment

has an undeniable truth: the child's gentle setting in 'The Lamb' is his true experience of life; while the 'lonely fen' from which an illusion of God rescues the lost boy, in *Innocence*, is a real wilderness. However, these landscapes are also symbolic of the states of mind *Innocence* and *Experience*. They are true perceptions of nature, but they are not nature itself.

3. These subjective perceptions of nature suffer transformations within the poems. In particular, in 'The Little Girl Lost' and 'The Little Girl Found' we see that they are restricted to the eyes of the different characters. So, Lyca is in a 'southern clime' where Summer endures permanently, surrounded by 'wild birds' and lying beneath a tree. Her parents are in the same landscape, but they see a 'desart wild' with 'pathless ways'. The legend of the poem prophesies that the 'desart wild' will become a 'garden mild'. So, the two contrasting landscapes exist simultaneously in the same place. Vision, or the lack of it, rules how we see nature.

4. Wild beasts appear in several of the poems. Blake does not mitigate their wildness, but he does criticise human fear of natural energy. When Lyca's parents meet the lion, their natural senses perceive the beast accurately: they perceive his power and size, the magnificence of his mane, and they see that he walks around them and sniffs. In the same way, at the end of the poem, lions still 'growl' and wolves still 'howl' as is their nature. However, the five senses can only perceive the physical. They do not perceive the essence. Only a different kind of seeing, which Blake calls 'vision' and which is not done with the 'senses' can understand and perceive the essence of nature. We looked at the moment of 'vision' when Lyca's parents see both a (physical) lion and a (visionary) 'spirit arm'd in gold'.

5. An effect of Blake's focus on subjective perceptions of nature is that nature itself is enigmatic. We cannot draw conclusions about nature's inherent goodness or evil, gentleness or violence, benevolence or malevolence. In these poems, nature itself simply is: it exists but does not have moral or emotional characteristics. This is a paradoxical effect, since all observers project intentions and emotions onto nature, intensively and constantly.

6. People also have a 'nature': natural emotions and desires. Blake

implies that these should be followed and expressed. We have met the obstruction, repression and distortion of desire in the poem 'The Angel'. The outcome is lies, hostility and a wasted life. We also witnessed the tyranny of distorted and selfish feeling, when Lyca's parents attempt to impose their own fear and misery on their daughter, using emotional blackmail.

7. The distortion of healthy feelings into negative ones – typically demands for pity, and defensive hostility – often focuses on emotions about sexuality. For example, we noticed that Lyca's parents are terrified into submission by the lion's display of masculinity, while their daughter's uninhibited natural development is accentuated when the lioness 'loos'd her slender dress'. The poem 'A Little Girl Lost' from *Experience* explicitly examines puritan fear and jealousy of sex, and its tragic consequences; but 'The Angel', which we have studied, also presents a potential love-relationship, destroyed by emotional dishonesty.

In our first two chapters we have built up a number of insights Into the *Songs*, and are developing a sound grasp of Blake's themes and methods. It is now time to carry this understanding forward to the more esoteric poems of Blake's oeuvre: the longer narratives commonly called the Prophetic Books. We will therefore take our conclusions about nature and look at them again in relation to one of the shorter Prophetic Books, *The Marriage of Heaven and Hell.*

Nature in *The Marriage of Heaven and Hell*

The Marriage of Heaven and Hell is an ironic, polemical work. Much of its meaning depends on grasping the reasons for Blake's ironic inversions of heaven and hell and angels and devils. If we think about it, we have already met the basis for Blake's reasoning, in the *Songs*.

In 'Earth's Answer' we heard of the 'Selfish father of men' with his 'cruel jealous selfish fear', and met the tyrannical oppression of a white-haired, authoritarian 'God'. In the 'Introduction' to *Experience* we met God cursing Adam and Eve, again in a critical context. So we already know what Blake thought of the Church's attitude towards nature and sexuality: he criticised it as intemperate, jealous and cruel.

In both 'The Lamb' and 'Night' we have seen Blake's ambivalent attitude to the simple faith of *Innocence*, with its idyllic dream of an afterlife. 'The Chimney Sweeper' poems in both collections go further. The moral prescription to be 'a good boy', which is the condition for Tom Dacre being allowed to dream of heaven; and the caustic phrase of *Experience's* sweep, that 'God and his Priest . . . make up a heaven of our misery' express Blake's anger at the Church. In Blake, the Church lies to support a cruel establishment. Priests promise heaven in return for obedience, and in doing so they lie to support the state and economic tyranny.

Blake's charges against the Church are two, then: first, he accuses religion of imposing oppressive and unnatural laws. Second, he accuses religion of feeding people's fears, so they remain imprisoned in their own despair, and of deluding people with false promises of heaven.

In *The Marriage of Heaven and Hell,* Blake ironically adopts the Church's terminology. He was well aware that his views were violently opposed by the establishment of his time. To most churchmen of the late eighteenth century, Blake's opinions were an evil, seditious threat to orthodoxy. To them, he represented the voice of Satan tempting people away from obedience to the Church. In these circumstances, Blake boldly adopts their name for him, and openly takes the side of 'the Devil' against 'angels'.

As a polemic, *The Marriage* deals with perceptions of nature more explicitly than is possible in the *Songs*. So, the differing perceptions of nature which are delicately woven into the poems we have studied, appear as broad satire and with a clear conclusion in *The Marriage*. In the fourth 'Memorable Fancy', an angel castigates Blake, speaking in the voice of an intolerant clergyman, deeply offended by the poet's unconventional ideas:

> 'O pitiable foolish young man! O horrible! O dreadful state! Consider the hot burning dungeon thou art preparing for thyself to all eternity, to which thou art going in such career.'
>
>   (K 155)

The angel's rhetoric is amusing, combining mannered exclamations, the archaic 'thou' and 'thyself', and poor diction (tautology in 'hot burning', the banality of 'going in such career'). Blake replies by asking that the angel show him his eternal lot, after which he will return the favour. The angel agrees, and they climb down through a stable, a church, a mill and caverns until they find themselves hanging from the roof of an immense subterranean space, and looking down. The description of hell Blake then gives is a masterpiece of satire, visually vivid and laughable at the same time. It culminates in this account of Leviathan:

> . . . at last, to the east, distant about three degrees, appear'd a fiery crest above the waves; slowly it reared like a ridge of golden rocks, till we discover'd two globes of crimson fire, from which the sea fled away in clouds of smoke; and now we saw it was the head of Leviathan; his forehead was divided into streaks of green & purple like those on a tyger's forehead: soon we saw his mouth & red gills hang just above the raging foam, tinging the black deep with beams of blood, advancing toward us with all the fury of a spiritual existence.
>
> (K 156)

In case we fail to recognise the falsely terrifying appearance of Leviathan, or do not catch the tone of pastiche in Blake's melodramatic phrases ('the sea fled away in clouds of smoke'; 'tinging the black deep with beams of blood'), we are directly reminded of the tyger, by the description of Leviathan's head 'divided into streaks of green & purple like those on a tyger's forehead'. Clearly, this description performs the same task as the awe-inspiring imagery in 'The Tyger': it is a picture of hell from the perspective of the terrified angel, but it is not the truth. Blake sustains the illusion, however, by his concentrated use of visual triggers ('fiery crest', 'golden', 'globes', 'crimson fire', 'clouds of smoke', 'streaks of green & purple'). Only the final phrase is openly and absurdly bathetic, dismissing all these concrete impressions in the one word 'spiritual'.

In the 'Memorable Fancy', the angel, again ironically, terrifies himself so thoroughly that he runs away, and in that moment the scene is transformed:

> & then this appearance was no more, but I found myself sitting on a pleasant bank beside a river by moonlight, hearing a harper, who sung to the harp
>
> (K 156)

The aggressive diction of 'crimson', 'fire', 'smoke', 'streaked', 'blood' seems to vanish along with the angel's vision, to be replaced by the gently plosive 'pleasant bank' and aspirant alliteration in 'hearing a harper . . . harp'. Here, the terrors of hell and the beast Leviathan are compared to the tales of bogeymen used to terrify children. When the terrified angel sees Blake again, he is astonished at the poet's escape from a terror he believes is a reality. Blake answers 'All that we saw was owing to your metaphysics'. Clearly, the angel's vision of hell is comparable to the construction put upon the lion's behaviour by Lyca's parents, when they imagine him sniffing 'to his prey': it is a perception created and ruled by fear, not the truth.

This passage has been our first foray into the reputedly esoteric and 'difficult' interpretation of Blake's Prophetic Books; and it has proved quite straightforward to identify the similarities between the fearful perceptions described in some of the *Songs* and this more explicit satire from *The Marriage of Heaven and Hell*. However, we should admit that this clarity has been achieved by being selective. For example, we passed over the two characters' journey to their subterranean cavern, without mentioning that they pass through a stable (alluding to the 'horses of instruction'), a church (religious orthodoxy), a vault (the tomb of passions) and a mill (industry, materialism and economic slavery) on their way. We have also ignored those parts of the 'Memorable Fancy' that allude to Swedenborg, a theologian and 'prophet' to whose sect Blake briefly belonged and whose doctrines he came to reject.

When you first approach the Prophetic Books, it will be sensible to adopt this 'selective' practice. Concentrate, first of all, on those passages which create Blake's meaning directly, by means of language, description and narrative. Recognise the elements you are familiar with from the shorter poems and gain a firm grasp of the themes first. Subsequently, an edition with a good commentary, or a library with a Blake concordance[5] will help you to look up the more esoteric allusions, and the significance of the allegorical machinery.

We have come to *The Marriage of Heaven and Hell* in the confidence that we can build on our work with the *Songs*, and understand. Let us put this assertion to a sterner test, by looking at an overtly polemical extract, Plate 14:

> The ancient tradition that the world will be consumed in fire at the end of six thousand years is true, as I have heard from Hell.
>
> For the cherub with his flaming sword is hereby commanded to leave his guard at [the] tree of life; and when he does, the whole creation will be consumed and appear infinite and holy, whereas it now appears finite & corrupt.
>
> This will come to pass by an improvement of sensual enjoyment.
>
> But first the notion that man has a body distinct from his soul is to be expunged; this I shall do by printing in the infernal method, by corrosives, which in Hell are salutary and medicinal, melting apparent surfaces away, and displaying the infinite which was hid.
>
> If the doors of perception were cleansed every thing would appear to man as it is, Infinite.
>
> For man has closed himself up, till he sees all things thro' narrow chinks of his cavern.
>
> (K 154)

What can we make of this passage? First, step back from some of the details, and make a statement about Blake's subject as a whole. At this stage we may not follow the reference to the end of the world, and we may not have digested the analogy between printing and cleansing 'the doors of perception'. On the other hand, certain elements of the passage, and some phrases, have given us a good idea of the subject. Blake is talking about a change. The world is limited at present, but something will happen in the future that will transform the world from 'finite' and 'corrupt' into 'infinite' and 'holy'. One memorable phrase, 'If the doors of perception were cleansed', tells us that this redeeming future change will have something to do with the way we see; with, if you like, 'vision'.

---

[5] Some useful reference works for this purpose are mentioned in *Further Reading* at the end of this book.

So, the subject is a future change of vision that will redeem the world from corruption. This is a general statement about the passage, and we can now look at some of the details more closely.

The passage begins with an allusion to the 'end of the world', the Apocalypse. Blake cheekily tells us that he has heard news of this from 'Hell', which continues the ironic inversion of the whole work. We understand that Blake is putting forward an anti-Church view in his ironic 'devilish' persona. Next, Blake refers to Genesis, and commands the Cherub guarding the tree of life to leave his post. The relevant verse from the Bible is:

> So he drove out the man; and he placed at the east of the garden of Eden Cherubims, and a flaming sword which turned every way, to keep the way of the tree of life.
>
> (Genesis 3, 24)

We have come across Genesis 3 before: it is the chapter in which Adam and Eve hear the 'word' walking in the garden (see the analysis of the 'Introduction' to *Songs of Experience* in Chapter 1). God curses them, and they are expelled from the garden. God's final act is to place the Cherubim and sword as a guard to keep mankind away from the tree of life. We know that Blake regards the curse and expulsion as the actions of a jealous, selfish God, intemperately wrathful about the natural desires of Adam and Eve. Blake now orders the guardian Cherub to leave his post; that is, he orders us to return to a state before the prohibition and the fall, a state where people have uninhibited access to knowledge and sexuality.

Removing the curse and prohibitive law, Blake then asserts, will transform the world from its present state of corruption, and reveal the 'infinite' in everything. Clearly, this is a call for an end to repression and prudery about sex: people should not be oppressed and obstructed, and their desires should have a natural, uninhibited outlet. Blake spells this out: 'This will come to pass by an improvement of sensual enjoyment'.

Blake's next paragraph identifies the major error he saw as causing the prevalent attitudes of embarrassment, disgust and repression about sex. Broadly, the Church has taught that we have a soul (or sometimes a mind or reason) and a body; that our body is bad and its impulses will lead us to sin and hell; and that our soul (or mind) must control and deny the body, helping us to be virtuous. We need only think of the mediaeval sins (gluttony, lechery, covetousness, avarice, etc.) to understand how, for centuries, people have been instructed to distrust and hate their bodies. We cannot be complacent in the present day, either: just think how frequently we still use phrases like 'restrain yourself', or 'don't get carried away'.

Blake rejected this antithesis of body and soul: he believed that body and soul are one, that we are whole, and that our bodies and souls must act in harmony together. So, he says 'But first the notion that man has a body distinct from his soul is to be expunged'.

Now we come to the analogy of printing. Blake used acid to eat away the metal around his text and designs: the action of the acid burned away everything else and left the script and design standing proud, ready to be inked and pressed onto paper. He likens this to the way superficial but misleading elements of the world, 'apparent surfaces', will be melted away so we can see the 'infinite which was hid'. This event is then rephrased as 'If the doors of perception were cleansed'. The 'doors of perception' must be the senses, and Blake's context implies that they need to be cleansed by acid, 'corrosively' in a violent and radical stripping away of false impressions. The comment that, in Hell, this method is called 'medicinal' gives us a hint of how violent and radical a change of vision Blake has in mind.

The opening of vision through a 'cleansing' of the senses, the reunion of body and soul, and the 'improvement of sensual enjoyment' will all come about from getting rid of the Cherub. In plain terms, the first act in Blake's planned revolution is to remove religious curses and laws. Blake's programme would have horrified an eighteenth-century cleric: here was a man openly encouraging immorality, openly declaring that he will bring down the law, and even daring to disagree with God's behaviour in the Garden of Eden. A clergyman would certainly think this a 'devilish' doctrine.

We have come across the tragic results of repressed sexuality in our study of the *Songs*, however. 'The Angel', in *Experience*, presents two distortions of desire, and a wasted life; and Lyca is subjected to tyrannical emotional blackmail from her parents, who are terrified of her sexuality. 'A Little Girl Lost', in *Experience*, further elucidates this theme. Here, Blake simply identifies the cause of all the divided selves and personal hypocrisies he saw around him (and we see around us) every day. It is interesting to note that modern psychology would agree: self-hatred, self-disgust, self-punishment, repressed urges, perverted impulses – these are all villains which lead people to fail in their relationships and their search for contentment. By setting the soul against the body, the teaching of the Church was responsible for creating painful division within people. By forbidding natural desire, the Church tyrannised over and perverted the population. We will return to these issues in the next chapter.

The passage on which we have commentated centres on the concept of 'vision', and this is an issue we are familiar with from the *Songs*. Lyca's parents pass through a sudden expansion of their 'vision' from the narrowness and error of their 'senses', to a new and wonderful perception. Clearly, at the moment when the lion licks them, they have their 'doors of perception' suddenly 'cleansed', so seeing the lion as a 'spirit arm'd in gold' is like seeing 'the whole creation . . . appear infinite and holy'. In this passage, Blake adds two further images for the senses. First, they are 'the doors of perception'; then 'narrow chinks' of man's 'cavern'. In *The Marriage of Heaven and Hell* Blake develops his idea, by placing the responsibility on man himself. The reason we only see through 'chinks' in a 'cavern', is that 'man has closed himself up'; and this reminds us of Earth who turns her back, and obstinately will not see dawn arriving. In another part of the *Marriage*, it becomes clear that if we use our senses as physical senses only, Blake believes we are 'closing' ourselves and thus – metaphorically – blinding ourselves:

> How do you know but ev'ry Bird that cuts the airy way,
> Is an immense world of delight, clos'd by your senses five?

> (K 150)

What have we gained from approaching a Prophetic Book? First, we have gained explicit confirmation of the opinions and feelings about nature we became aware of from analysing shorter poems. Secondly, we have been able to reach firmer conclusions on two questions which were hinted at in the *Songs*, but which are much more plainly urged in the polemical work. First, the limitation of the five senses, which in the *Songs* appears to be a 'normal' state before the characters are suddenly exposed to 'vision'. Now that we have followed this idea to the *Marriage*, we understand a great deal more about it: that the physical use of the senses is like a prison or a blindfold, for which we are held responsible; and that opening or 'cleansing' our senses will be a violent process. Secondly, the hints towards uninhibited sexuality, and against prudish restraints, which were present in Lyca's nakedness, and implicitly in the story of the 'maiden Queen' in 'The Angel', have become strong and explicit. Blake advocates 'an improvement in sensual enjoyment'. We have also learned more about the origin of these problems: Blake traces them to the puritanical God-figure of the fall and expulsion in Genesis, and to the error of Church teaching, in making the division between body and soul.

Finally, we are beginning to appreciate the complex interlocking of Blake's thought. This is a peculiarly Blakean characteristic. On first meeting a poem, we respond to an expressed or conveyed emotion – a state of fear, or delight, whatever it may be. The more we investigate, however, the more we appreciate that this poetic 'state' is integrated into a coherent analysis. The 'state', or feeling, seems to be at both ends of the process at once: it provides the motive for analytical thought, to find out how it came about; and it is the end of a process of thought, the result of reasons which have necessarily produced it. So, for example, we feel the sudden despair of '. . . the time of youth was fled / And grey hairs were on my head' at the end of 'The Angel'. There is a devastating realisation that life has been wasted. Now we can ask and answer questions:

What went wrong?

She hid her pleasure.

Why?

Because pleasure was frowned on, and went against her self-image as a 'maiden Queen'.

Why was pleasure frowned on?

Because the Church said so.

Why did the Church say so?

To keep her from being free, out of jealousy.

Why was the Church jealous?

Because it is an old, white-haired, impotent institution.

How did the Church teach this?

By persuading her that body and soul are opposed to each other.

Then we find we could start again in the other direction. This time, I shall journey through the reasons a little more briefly:

What will follow from teaching division of body and soul?

Hatred of the body, banning all sensual pleasure.

What will people do if pleasure is banned?

They will distort, hide and pervert their impulses.

How will they behave?

Emotionally demanding, repressed, dishonest, hostile and defensive.

How will they feel?

Miserable and futile.

So, the chain of reasons is continuous and can lead us both back from the 'life-experience' of the poem, to an original cause; and forward from the cause, which can predict, as an inevitable consequence, the 'life-experience' of the poem.

Conclusions

We now have certain 'visions' of nature to consider, and it is worth recording two points about these sudden insights, which occur when the 'inner' eye breaks free from the prison of the 'senses' and sees to the essence of the world about us.

1. First, the moments of 'vision' we have found are all positive. When Lyca's parents see the lion in his visionary character, they see 'a spirit arm'd in gold'; and they forget their fear. When Blake breaks the false vision of Leviathan, a truth of calm and beauty is revealed, upon a 'pleasant bank' and listening to a harper. When God created the tyger, the stars 'threw down their spears / And water'd heaven with their tears' of wonder and joy, not sadness. In *The Marriage of Heaven and Hell*, Blake gives a further name to this visionary revelation: when the apparently 'finite &

corrupt' world is transcended, what is revealed – the true essence of nature – appears 'infinite and holy'. In the same passage, 'infinite' is used twice more to characterise what nature truly is.

This answers one of our questions: Blake is an optimist, and believes that nature is inherently good, inherently wonderful and divine. However, we should notice the word 'infinite'. Nature is not in any sense limited, and this means that nature's power and frightful appearances are as infinite as its shining benevolence and joy.

Bright and powerful colours – gold, burning and shining – as well as deep extreme emotions (for example the 'deep surprise' of Lyca's parents) are connected to these positive visions of true or infinite nature. There may still be some confusion between these genuine moments of revelation and the positive dreams of heaven depicted as a childlike faith in the *Songs of Innocence*. However, we are learning to distinguish the ambivalent but temporarily reassuring dream of a God 'like his father in white' who rescues the little lost boy in *Innocence*, from the altogether more robust and assertive statements Blake reserves for 'true' vision.

2. Secondly, what circumstances bring about the sudden revelation of a 'vision'? On each of the three occasions that we have studied, the moment of 'vision' coincides with a climax of emotions. In his poem to Thomas Butts, Blake describes himself as over-whelmed by the dazzling beauty of the morning: 'Amazed and in fear / I each particle gazed', and he is 'astonished, amazed' to underline the heightened state of his emotions. In *The Marriage of Heaven and Hell*, the angel's vision of Leviathan has built up vivid power as the monster approaches, and at the moment of climax terror is so overwhelming that the angel himself flees, whereupon 'vision' occurs. This same close relationship between extreme fear and vision occurs in the case of Lyca's parents, who cringe to the ground in extreme fear before realising 'with deep surprise' that the lion is 'a spirit arm'd in gold'. The more theoret-ical analogy in *The Marriage of Heaven and Hell*, between acid eating away the metal around Blake's engravings on the printing plate, and the cleansing of the inner eye or the burning away of impediments to vision, implies a similar conclusion: that

achieving vision is a violent, radical and – initially at least – frightening process.

Methods of Analysis

In this chapter, we have continued to approach each poem in the manner demonstrated and described in Chapter 1. However, we have added some further features to our analytical 'armoury':

1. We have pursued a particular question: we have investigated the presentation of nature in Blake's poems. This has given us a clear goal to aim at, and at each stage our interest in understanding a specific theme enabled us to formulate clear questions and then seek answers to them.

2. At the start, we also brought forward what we had learned about *Innocence* and *Experience* from Chapter 1. The different coexistent perceptions we noticed in Chapter 1 relate to the theme of nature. Thinking about this relationship at the start of the present chapter also helped us to clarify the kind of theme we were investigating. We therefore began with the understanding that we would look at *perceptions of* nature, hoping to discover what ideas and implications about nature itself lie *behind the competing perceptions.*

3. We have made a 'jump' from the *Songs of Innocence and Experience*, moving on to one of the Prophetic Books where the reasoning that underpins Blake's view of the world is made more explicit, but where interpretation can often appear more difficult because of the allegoric and allusive form of the writing.

4. We approached *The Marriage of Heaven and Hell* selectively, deliberately ignoring elements in the Prophetic Book where interpretation would be dense, or references would need to be looked up. Instead, we searched for, and found, confirmation and extension of ideas and motifs we had already found in the *Songs.*

5. In this selective approach, we also focused on naturalistic rather than polemical passages in the *Marriage*. We can approach these passages with the same concentration on language and effects as

we can apply to the poems, or to other prose works. Working out the more complex allusions and names, with the help of a good reference-work, can be deferred to a later stage, after a sound understanding of Blake's work as a literary creation is in place.

6. We are actively drawing comparisons between Blake's works, and this begins to draw his ideas on several different topics together into a single philosophic entity. For example, we likened the angel's inability to see the 'pleasant bank' and 'harper', and his insistence on his vision of hell, to Earth's refusal to 'turn' toward the morning, in 'Earth's Answer'; and we related Blake's command for the Cherub to leave his post to the punishing God of both 'Introduction' and 'Earth's Answer' in *Experience*. Similarly, we connected Lyca's nakedness to the phrase 'an improvement of sensual enjoyment'. We could call this active seeking of comparable moments, and then thinking about them and the themes they exemplify, a process of 'networking' in Blake's works. Networking, both between the *Songs* and between them and the Prophetic Books, will become an increasingly rewarding approach as we continue to study.

Suggested Work

1. Nature as subjective perceptions and imaginative vision is a per-vasive theme: it informs all the *Songs* either directly or indirectly. Using the approach demonstrated in this chapter, complete your study of the 'Lost' and 'Found' poems from *Songs of Innocence and Experience* by studying 'A Little Boy Lost' (K2, 50) and 'A Little Girl Lost' (K2, 51). These two poems focus on religious zeal and sexual oppression, and you will be able to carry the con-clusions we have reached in this chapter directly into studying them.

2. Read Blake's poem *Auguries of Innocence* (K 431–4). This poem was written a decade after the *Songs*, in about 1803, and is not symbolically difficult. However, the opening quatrain is a cele-brated statement of imaginative reality. In studying this poem, two analytical tasks may be enlightening:

a) List and annotate any connections between *Auguries of Innocence* and the *Songs* we have studied which come to your mind.

b) Compare the use of 'heaven' and 'God' in *Auguries of Innocence* to their use in *The Marriage of Heaven and Hell*. This will help to distinguish between ironic and non-ironic uses of spiritual terms in Blake, and will further clarify the shifting perspectives on 'heaven', 'God' and 'Lamb' we find in *Innocence* and *Experience*.

3

Society and its Ills

We have already strayed into the territory this chapter will investigate. We have made passing references to the two 'Chimney Sweeper' poems, for example, and we have begun analysing Blake's criticisms of the established Church, which he saw as a hypocritical institution supporting a corrupt and unjust status quo. So we know that Blake held subversive beliefs, and was indignantly angry at injustice, oppression and tyranny. In this chapter we will begin by studying six of the *Innocence* and *Experience* poems, then move on to look at extracts from three of the Prophetic Books – *The Marriage of Heaven and Hell* again, as well as *The First Book of Urizen* and *Europe, A Prophecy*.

'The Chimney Sweeper' (*Songs of Innocence*)

Here is 'The Chimney Sweeper' from *The Songs of Innocence*:

'The Chimney Sweeper'

When my mother died I was very young,
And my father sold me while yet my tongue,
Could scarcely cry weep weep weep weep.
So your chimneys I sweep & in soot I sleep.

Theres little Tom Dacre, who cried when his head
That curl'd like a lambs back, was shav'd, so I said,

Hush Tom never mind it, for when your head's bare,
You know that the soot cannot spoil your white hair.

And so he was quiet, & that very night,
As Tom was a sleeping he had such a sight,
That thousands of sweepers Dick, Joe, Ned & Jack
Were all of them lock'd up in coffins of black,

And by came an Angel who had a bright key,
And he open'd the coffins & set them all free.
Then down a green plain leaping laughing they run
And wash in a river and shine in the Sun.

Then naked & white, all their bags left behind,
They rise upon clouds, and sport in the wind.
And the Angel told Tom, if he'd be a good boy,
He'd have God for his father & never want joy.

And so Tom awoke and we rose in the dark
And got with our bags & our brushes to work.
Tho' the morning was cold, Tom was happy & warm.
So if all do their duty, they need not fear harm.

(K2, 12)

The story of this poem is clear on first reading. The speaker is a sweep who was sold when very young. A second sweep, a new recruit called Tom Dacre, is upset at first because his head is shaved. He is comforted, first by the poem's speaker, then by a dream of heaven and an angel. At the end of the poem, Tom Dacre is happy in his new life as a sweep.

The metrical brilliance of this poem lies in its variations on a predominantly anapaestic pattern. There are several different kinds of variation employed, and we will only notice three before moving on to our main interest in this chapter, the political and social conundrum with which Blake challenges us. First, Blake slips occasional iambs in among his anapaests, which gives a lingering, hanging delay to the iambs: they lack the expected 'patter' of an anapaest. This variation adds a mournful ring to the mother's death and the sweep's extreme youth in the first line: 'When my **moth** / er **died** / I was **ver**

/ y **young**'. Secondly, Blake adds stresses in some lines. For example, the speaker's enthusiasm for Tom's dream spills over as he enumerates all the sweeps: 'That **thou** / sands of **sweep** / ers **Dick**, / **Joe**, **Ned** / & **Jack**', and an extra bounce enlivens the release as '**leaping laughing** they **run**'. The most outstanding example of extra stresses comes in the third line, where the child sweep cries out his misery and his trade simultaneously through the streets, in a way that seems to block the running anapaests completely, and stop the whole story in its tracks: 'Could **scarce** / ly cry **weep** / **weep weep weep**'. The third effect Blake employs is complete regularity. Again, Blake achieves more than one effect by means of regular anapaests. So, for example, the contrast between metrical obstruction in the proviso '**if** he'd **be** a **good boy**', and the succeeding regular line 'He'd have **God** / for his **fath** / er & **nev** / er want **joy**', adds a rapid glibness to the angel's spurious promise. On the other hand, the combination of regularity with monosyllables and off-rhyme in lines 21 and 22 lends a drumming monotony to the rhythm, conveying the weary drudgery of the sweeps' lives.

However, much of Blake's metrical artistry is deployed simply in the service of naturalness: this poem creates an expressive but unaffected voice, and convincing dialogue. Look, for example, at the sweep's conversational rhythm in '**Hush Tom** ne**ver mind** it'. Much of the impact of the poem's uncompromising content resides in the very ordinariness of the sweep's voice which tells us the story. The stark and matter-of-fact relation of the sweep's childhood in the first stanza, with its ghastly acceptance of inevitable consequence in 'So your chimneys I sweep', chillingly provokes the reader's outrage.

Looking back at our brief study of rhythm and tone in this poem, we can say that we have identified two contrasting (but equally natural) tones of voice. First, we have found the chillingly matter-of-fact voice of the opening stanza, fatalistic and bleak; and we can connect the weary drudgery of lines 21 and 22 with this. Secondly, we have noticed a build-up of enthusiastic excitement in the account of Tom Dacre's dream, a mood ushered in by the angel's double-stressed 'bright key', sustained by the multi-stressed list of 'Dick, Joe, Ned & Jack', made to gambol and bounce in 'leaping laughing they run', and sprinting at pace through the regular 'And **wash** in a river and **shine** in the **Sun**', enhanced by the brightness of the sibilance.

When we consider the content of 'The Chimney Sweeper', it falls into these two contrasting perceptions: on the one hand, a factual depiction of the sweeps' lives that is clear and shocking; on the other hand, an intoxicating picture of the promised afterlife in Tom's dream of an angel. Blake's conclusion is the final couplet. Here, two strong caesurae bisect the lines to give the finality of antithesis to both statements. The first provides a bald contrast between the actual situation and Tom's comforting faith, a microcosm of the poem as a whole which flatly juxtaposes these two perceptions throughout. The final line, introduced by a spurious appearance of logic in 'So . . .', sets out the Church's deal with oppressed people. We can paraphrase this as 'If *you* submit to misery and don't make trouble, *we* will give you a dream'.

What are the characteristics of the two contrasting 'truths' in this poem? We have used the words 'bleak', 'fatalistic', 'stark' and 'uncompromising' to denote the portrayal of the sweeps' actual situation. Blake endows the description with these qualities in two ways. First, he avoids elaboration and gives a matter-of-fact account. For example, notice that 'my father sold me', and 'we rose in the dark / And got with our bags & our brushes to work' are plain statements of fact, without emotive content. Secondly, Blake encourages a sense of fatalism by the repeated use of the conjunction 'so', and by the logic of the sweep's comforting words to Tom. We notice that each stage of the story is connected to the next by 'so' (lines 4, 6, 9, 21 and 24). Each stage in this grim story is thus presented as an inevitable consequence of the last: the speaker shows no consciousness that the ghastly train of events could be altered or avoided in any way. The logic of his comforting words to Tom is equally chilling. We notice that one idea, the idea of Tom not becoming a sweep, is utterly excluded from his mind: he cannot and does not think about it at all. The other variables – fair hair, baldness and soot – are dealt with logically. The awful conclusion, that Tom will be happier bald, is the outcome of this fatalistic exclusion in the speaker's mind.

Blake, then, has excluded all possibility of change, and all emotion, from his account of the sweeps' lives. As readers, we are invited to bring our own morality into the equation. It is clear that Blake expects all fair-minded people to experience the revulsion and outrage we feel at the start of the twenty-first century: the child sweeps were a social obscenity, a scandalous system of child slavery within a society claiming to be 'civilised'. However, we should go further than this, to imagine the direct challenge to conscience this poem presented at the time. Notice that the speaker says '*your* chimneys I sweep' (my italics): Blake's contemporaries employed master-sweeps, the slavers, who sent small children up the flues. We should think about the present-day equivalent. This would be something like a fourteen-year-old factory worker on starvation wages and an eighty-hour week somewhere in Korea, Thailand or Taiwan, addressing us directly: 'So *your Walkman* I assemble'. We, as readers, are addressed directly and treated as contributors to the unjust system. We are not receiving Blake's message in the way it was intended, if we feel complacent because there are no child sweeps nowadays.

The other perception in the poem is Tom's dream. We have seen that this is exciting and related enthusiastically, in rhythmically intense verse. At the same time, we notice that it is strictly relegated to a time after death and another world, not this one. The sweeps begin 'lock'd up in coffins of black'. The angel of this poem is similar to those of 'Night': unable or unwilling to alter the harsh facts of life in this world, only active in an idealised afterlife. We could take a cynical attitude to Tom Dacre's dream and simply think of it as a lie, but Blake's poem does not give us authority to dismiss the dream of heaven in this way, just as we had to both recognise the limitations of the lion's 'New worlds', and suspend our disbelief in the poem 'Night'. In 'The Chimney Sweeper', we are not invited to decide on the truth or falsity of Tom's dream. Instead, Blake emphasises its truth *for Tom*. The dream's influence over the upset sweep is undeniable, for despite the cold morning 'Tom was happy & warm'.

The problem this presents to us is the social dilemma of *Innocence*. We are faced by scandalous cruelty and injustice, and the religious propaganda that sustains injustice. We feel an urge to change things – to help the sweeps gain their freedom, perhaps to

attack the heartless father, the master-sweep, the employers (ourselves), the 'angel'-Church with its moral blackmail: there is no
shortage of villains in this picture. The problem is that the victim is
happy, and the other sweep, the speaker, clearly cannot conceive of
any other life. Our dilemma is, should we, or should we not, make
people miserable by telling them? Should we tell them that they are
obscenely exploited? What do you do with a happy victim, like Tom
Dacre at the end of the poem: make him unhappy, or leave him as
he is?

Blake's 'The Chimney Sweeper' embodies this problem in both of
its contrasting views. Our dilemma is deepened by both the speaker's
fatalism and limited outlook, and the eager energy of Tom Dacre's
dream. We should notice that Blake has gained this disturbing effect
by again keeping his poem strictly within the limits of *Innocence*'s
perception. We have come across the same divided perceptions, and
the same problem before, in the poem 'Night'; but in the sweeps'
case the division between perceptions is more stark, and provokes
more outrage in the reader.

What is the relation between dream and reality in this poem? We
have pointed out that the two perspectives are repeatedly and flatly
juxtaposed throughout the poem, and in these terms the speaker
does not suggest any relation between them: they are both 'facts',
one objective and the other subjective, and that is all. However, the
angel and then the speaker, who accepts the angel's message, both
propose a conditional relationship, and the horrific symmetry of this
condition is emphasised in the antithetical structure of the final
couplet. The angel's and speaker's message is that you should 'be a
good boy' and 'all do their duty'; in other words, submit to misery
and poverty without complaint. Then, in return, you will be given
an optimistic dream. Of course, we notice that this deal excludes the
same idea the speaker excluded from his words of comfort: the idea
that we could change and better our existence in *this* world. The flat
juxtaposition of dream and reality in the rest of the poem highlights
the lack of any real relation between the two. Whether we believe in
heaven or not, Blake implies, we could still – separately – destroy the
moral obscenity of children being sold into slavery.

'The Chimney Sweeper' (*Songs of Experience*)

'The Chimney Sweeper' in *Experience* develops the same situation, but introduces a new perspective:

'The Chimney Sweeper'

A little black thing among the snow:
Crying weep, weep, in notes of woe!
Where are thy father & mother? say?
They are both gone up to the church to pray.

Because I was happy upon the heath,
And smil'd among the winters snow:
They clothed me in the clothes of death,
And taught me to sing the notes of woe.

And because I am happy, & dance & sing,
They think they have done me no injury:
And are gone to praise God & his Priest & King
Who make up a heaven of our misery.

(K2, 37)

We can begin by trying to define the different perspectives on the sweep's lot that are expressed in this poem. Here, we come across three views of the sweep's situation: an observer's, his own, and that of his parents. It is clear from first reading that the observer feels pity and outrage; that the sweep understands how he has been exploited; and that his parents are self-justifying, salving their consciences.

The metre is a combination of iambs and anapaests again; but in this poem there is a majority of iambs, so the poem hangs and beats more slowly than the one from *Innocence*, giving an effect of weariness. Blake repeats and metrically isolates the word 'weep' in the second line, as he did in the earlier poem; but this time he adds an explicit comment, calling the sweep's cry 'notes of woe', a comment repeated by the sweep himself at the end of the second stanza. The final word, 'misery', breaks the metre completely. It is as if this word cracks through the pretence of the parents' made-up 'heaven', and the metre of the poem, like a final fragmenting of false dreams and false coverings. However, the weary tone of the whole poem, and the ominous rhyme-words Blake has used ('snow' [twice], 'woe' [twice], 'death', 'injury' and 'misery') insistently undermine the validity of any made-up 'heaven'.

We can now look at the poem's three perspectives more closely. The observer's perspective evokes pity, calling the sweep a 'little black thing' crying 'notes of woe'. Blake chooses the simplest possible way to convey how disturbed the observer feels. The observer's question, 'Where are thy father & mother? say?', conveys his need to find an explanation for the sweep's condition, and his need to apportion blame. In fact, the observer acts out our role as readers: he is upset by destitution, and he reacts by trying to find a culprit in order to vent his feelings.

The parents' perspective is in three stages. First, we are told (stanza 2) that they sold their boy into misery *because* he was happy. This is a more extreme instance of the attitude of Lyca's parents in 'The Little Girl Lost', who order her to be miserable because they are: this implies jealousy of the child's happiness – they find his innocence intolerable. The second stage the parents pass through (lines 9 and 10) is to absolve themselves from guilt, on the grounds that their son is still happy. This stage in their feelings is crucial, as it re-states the dilemma of the *Innocence* poem, but from another point of view. The earlier poem asked: 'what do we do about a victim who is clearly in ghastly circumstances, but who is nonetheless happy?' One answer is to do as these parents do: shrug off responsibility and guilt, and deny that the evil exists simply because it does not hurt. By re-stating the question and answering it in this way, Blake is complicating the reader's response to the two poems. The parents appear to answer the observer's needs: they are clearly to blame, so we feel that we are on the trail of a scapegoat, a proper target for our anger and indignation. At the same time, the denying response to social injustice is closed off from us. We cannot now answer the first poem by saying 'why make the poor mite miserable? It is better to leave him happy, as he is'.

The third stage of the parents' perspective suddenly multiplies our targets for us. The parents' psychology is clear: they are pleased because they do not have to feel guilty. They do not feel guilty because they are persuaded that their son will go to heaven. They are grateful to the whole establishment, Church and state, which enables them to salve their consciences. The sweep is clear that Church, state and parents collude in a hypocritical lie: they 'make up' a heaven where, in fact, there is 'misery'.

The sweep's perspective is the most problematic. On the one hand, he is outspoken about the life he has been sold into. He wears 'the clothes of death' and cries 'the notes of woe'; it is only his parents who 'think' they have not harmed him; and the establishment invents heaven where the fact is 'misery'. On the other hand, he remains happy both before and after being sold as a sweep. Notice that the sweep's happiness was never affected by adversity ('I . . . smil'd among the winters snow'); and that 'I am happy, & dance & sing' is in the present tense. This poses a further question for us. This sweep is clearly not under the delusion of Tom Dacre's dream: he recognises his dreadful life, and rejects Church teaching categorically. Why, then, is he still happy?

The sweep's attitude seems to be something new. We have met figures whose minds are limited to the perspective of *Innocence* (for example, Tom Dacre and the speaker in the earlier poem; and the little boy who questions the Lamb, deducing a gentle creator from his gentle experience of life) and we have met figures imprisoned within the viewpoint of *Experience* (for example, Earth in 'Earth's Answer', or Lyca's parents in 'The Little Girl Lost'). This sweep, who clearly understands both *Innocence* and *Experience*, and remains happy despite his knowledge, represents a new perspective.

We will pause here, to summarise what we have found about the social and political actions of these poems.

First, Blake presents a thorough and radical analysis of society, in many ways similar to that of Marxism, or socialism. The established authorities exploit and oppress people. These authorities include the 'King' or state, the Church and its priests, and implicitly ourselves – the bourgeois reader who contributes to and benefits economically from a corrupt status quo. The materialist motive for this exploitation is stated when the child is 'sold'.

Secondly, Blake presents the scandal of social injustice in a complex form: there is a failure of love, or jealousy of innocence, in the sweeps' parents; the Church colludes with this by insisting on obedience, providing a dream of heaven, and absolving the parents from responsibility; the other victim also colludes, being unable to imagine any different existence. In short, it is a whole social system that is unjust and corrupt, and trapped within the narrow, frightened viewpoint of either *Innocence* or *Experience*: there is no comfortable scapegoat, but many contributors to the evil. This said, it must be acknowledged that the tyrannical agency these two poems criticise most is the Church.

Thirdly, Blake concentrates to a great degree on problems of understanding. Both poems juxtapose different limitations of viewpoint, and both develop the central role of understanding in any possible improvement or reform. Karl Marx, the so-called 'father of communism', identified education as a crucial stage in a society's progress towards equality. In his analysis of social classes, he predicted that the middle class would become increasingly idealist, and would therefore educate the working classes and actively lead them towards rebellion and the assertion of their economic power. In the case of Blake, the structure of the *Songs*, founded on the opposition of two fatally limited perspectives, emphasises that he places the question of understanding, and seeing clearly, at the heart of any hope for change.

Finally, we must recognise that these are active, campaigning poems. They may be beautifully crafted, psychologically true (see, for example, the portrait of the sweep's parents' attitudes in the *Experience* poem) and provide aesthetic pleasure, but they also provoke us, manipulate our responses as readers, and attack our complacency in a radical and active manner. These poems present us with problems, and leave us feeling both indignant and uneasy. The target for our outrage is the whole system, because the whole system inflicts the suffering we pity. Clearly, Blake has a political purpose in these poems.

This perceived political aim in Blake's poems will lead us to look at the role of poetry and prophecy later in the chapter. We will now move on directly to look at the 'Holy Thursday' poems, which focus on the issue of charity. For the purposes of our analysis, we can take both poems more-or-less together.

'Holy Thursday' (*Songs of Innocence*)

Here is the poem from *Songs of Innocence*:

'Holy Thursday'

Twas on a Holy Thursday their innocent faces clean
The children walking two & two in red & blue & green
Grey headed beadles walkd before with wands as white as snow
Till into the high dome of Pauls they like Thames waters flow

O what a multitude they seemd these flowers of London Town
Seated in companies they sit with radiance all their own
The hum of multitudes was there but multitudes of lambs
Thousands of little boys & girls raising their innocent hands

Now like a mighty wind they raise to heaven the voice of song
Or like harmonious thunderings the seats of heaven among
Beneath them sit the aged men wise guardians of the poor
Then cherish pity; lest you drive an angel from your door

(K2, 19)

This poem describes an annual procession, when thousands of the poorest children in London were marched from charity schools to St Paul's. There, they took part in a church service as a demonstration of their piety, while their patrons looked on. Blake adopts an ambivalent tone, as befits the poem in *Innocence*. So, the beadles are 'Grey headed' and have 'wands as white as snow' – the attributes of senile impotence and puritanism – and they sit symbolically 'Beneath' the children; yet the explicit comment in the poem calls them 'wise guardians of the poor'. In the context, this is ambiguous: is their wisdom in guarding the poor due to kindness, or self-interest and the defence of the establishment? The final line is equally ambiguous, addressed directly to the reader and leaving open whether we should pity the children for being poor, or for being regimented and exploited in a public show of piety.

'Holy Thursday' (*Songs of Experience*)

Here is 'Holy Thursday' from the *Songs of Experience*:

'Holy Thursday'

Is this a holy thing to see,
In a rich and fruitful land,
Babes reducd to misery,
Fed with cold and usurous hand?

Is that trembling cry a song?
Can it be a song of joy?
And so many children poor?
It is a land of poverty!

And their sun does never shine.
And their fields are bleak & bare.
And their ways are fill'd with thorns
It is eternal winter there.

For where-e'er the sun does shine,
And where-e'er the rain does fall:
Babe can never hunger there,
Nor poverty the mind appall.

(K2, 33)

In this poem, criticisms which are implied by the ambivalent subtext of the *Innocence* poem are expressed. Blake contrasts the bounty of nature in 'a rich and fruitful land' with the misery and poverty of the children. Rhetorically, the speaker adopts a pose of incomprehension in order to drive home the point that plentiful nature and poverty in the same world do not make sense together, and the situation is unnatural.

The poem opens with a powerful rhetorical question expressing astonishment at plenty and poverty. Three further questions in the second stanza introduce the only element of an implied and different perspective in this powerful outraged poem. The speaker is amazed to find plenty and poverty together in the world; he is then even more amazed to hear the children singing, and the question-form leaves it up to the reader to choose whether the children do, really, sing a 'song of joy' or whether they only manage a 'trembling cry' hardly recognisable as music. The suggestion that they might sing with joy despite their condition implies an attitude similar to that of the chimney sweeper of *Experience*. His continued happiness and avowed 'misery' were equally unexplainable. However, in this poem, we cannot be sure that this is what Blake implies: the question may well be bitterly ironic because their forced songs praising God are not joyful. We bring our own answers to the reading here, helping to 'make' the poem.

Having failed to comprehend the world in front of him, the poet therefore describes two natural worlds in the final two stanzas. First, he asserts that the children's world is 'bleak & bare' and sunless in an 'eternal winter': it must be, because they are poor. Then, he asserts that in a world with sunlight and rainfall, poverty is impossible.

The metre is a varied iambic, often leaving out the unstressed first syllable for a strong, natural emphasis at the start of the line (as in '**Babes** re**ducd** to **misery**') and invariably ending on a stressed (or 'masculine') rhyme. The tone of the whole is heavy and powerful, the lines cut off harshly. This contrasts with the lilt of occasional anapaests, and long hexameters, which give a bouncing or steady marching rhythm, in the poem from *Innocence*. Notice that in the earlier poem, the word 'innocent' provokes anapaests in both line 1 and line 8.

Both poems are rich in natural and seasonal imagery. The *Innocence* poem compares the children to 'Thames waters', 'flowers', 'multitudes of lambs'; and their song to 'a mighty wind' and 'harmonious thunderings'. This last juxtaposition hints ominously at a subtext. The mass of deprived children represents a threatening power: perhaps a coming storm the beadles and the establishment will be unable to control, in other words a revolution. It certainly suggests that the children's song is a natural force of far greater power than the pathetic beadles who sit 'beneath'. We have already remarked that the beadles' sticks 'as white as snow' are an emblem for their senile impotence; additionally, the 'white' and 'grey' of the beadles contrasts with the bright colours of the children's clothes. So, in the *Innocence* poem, imagery enhances the subtext: the suggestion of a more critical and conflictual analysis of the event than is verbally expressed.

In the *Experience* poem, the imagery is plain, and uses archetypal natural things: sun, rainfall, natural growth, and the seasons. The one extended metaphor asserts the subjective truth of the world from the children's point of view: stanza 3 depicts their lives as 'eternal winter' and 'fill'd with thorns'. Again, the meaning and effect are powerful and plain.

Combined, the two poems convey a sense of two powerful forces. In the first poem, imagery and the ambivalence of the final line suggest that there is a natural force within these oppressed children that would be 'mighty', capable of sweeping aside the authorities and their feeble 'wands'. This force is able to thunder among 'the seats of heaven'. In the second poem, the speaker's angry indignation is coupled with the point that poverty is an offence against nature. Anger, and nature itself, will surely right the situation.

We should notice, however, that the poem from *Experience* is characteristically analytical and uncompromising. It was generally accepted throughout the nineteenth century, and is still accepted by societies and governments today, that charity is a 'good thing': giving to charity is approved, and is regarded as a duty of the haves to the have-nots. In the present day, large international institutions channel charity from developed countries to famine relief and other huge projects in the third world. For Blake, charity was an evil. Why, he asks, does charity exist? Only because there is inequality and injustice. What, then, should we do? He emphatically tells us that we should not have charity, giving a little bit so poverty is *not so bad*, or *a little better*. Blake looks for the cause of the evil, and urges us to stamp out that. Put simply, charity only lessens the symptoms, it does not cure the disease, which is inequality.

The uncompromising anger of Blake's stance in 'Holy Thursday' in *Experience* is revolutionary. The poem suggests that there will not be a better world until private property – the very basis of the capitalist state, protected by laws and supported by religions for centuries – is abolished. Only then will we all equally share the sunlight and rainfall, and live in a world where 'Babe can never hunger'.

Analysing this 'pair' of poems has underlined the investigative, analytical qualilty of Blake's social and political thinking. In 'The Chimney Sweeper' of *Experience* we found that the search for blame began at the sweep's parents, but quickly widened to draw in the entire establishment, and the socio-economic system. Here, we find the poet attacking and dismissing charity: it is the underlying cause Blake seeks. He is not interested in tinkering with the system, helping a bit here and reforming a bit there. He goes for the underlying cause, urging us to look at it squarely, then eradicate it.

'The Garden of Love'

The two poems we will consider now are both from the *Songs of Experience*. The first is 'The Garden of Love':

> I went to the Garden of Love.
> And saw what I never had seen:
> A Chapel was built in the midst,
> Where I used to play on the green.
>
> And the gates of this Chapel were shut,
> And Thou shalt not, writ over the door;
> So I turn'd to the Garden of Love,
> That so many sweet flowers bore,
>
> And I saw it was filled with graves,
> And tomb-stones where flowers should be:
> And Priests in black gowns, were walking their rounds,
> And binding with briars, my joys & desires.

(K2, 44)

The title and first line of this poem immediately tell us that the story is a metaphor to be interpreted, not literal. The speaker goes to the garden where he played as a child, and finds it changed; but clearly the 'Garden of Love' represents childhood, innocence, and natural development as a whole; while the present priest-infested place with its chapel and tomb-stones represents the world as perceived in adulthood, a world in the perception of *Experience* dominated by Church laws.

The metre is anapaestic, and in this poem Blake uses the regular pattern almost throughout, thus achieving the maximum effect with two significant moments of irregularity. The first of these occurs in line 6, when three successive stresses, all thick with consonants and two of them ending in hard 't', batter the rhythm virtually to a halt: 'And **Thou shalt not**, writ over the **door**'. It is a harsh and destructive interruption to lilting anapaests, and conveys how aggressively Church law has invaded a once-joyful and natural spot. 'Thou shalt not', of course, is the opening of each of the Ten Commandments in the Bible.

The second strong variation of metre occurs in the final two lines. Two elements of the metre change suddenly. First, the lines are unexpectedly longer, quatrameter lines, whereas the poem has consisted of trimeter lines up to this point. This forces us to read for longer than we have planned, so when reading aloud we may find breath short in the extra final foot. The sudden lengthening conveys the weary oppression, and dull pointless repetition of priestly rule, and the priests' own futile sentry-duty, their 'rounds'. The weary drudgery Blake seeks to convey here is enhanced by the second metrical effect, where the second syllable of the second and fourth feet of each line asks to be stressed as much, or almost as much, as the final syllable. This creates a metrical unit 'de-**dum-dum**', containing two stresses. The amount of stress placed on the middle syllable varies within these lines, but arguably all of them carry extra weight to some degree:

And **Priests** in **black gowns**, were **walking their rounds**,
And **bind**ing **with briars**, **my joys** & **desires**.

The doubling of stresses in most feet here gives further heaviness and weariness to the rhythm. Repetition and dull drudgery is further enhanced by regularly spaced commas making two strong caesurae, and by internal rhyme (gowns / rounds, briars / desires). Apart from these two powerful effects conveying the destructive oppression of the Church, and a slight lingering of metre at '**sweet flow**ers' (line

8), the poem is made up of regular anapaests with an occasional iamb.

Just as Blake's metrical effects go for power, the imagery is strong and plain. A clear colour contrast is established between 'green' and 'flowers' on the one hand, and both the darkness of 'graves', the greyness of 'tombstones', and the priests' 'black gowns' on the other. The picture of the present – a graveyard filled with black-gowned priests and dominated by a forbidding chapel – increasingly fills the poem, so that the verse seems to become darker and darker as we read, through grey stones and dark earth to the eventual 'black' of line 11. In short, every element of the poem contributes to a sense of increasing despair, darkness and oppression.

Blake's subject is the loss of innocence, and his particular target is the denial of natural sexuality. It was the 'Garden of Love', and 'play' seems to refer to the innocent, uninhibited discovery of sexuality between children. However, the speaker is now aware of Church law, and sex is surrounded by bans, punishment and statutes which are enforced by a watchful priesthood. Some commentators take interpretation further, seeing the graves surrounding the chapel as a symbol for dead and buried instincts. Certainly innocence, 'play' and joy have been murdered by the negative commandments, and the graves indicate the deaths of pleasure and beauty.

The strong message of 'The Garden of Love' is enforced by the design, in which a boy and girl are praying, instructed by a black-gowned, bald monk, beside an open grave. The leaning tombstone repeats the children's pose in stone, indicating the petrified death their lives will now become. At the bottom of the plate, a turfed grave-mound is bound with criss-crossed briars repeating the diamond leading of a church window at the top right, and this is the grave of 'joys & desires'. The text is treated as underground: in place of Blake's usual plant-borders, this text is bordered by worms.

The content of this poem adds to our grasp of Blake's political agenda. Here he clearly opposes the rules governing sexuality in society. In place of chastity, shame and marriage, Blake advocates a natural development of sexual feelings, uninhibited by any rules or bans. This sounds like a campaign for what has more recently been called 'free love', but we should be careful of drawing over-facile conclusions. Sex is such a heavily-stereotyped and socialised subject, both in Blake's time and our own, that it is all too easy to imagine that he advocates promiscuity, a sort of anarchic sensual indulgence. This is not Blake's point at all.

At this point, it is often useful to think back to the other poems you have studied and look for other contributions to the theme, which will fill out your understanding. In our case, we can bring to mind three other texts in particular which help us with Blake's attitudes to sex.

First, remember 'The Angel' which was analysed in Chapter 2. This poem helps answer the question 'what is wrong with the Church's rules? Why are they so evil?' 'The Angel' tells us the story of what happens after natural sexual feelings have been murdered and buried underground (or repressed). In 'The Angel' these feelings have become selfish, perverted, dishonest, and eventually destructive. So, referring to 'The Angel' tells us why Blake opposed the repression and prohibition of sexuality.

Secondly, think back to our study of the 'Introduction' and 'Earth's Answer' from *Songs of Experience*, in Chapter 1. In those poems we found Blake criticising the God of Genesis who expelled and punished Adam and Eve. We remember that Earth calls this angry, anti-sex God a 'selfish, jealous' and 'cruel' father of men. Recalling these poems broadens Blake's criticism of repressed sexuality, suggesting that the personality of the oppressor is crucially flawed – that the Old Testament God is himself warped by fear, jealousy and an unnatural resulting cruelty.

Finally, in Chapter 2 we came across this statement from *The Marriage of Heaven and Hell*, saying that an 'improvement of sensual enjoyment' will come about: 'But first the notion that man has a body distinct from his soul, is to be expunged'. This increases our understanding considerably. Any ideas of promiscuity or sensually indulgent orgies of 'free love' are not Blake's, because they make the same mistake as Church law, in reverse. The Church wants *only* the soul, orgies are *only* for the body. This is clearly not Blake's meaning: his belief is in complete love by complete, 'whole' people who act with their physical and spiritual selves in unity. This is why the notion of separate bodies and souls should be 'expunged'. In *The*

Marriage of Heaven and Hell, Blake called for the Cherub and flaming sword to leave their place guarding the tree of life. This suggests a return to a state of innocence, before the Fall; but with a difference. In Blake's Eden, people could eat apples with impunity.

Finally, we are beginning to notice that the theme of nature we began studying in Chapter 2 is still with us, and continues to grow in significance. In the 'Holy Thursday' poems, we noticed that the power of the children's song is expressed as a natural energy ('mighty wind' or 'harmonious thunderings') and that the *Experience* poem strongly evokes nature's bounty. We remarked that nature and the natural are depicted as a standard of generosity, goodness and truth. In contrast, the tyrannical and unjust system makes a nonsense of nature. In 'The Garden of Love', flowers and the 'green' are evoked to convey the natural development Blake advocates; and the chapel-and-grave-filled present is clearly a perversion of the garden, an antinatural oppression. So, the significance of nature is being underlined again and again, as a basic truth underpinning the different social and political targets Blake focuses on in different poems.

'London'

We can now turn to the last of the short poems we have space to study in this chapter, 'London', from *Songs of Experience.*

'London'

I wander thro' each charter'd street,
Near where the charter'd Thames does flow
And mark in every face I meet
Marks of weakness, marks of woe.

In every cry of every Man,
In every Infants cry of fear,
In every voice; in every ban,
The mind-forg'd manacles I hear

How the Chimney-sweepers cry
Every blackning Church appalls,
And the hapless Soldiers sigh
Runs in blood down Palace walls

But most thro' midnight streets I hear
How the youthful Harlots curse
Blasts the new-born Infants tear
And blights with plagues the Marriage hearse.

(K2, 46)

'London' is another clear poem expressing bitter indignation against the state of society. The metre is predominantly regular, and has the iambic's strong steady beat. Similar in effect to the tripled stresses on 'Thou shalt not' we noticed in 'The Garden of Love' is the phrase 'The **mind-forg'd manacles**' in line 8. Here, however, the length of vowels and multiple consonant endings of 'mind-forg'd' give the phrase a less sudden, chopping brutality than 'Thou shalt not'. 'Mind-forg'd' is reminiscent of some phrases from 'The Tyger' which convey pain endured and sustained physical effort, such as 'dare sieze' and 'dread grasp'. Elsewhere, Blake sometimes omits the unstressed first syllable of the line to add impact with a stressed opening word: he does this with 'Marks' (line 4), 'Runs' (line 12) and 'Blasts' (line 15).

The speaker's voice in this poem, as in the 'Holy Thursday' poem from *Experience*, is not clearly distinguishable from Blake himself: he wanders the streets of London, a world corrupted and dominated by the narrow views of *Experience*, and reacts with shock and outrage; but the poem's power comes from the daring use of imagery which combines or juxtaposes different qualities.

In the first two lines, a world where even nature is bought and sold is revealed in the progress from 'charter'd [contracted, hired] street' to a bitter combination of nature and commerce: 'charter'd Thames'. The pun on 'mark' and 'marks' then hints at abstracts becoming concrete – the first 'mark' means 'perceive' or 'notice', but the 'Marks of weakness, marks of woe' are physical signs of suffering in the faces of those around him.

The second stanza builds the sounds of suffering in a law-bound society ('in every ban') and condenses them all into one image: 'mind-forg'd manacles'. Blake does not specify whose mind imprisons people, whether it is the fear and false belief in their own minds, or the minds of oppressors who invent laws and lies. If we consider the two poems about chimney sweepers we have already studied, or our analysis of 'Earth's Answer' in Chapter 1, we know that Blake portrays both sides of this question in his *Songs*: people's fears and fatalism imprison them in a false despair; the Church offers them a false deal in which obedience is exchanged for faith. This image repeats the transition from abstract to concrete rapidly and shockingly, by combining 'mind' with 'forg'd manacles'; at the same time, as we have remarked, the triple stress lengthens and weights this phrase with suffering and effort. Blake then passes directly back to the literal, in 'I hear', reminding us, after the sudden concrete image of cold iron and chains, that his real subject is cries of pain and misery.

Blake's success in presenting powerful concrete images for his subject-matter, and moving unhindered between abstract concepts and strongly physical objects, is like an assertion in itself. The effect is to add a further statement to the poem's meaning: the imagery seems to say to us 'you think mental imprisonment, manipulation and psychological oppression are abstract concepts; but they are not. They are just as much a prison as piles of stones and iron bars. When you cannot reach a thought, because it is beyond your mental bars, you are, *really*, in prison.'

The same technique renders the political points of the third stanza vivid. The Church is presented as a church, a building, which is 'blackning' being covered with both soot, and the colour of death, which is also symbolic of the sweeps' lightless lives. 'Blackning', then, combines concrete and abstract in one word. The 'hapless Soldiers sigh' is his last breath as he dies on the battlefield, and in a vivid concrete image this 'Runs in blood down Palace walls'. The political point is that the King uses the lives of his soldiers to maintain his luxury life, but of course British soldiers were not fighting at the King's palace – in Blake's time they died in America or India, in Spain, Belgium or France. Blake daubs the palace wall with the gore of war to enforce the radical political point he is making; and this image seems to say 'you may think the King does not _really_ want his soldiers to die; but that is not true – _really_, the King lives on their blood'.

The images in the final stanza are of infection, disease and death. The harlot's curse 'blasts' (infects) a baby's tear and 'blights' marriage with 'plagues'. Two elements from earlier in the poem recur here. First, the harlot is love for sale, and therefore repeats the unnatural motif of a 'charter'd' world from the opening two lines. Secondly, her voice becomes a physical disease in a way reminiscent of the cries turned concrete in stanza 2. Finally, marriage is asserted to be a 'hearse', a vehicle carrying the dead.

We could call the images in this poem 'metaphorical assertions': they are more aggressive than a comparison, and amount to the assertion that this (abstract) thing _is_ that (concrete) thing. In the final stanza Blake has used his technique to further develop his analysis of social attitudes to sex. The stanza divides sexual love into two: a coarse physical pleasure for sale on the one hand, and the deadness of a loveless, institutionalised 'marriage hearse' on the other. They are, of course, interdependent: men in commercial, love-less marriages buy their sex from prostitutes, and whores cannot aspire to be wives.

In Blake's analysis, then, society provides two institutions which enable sexual relations between men and women: prostitution and marriage. This observation makes convincing sense to us as readers, particularly when we think of the arranged marriages of Blake's time. However, we have found that Blake habitually goes beyond the symptoms of evil, seeking to identify the cause and calling for its eradication. So again, it is helpful to consider the picture given here in the context of other texts we have studied. Is there an underlying principle behind the criticised evil depicted?

The division between prostitution and marriage may remind us of the Church's separation of body and soul, that Blake will 'expunge'. We can suggest that the unnatural division of love between the 'pure' and cold (marriage hearse), and the physical and dirty (harlot) is a consequence of Church teaching because the Church exalts the soul and denies the body.

In the chimney sweeper poems, Blake's target was social cruelty and hypocritical Church teaching which sustains cruelty; in the 'Holy Thursday' poems, the target was economic injustice and charity; in 'The Garden of Love', the target was Church repression of sex. What are the targets of 'London'? The answer seems to be all of these and more. The 'chimney-sweepers cry' is mentioned in this poem as well, but in the context of a general attack on the **economic system** because the streets and nature are equally 'charter'd', the harlot sells sex, and the palace represents luxury enjoyed by the ruling class at others' expense. **Church hypocrisy** is attacked again in 'Every blackning Church', and more generally in 'every ban' – another reference to Church laws – as well as implicitly in the attack on marriage as a dead institution. **Oppression, injustice** and **suffering** are attacked again in 'Marks of weakness, marks of woe', but this time Blake's picture is not confined to one group, sweepers or the charity children: it is in 'every face I meet' and 'every voice'. In 'London', then, a whole suffering population is evoked. **The State** is attacked in the person of the King, whose palace represents economic injustice as well; but also, more generally, 'every ban' refers to state laws as well as religious ones, and marriage is a legal, social and economic as well as a religious institution. **Militarism**, and what we can call **imperialism** are attacked by the image of blood on palace walls: Blake dismisses honour, glory and patriotism, saying that the purpose of war is to protect the luxury lifestyle of a ruling class.

In short, the poem 'London' and the group of poems we have studied in this chapter represent a comprehensive attack on the political and religious establishment. Blake not only highlights the particular phenomena that provoke outrage or disturb complacency – such as the chimney sweeps' lot, or children in poverty – in these poems he launches an assault on the very bases of an oppressive society: **capitalism**, **organised religion** and **military power**. By implication, Blake's call is for us to sweep away these underlying causes, the bases on which society is ill-founded. So, these are not merely poems of **indignation** or **reform**. Because they call for a fundamental change, they are **revolutionary** works.

So far, we have sought to itemise Blake's targets in political terms. We conclude that he launches a comprehensive attack on society in these poems. However, we have found that Blake always sought to define the underlying evil behind all particulars, so we can also take a different approach. Is there one single focus of attack against which Blake directs his energy? To answer this question, we try to think of the poems we have read and studied as a group, and consider whether there is a principle they have in common, something that binds them together with the force of an universal idea.

When I consider Blake's attacks on society, I am struck by more than one salient point. First, I recognise that the Church figures prominently throughout: Blake expresses a constant abhorrence of its influence, and is outraged at its hypocrisy. Secondly, the theme of natural liberty and unnatural constraint appears everywhere. Finally, each evil we meet is related to economic power. These prominent themes are, of course, inter-related, since all contribute to one outcome: the preservation of the ruling establishment. Perhaps Blake's most inclusive expression of his 'vision' of society is a poetic one, which conveys not only the abhorrent hypocrisy and enslavement he saw around him, but also the poet's sympathy for those imprisoned within the system: the metaphor of 'mind-forg'd manacles' includes a great deal of what we have found in this chapter, from the heart-rending perspectives of 'The Chimney Sweeper' in *Innocence* to the bewildered speaker of 'The Garden of Love' and the 'trembling cry' of poor children singing in 'Holy Thursday'. To complete the idea, we only need to remember that it is all in aid of a 'charter'd', or commercial, world.

Toward the Prophetic Books

We have analysed a series of short lyrics from the *Songs of Innocence and Experience* which highlight suffering and injustice, and attack the society of Blake's time. He identifies underlying causes, and these basic errors in society are the targets of his attack. The emotional drive of these poems is powerful: indignation, anger, pain and sympathy drive them to challenge our complacency. By implication, then, the short lyrics call for a revolutionary change: Blake wishes to shock his readers from their apathy and enlist them as allies in rebelling against the status quo. However, as yet we have only a broad idea about what he wants to put in place of the corrupt system. At this stage we can summarise what we already know from the *Songs* about Blake's positive 'vision'. Again, we try to do this by thinking about all we have studied so far, as a whole, and looking for the prominent positive themes. This will give us a clear foundation of ideas to identify and pursue in some of the Prophetic Books.

Thinking about the poems we have studied so far, there appear to be five main positive themes:

1. **Nature.** We have found that the theme of nature is much more than one of natural beauty or landscape. Nature has a funda-mental significance in Blake. It includes both beauty and fear or awe (see 'The Tyger'); it is invoked in human life and develop-ment as well as in plants and animals (so, for example, false per-ception of nature is a 'mind-forg'd manacle' for Lyca's parents in 'The Little Girl Lost'; and the transformation of 'The Garden of Love' into a graveyard is anti-natural); and nature has a potential power infinitely greater than the oppressive establishment (so the children's song in 'Holy Thursday' is like a 'mighty wind'). Clearly, nature and natural development are portrayed as good, positive forces, while most of the evils Blake attacks can be seen as oppressions or perversions of nature.

2. **Innocence.** There is clearly a positive force, a sort of redemptive power, in the Innocent. However, it is still ambivalent since the 'innocent' so often also becomes the 'deluded' or ignorant. Nonetheless, we have met suggestions that a kind of 'innocence' may be able to survive the negative prison-world of *Experience*. We have met the unaccountable happiness of 'The Chimney Sweeper' from *Experience*, who understands his misery but remains happy; the 'vision' of Lyca and her parents, which makes the parents' fears disappear; and the power implied in the poor children's song in 'Holy Thursday': their 'innocence' and the joy of their song – again despite their oppressed physical conditions – may thunder 'the seats of heaven among'. Finally, we can remember the determination of the Bard, in the 'Introduction' to *Experience*: he asserts that the night of fear and materialism is 'worn', and that 'the morn / Rises from the slumberous mass'. By

implication, if Earth had the courage and optimism of this different kind of 'innocence', she too would be able to see a hopeful future, and would have the strength to throw off her chains.

3. 'Vision'. We have found moments which reveal essential insights, and on these occasions the 'mind-forg'd manacles' dissolve. Vision, in fact, can defeat all oppressive, hypocritical and tyrannical forces. The prominent example of this that we have met is narrated in 'The Little Girl Found', when Lyca's parents suddenly perceive the essence of the lion as 'a spirit arm'd in gold', and all – landscape, emotion and all other restrictive attitudes – is transformed. In *The Marriage of Heaven and Hell* we have read a more theoretical account of the power of 'vision'. The idea is connected to escaping from the prison of the five senses (the 'narrow chinks of his [man's] cavern') so that 'the doors of perception' are 'cleansed'. Then, the world will become 'infinite and holy' instead of 'finite & corrupt'. The theme of 'vision' focuses on individual subjective experience: a new way of seeing the world would need to open up within each person. So this theme suggests a kind of **self-liberation** through revelation, or imaginative seeing.

4. **Cyclical change**. We notice that many of the symbols which present change are what we call 'cyclical' symbols: of day and night, the seasons, growth and death of plants, and so on. In the poems we have studied, the movement of *Innocence's* day into *Experience's* night is constant and inexorable (see, for example, 'Night' from *Innocence*); and this is closely related to the development of people through childhood, youth, maturity and old age. The only unchanging 'immortal day' we have met is presented ambivalently in the poem 'Night'; predominantly, these poems present a picture of continuous cyclical changes, with the implication that these cycles will continue to be repeated. So, after entering the night of *Experience*, it is natural that there will be a new day, as the Bard prophesies in 'Introduction'. On the other hand, this also implies that there will be another night, and another day, in continuing cycles.

5. In connection with the 'cycles' we have noticed, we should consider **youth** and **age**. Thinking of the poems we have met, we can

remember numerous figures associating old age and oppressive or misleading authority. For example, we remember the grey-haired, impotent beadles of 'Holy Thursday'; the imbecilic 'old John with white hair' who leads the children back into childhood, away from knowledge, in 'The Ecchoing Green'; and the 'Cold and hoar . . . selfish father of men' who keeps Earth 'chained in night' in 'Earth's Answer'. Youth, on the other hand, is presented in a number of different forms, ranging from the pure innocence of the speaker in 'The Lamb' to the potential 'mighty' power of children in 'Holy Thursday', and the untouchable strength of happiness in *Experience*'s sweep. Clearly, there is a further future story implied: the white-haired old men will not survive for ever, and youth will take over. However, the outcome of this struggle is still to come. We have only found one, very positive, version of this future story: the redemption of her parents by Lyca, in 'The Little Girl Found', and we remember that this vision is presented as 'In futurity, / I prophetic see' – a projection beyond the present time of the *Songs*.

Blake's Prophetic Books have a reputation as difficult esoteric works, in which his private symbolic mythology baffles the reader. It is true that these works are often densely filled with references and allusions, and with invented symbolic names. Our contention, however, is:

1. We can approach the Prophetic Books from *Songs of Innocence and Experience*: the understanding we bring from the short lyrics will enable us to grasp Blake's meaning, if we make proper use of it.
2. There are elements and passages in the Prophetic Books which are accessible to study.
3. We can glean a great deal from the Prophetic Books, with a sensible, selective understanding of Blake's symbols. We can defer looking up the more intricate and secondary references to a later stage of study.

We tested this contention to some degree in Chapter 2, when we studied two short passages from *The Marriage of Heaven and Hell*. In the remainder of the present chapter, we will subject the method to a sterner test, taking longer passages from both *Europe, A Prophecy* and *The First Book of Urizen,* for detailed study.

The Prophetic Books

Europe, A Prophecy

We will print our first extract in full, taking quite a lengthy sample from *Europe, A Prophecy.* This will enable us to approach the analysis in clear stages that demonstrate how to obtain a toe-hold on these texts and begin to climb. Later extracts from the Prophetic Books will be treated more briefly and selectively.

Here are plates 10, 11 and 12 of *Europe,* complete:

Plate 10:
In thoughts perturb'd, they rose from the bright ruins, silent following
The fiery king, who sought his ancient temple, serpent-form'd
That stretches out its shady length along the island white.
Round him roll'd his clouds of war; silent the Angel went,
Along the infinite shores of Thames to golden Verulam.   5
There stand the venerable porches that high-towering rear
Their oak-surrounded pillars, form'd of massy stones, uncut
With tool, stones precious, such eternal in the heavens,
Of colours twelve, few known on earth, give light in the opake,
Plac'd in the order of the stars, when the five senses whelm'd   10
In deluge o'er the earth-born man, then turn'd the fluxile eyes
Into two stationary orbs, concentrating all things;
The ever-varying spiral ascents to the heavens of heavens
Were bended downward, and the nostrils' golden gates shut,
Turn'd outward, barr'd and petrify'd against the infinite.   15

Thought chang'd the infinite to a serpent, that which pitieth
To a devouring flame, and man fled from its face and hid
In forests of night: then all the eternal forests were divided
Into earths rolling in circles of space, that like an ocean rush'd
And overwhelmed all except this finite wall of flesh.   20
Then was the serpent temple form'd, image of infinite
Shut up in finite revolutions, and man became an Angel,

Heaven a mighty circle turning, God a tyrant crown'd.

Now arriv'd the ancient Guardian at the southern porch
That planted thick with trees of blackest leaf & in a vale   25
Obscure, enclos'd the Stone of Night; oblique it stood, o'erhung
With purple flowers and berries red, image of that sweet south
Once open to the heavens, and elevated on the human neck,
Now overgrown with hair and cover'd with a stony roof.
Downward 'tis sunk, beneath th'attractive north that round the feet,   30
A raging whirlpool, draws the dizzy enquirer to his grave.

Plate 11:
Albion's Angel rose upon the Stone of Night.
He saw Urizen on the Atlantic;
And his brazen Book
That Kings & Priests had copied on Earth,   35
Expanded from North to South.

Plate 12:
And the clouds & fires pale roll'd round in the night of Enitharmon,
Round Albion's cliffs & London's walls: still Enitharmon slept.
Rolling volumes of grey mist involve Churches, Palaces, Towers;
For Urizen unclasp'd his book, feeding his soul with pity.   40
The youth of England, hid in gloom, curse the pain'd heavens, compell'd
Into the deadly night to see the form of Albion's Angel.
Their parents brought them forth & aged ignorance preaches canting,
On a vast rock, perceiv'd by those senses that are clos'd from thought:
Bleak, dark, abrupt it stands & overshadows London city.   45
They saw his boney feet on the rock, the flesh consum'd in flames;
They saw the Serpent temple lifted above, shadowing the Island white;
They heard the voice of Albion's Angel howling in flames of Orc,
Seeking the trump of the last doom.

Above the rest the howl from heard from Westminster, louder & louder: 50
The Guardian of the secret codes forsook his ancient mansion,
Driven out by the flames of Orc; his furr'd robes & false locks
Adhered and grew one with his flesh, and nerves & veins shot thro' them.
With dismal torment sick, hanging upon the wind, he fled
Grovelling along Great George Street thro' the Park gate: all the Soldiers   55
Fled from his sight: he drag'd his torments to the wilderness.

Thus was the howl thro' Europe!
For Orc rejoic'd to hear the howling shadows;
But Palamabron shot his lightnings trenching down his wide back;
And Rintrah hung with all his legions in the nether deep.   60

Enitharmon laugh'd in her sleep to see (O woman's triumph!)
Every house a den, every man bound: the shadows are fill'd
With spectres, and the windows wove over with curses of iron:
Over the doors "Thou shalt not," & over the chimneys "Fear" is written:
With bands of iron round their necks fasten'd into the walls   65
The citizens, in leaden gyves the inhabitants of suburbs
Walk heavy; soft and bent are the bones of villagers.

Between the clouds of Urizen the flames of Orc roll heavy
Around the limbs of Albion's Guardian, his flesh consuming:
Howlings & hissings, shrieks & groans, & voices of despair   70
Arise around him in the cloudy heavens of Albion.

(K 241–3)

This is an extract from a longer poem, so we need a general idea of
the story to begin with. *Europe* is dated 1794 on the title-page. The
part of the poem we are looking at is framed between two historical
events: first, the American War of Independence, when the
American colonies defeated the British and won independence;
second, the French revolution and events in France between 1789
and 1793.

We know that Blake hated the ruling class and the established
Church in England. We have seen them depicted as tyrants in the
Songs, and the present extract continues Blake's enmity against the
establishment, and his desire for the English people to throw down
the oppressors (King, Queen, Parliament, Church). This extract tells
the story of the British ruling class, between their defeat at the hands
of the American colonists and the time when the banner of liberty
was raised across Europe while the French overthrew their monarchy
and executed their ruling class. In Blake's view, the government had
a warning at the hands of the Americans: their militarism had failed,
and liberty won the day. Blake imagined that the roof of parliament
fell down on the government following the defeat in America ('One

hour they lay buried beneath the ruins of that hall; / But as the stars rise from the salt lake they arise in pain . . .', *Europe*, plate 9, K 241). The first line of our extract, 'In thoughts perturb'd, they rose from the bright ruins . . . ', then, refers to the British government.

This is the historical context of the extract. However, it is obvious that we will need more information before we can grasp what is happening in the poem. There are a number of Blakean names, for example, and we do not know what they stand for. It is at this point that a novice reader wants to look up all the names. However, it is just at this crucial stage when it is vital to do further work on the poetry first: keep the reference books closed for the time being, and put up with confusion for the present.

There are two sound reasons for this advice. First, there are several Blakean names in the extract, but so far we do not know which ones are the most important. If you look up all of them, your mind will be cluttered with references, some of which are not relevant to the current extract. To demonstrate this, look at the following explanation of Palamabron (see line 59 of the extract):

> PALAMABRON symbolizes the poet's Pity for the oppressed, and in *Milton* plays the role of Blake himself in his quarrel with Satan-Hayley. Enitharmon compares him to the greathearted Judah, ancestor of Jesus (*Jerusalem* 93:14). Though he is 'the strongest of Demons' (*Milton* 7:47), he is 'mild & piteous' and 'good natur'd' (*Milton* 24:11; *Four Zoas* viii:391). His position is East; he is under Luvah and London (*Jerusalem* 74:3); but when the Zoas shift, he is found in the West (*Jerusalem* 54, design).[1]

This is only the first paragraph of six in the 'Palamabron' entry in a Blake reference-work. The new reader will be baffled by the number of other names mentioned (we know nothing so far about Hayley, Enitharmon, Judah, Luvah and the Zoas). Notice, also, that the expert refers to three poems, *Milton, The Four Zoas* and *Jerusalem*, and **none of them is the poem we are studying**. So, looking up the reference has befuddled our heads with a lot of names we don't

---

[1] Damon, S. Foster, *A Blake Dictionary: The Ideas and Symbols of William Blake*, Brown University Press, Providence, Rhode Island, 1965, p. 321.

understand; and we still know nothing about Palamabron's role in *Europe*.

Secondly, we are looking for a grasp of the poetry itself. We will achieve that by focusing on how it works. Information we look up slips out of our minds easily because it is only a disembodied label. In poetry, on the other hand, we learn from narrative and concrete imagery: it sticks in our minds. Additionally, remember that we bring a great deal of insight from the *Songs*. If we build on that instead of running to the reference-books, our grasp will consequently be more secure.

We can begin by working out as much as possible from the poetry. Let us look at each of the 'characters' in turn, and assemble as much as possible from the way they appear in the extract.

[1] **The 'fiery King'** is mentioned in line 2. From the sense of the lines, this is clearly the same person as the 'Angel' of line 4; and this in turn must be the figure referred to as the 'Guardian' in line 24, and '**Albion's Angel**' in line 32. Start by looking at the name itself: 'Albion' is an ancient name for Britain, and we know from *The Marriage of Heaven and Hell* that an 'Angel' may be a deceptive, Church-dominated hypocrite: one of the tyrants in Blake's world. If we put these together, we have 'Britain's tyrant'. This would suit the opening narrative: the members of the government crawl out from the ruins of their fallen parliament and follow their king or leader to various places in England 'Along the infinite shores of Thames to golden Verulam' (Verulam was a Roman site near to present-day St Albans, traditionally a religious centre). There is no need to be more specific, but we should notice that Blake compiles this figure out of a parliamentary leader (that would be the prime minister), a 'King', and elements of religion (Verulam – but also the fact that he 'sought his ancient temple'). So, **Albion's Angel** (also 'fiery King' and 'Angel') is the leader of Britain's government including monarchy, state and Church.

Now we can look at the extract, and see the role 'Albion's Angel' plays in the narrative. What does this character do? First (lines 2–23) he goes to Verulam and finds the 'ancient temple, serpent-form'd' that he sought. At the end of this part of the story, Blake sums up:

Then was the serpent temple form'd, image of infinite
Shut up in finite revolutions, and man became an Angel,
Heaven a mighty circle turning, God a tyrant crown'd.

We remember Blake's call for things to be 'infinite & holy' in *The Marriage of Heaven and Hell*, so the 'serpent temple', making the 'infinite . . . finite', or limited, must be negative. Our knowledge of the *Marriage* and the *Songs* also tells us that an 'angel' is part of the Church's big lie, deceiving and oppressing the people. If we take this thought further, we can suggest that 'heaven' – i.e. where 'angels' live – stands for the world of luxury and palaces in which the ruling class pampers itself: heaven, then, is mansions and palaces, places of power. The 'God' of this passage is clearly the oppressive tyrant we have met before: not a real God, but one invented by lying priests to support their power and legitimise their unnatural laws. So, in God becoming 'a tyrant crown'd' we recognise the same invidious, cruel co-operation between different branches of the establishment (state, king, Church) we met in 'The Chimney Sweeper': 'God & his Priest & King / Who make up a heaven of our misery'. During the forming of this 'serpent temple' we notice that the physical senses have overwhelmed everything else (the nostrils 'shut . . . barr'd and petrify'd'; the eyes 'stationary') and people have fled into 'forests of night'. We recognise much of this picture of oppression from the *Songs of Experience* and the *Marriage*. Blake is again describing a corrupt world, dominated by fear, limited by the physical senses, and deprived of vision.

Next, **Albion's Angel** finds the 'Stone of Night'. In lines 26–31, we gain some idea of what this 'stone' might be. We read that it was once 'open to the heavens, and elevated on the human neck', but it has now sunk down, has a 'stony roof' and is overgrown with hair. This imagery sugggests a human brain, and Blake tells us that it was once open and is now enclosed, imprisoned beneath stone. This adds to the images of 'barr'd' and 'petrify'd' senses – it is a further image of limitation, imprisonment, oppression. South and North may confuse us in this passage, as they are the wrong way around. However, since the whole of the picture so far is of evil and error, including Blake's characteristic irony of oppressive 'angels' and 'heavens', it should not surprise us that the compass is also upside-down.

Then, **Albion's Angel** stands on the 'Stone of Night' (in other words, the imprisoned intellect) and sees a figure called 'Urizen' who opens a book (see lines 32–6). Much of the rest of the action in our extract involves this 'Urizen' and other characters called 'Orc' and 'Enitharmon'. We can tell that there are further pictures of fear and oppression. See, for example, lines 41–5, where the 'youth of England' see the fearful dominance of the Angel standing upon his stone; and the picture of oppression in lines 62–7, where we recognise the dominance of Church law in 'Over the doors "Thou shalt not", & over the chimneys "Fear" is written' – imagery we met in 'London' from *Experience*.

We also find elements pain and defeat associated with **Albion's Angel** himself. For example, his bony feet on the rock have their 'flesh consum'd in flames' (line 46) and he is 'howling in flames of Orc' (line 48); and in the final lines 'the flames of Orc roll heavy / Around the limbs of Albion's Guardian, his flesh consuming', and sounds of pain and despair fill the 'Heavens of Albion'. Remember that these 'heavens' are courts and palaces. The clear implication is that the British government ends this extract under attack and fighting, far from dominant or secure.

Now that we have traced the story of **Albion's Angel** in this extract, it is worth trying to summarise. Here is an attempt to give a brief outline of what we have found: *The British governing class rises from being rocked by defeat in America, and uses its ancient religion to rebuild its dominance and oppress the people. However, at the end of the extract flames which are now burning 'throughout Europe' begin to threaten and consume the British governing class.*

The 'flames' in the last part of our extract must refer to revolution and overthrow in France and elsewhere in Europe. Blake sees the British government fighting with all its old weapons of tyranny and religious oppression, trying to sustain its power against a swell of revolution from Europe which threatens to overwhelm it.

[2] **Urizen**. This figure is introduced when Albion's Angel climbs onto the Stone of Night. We will again look at the poetry to formulate some idea of what 'Urizen' might be. First, Urizen has a 'brazen Book' which 'Kings & Priests had copied on Earth'. If we think back to the Sweep's 'God & his Priest & King', we can guess that Urizen might

therefore fill the role of 'God'. Call to mind our analyses of the poems from *Experience*: the 'God' Blake means is not a *true* God, but the aged selfish tyrant the Church imposes, who excuses child-slavery and commands priests to bind 'my joys and desires'. We remarked that this is the same kind of God as the one Earth fears, in 'Introduction' and 'Earth's answer': the angry God of Genesis, who curses and punishes Adam and Eve and is called 'cruel jealous selfish' by Earth.

Can we support this theory from the present extract? Looking again at the relevant passages, we find that Urizen has 'clouds & fires pale' which become 'Rolling volumes of grey mist' and hide people in 'gloom'. At the end of the extract the 'clouds of Urizen' are associated with the 'cloudy / Heavens' of Albion. This conveys a sense of mystery, blindness, and in 'grey mist' suggests old age (supported by the image of the establishment as 'aged ignorance preaches, canting'). It seems likely that our guess is leading us in the right direction, and that 'Urizen' stands for aged, white-haired and cruel tyranny – a God of harsh laws, who is used to frighten the people into submission.

[3] **Orc**. Orc is the most unknown figure in this extract. He is associated with 'flames' every time he is mentioned, and he is clearly the enemy of both **Urizen** and **Albion's Angel**. The Angel is caught between 'clouds of Urizen' and 'flames of Orc'; and Orc's flames are consuming the tyrant Angel, causing all the fear ('Howlings & hissings, shrieks & groans, & voices of despair') in the palaces of the ruling class ('the cloudy / Heavens of Albion'). We also notice that Orc 'rejoiced' to hear howls of pain from the ruling classes throughout Europe – so we can speculate that Orc is a revolutionary energy, hating the ruling class.

[4] **Enitharmon** is female and asleep. We cannot tell a great deal about her from this extract, and her name is no help. In this situation, simply place her in the conflict. Clearly, Enitharmon is on the side of the oppressors, since she 'laughed in her sleep' to see the oppression of society, vividly described in lines 61–7.

[5] **Palamabron**. We do not know how he fits in, or even which side he might be on, since he attacks 'his' wide back, but we cannot be sure whether the 'he' is Orc or the 'Guardian' whom Orc has attacked.

[6] Rintrah. We do not know how he fits in, either. He has military associations, having 'legions', but they are not yet in the fight.

So far, we have used the poetry to build up a picture of the character and actions of each figure in the extract. We have made interpretative use of imagery, suggesting for example that 'grey' hints at old age, and that 'mists' imply mystery, hiding the clear light of truth. This method of approach has given us a grasp of the overall story and its dominant theme: a violent conflict between tyrannical oppression and a wild revolutionary energy. There are two characters whose significance we cannot guess (Palamabron and Rintrah) and another about whom we know very little (Enitharmon). On the other hand, we understand what 'Albion's Angel' stands for; and we have sensible theories about Urizen and Orc.

It is now time to use a reference-book; but all we want to do, for this extract, is confirm the interpretations of Urizen and Orc that we have advanced as theories. We have suggested that Urizen stands for a jealous, selfish and cruel authority: tyranny that rules by restrictive laws and fear. We also remember from the *Songs* that this kind of 'God' separates body and soul, then demonises the body, hating and banning sex. In K. P. and R. R. Easson's commentary on *The Book of Urizen*,[2] we read that 'Urizen is the adversary; through Urizen Blake exemplifies all the errors of a reasoning mind and the reality it builds, the fallacious reality which obscures and obstructs the path to infinite perception' (p. 67). They continue: 'The history of the adversary, Urizen, Blake saw catalogued in the history of religion, especially in the history of the Judeo-Christian religion. The fundamental error in Christian myth, Blake thought, was the narrative of the Fall of Man . . . Urizen is the god who falls, the god of the fall, and the god who perpetuates the fall through his "Net of Religion".' (p. 70). This adds to our conception of Urizen; but it also confirms our theory. Urizen *is* a reactionary, oppressive force, associated with the tyrant God who curses Adam and Eve for disobedience, the jealous oppressor of Earth in 'Earth's Answer', and the cruel deceiver who 'makes up a heaven' of the sweep's misery.

---

[2] Blake, William, *The Book of Urizen*, ed. and with a commentary by K. P. Easson and R. R. Easson, London, Thames & Hudson, 1979.

We connected Orc with the revolutionary upsurge in France, a force for liberty threatening to overthrow the established ruling classes. When we look up this name, we find that 'ORC is Revolution in the material world. He is the lower form of Luvah, the emotions', and that 'The relationship of Urizen and Orc, or convention and revolt, is that of the Contraries, without which progression is impossible. Their warfare goes back to the original antagonism of Urizen and Luvah. Urizen, by suppressing Luvah, only forces him into the lower form of physical revolt [Orc] . . .'.[3] This certainly confirms our guess that Orc stands for revolutionary force; his 'flames' must therefore be the destructive violence of rebellion. Here again, looking up a reference has added to our understanding because it has introduced the idea that Urizen and Orc are 'contraries': they are parts of a whole, and their conflict, which dominates our extract, is a struggle which will lead to progression.

On the other hand, looking up Orc and Urizen has complicated matters by mentioning another name – a figure we have not met before, Luvah, who apparently, and confusingly, stands for 'the emotions' and somehow becomes Orc. This introduces a characteristic of Blake's mythology that students often find difficult to master: characters change their names and turn into other characters. So, Luvah becomes Orc, as we have been told. Once we understand why characters change into one another, however, the system becomes easier to follow and expresses Blake's meaning far more fully. The answer is simply this: Blake's names belong to states: states of consciousness, development, perception; they do not belong to individual people. So, when a figure passes from one state of consciousness into another, their name changes. Indeed, even a part of a figure – one aspect of the personality – will have the name of that aspect, that mood. The reader therefore needs to be flexible, ready to follow these transformations of figure into figure, state into state; and the reader gains insight from understanding how and why these changes happen.

So far, we have assumed that the figures in this poem are like people, who carry their names with them whatever happens. We

---

[3] Damon, S. Foster, *op. cit.*, pp. 309–11.

could call this a mechanistic, or static, interpretation. However, Blake's ideas are not static. Blake's ideas are dynamic, which means that they are about forces and counter-forces (for example, the paired concepts he calls 'contraries') which act on each other. They have conflicts, their relationships change, and they produce outcomes which lead to further transformations and changes, further conflicts, and so on. So, we need to go a stage further than grasping Urizen's and Orc's 'characters', as we have done so far. We need to understand the dynamic whole, because the battle between Urizen and Orc is a temporary part of a whole cycle.

This becomes clearer if we tell part of the story. We begin with Blake's most universal figure, Los. Los is very widely and inclusively representative in Blake's mythology. He is sometimes called 'poetry', 'the human imagination', or a 'prophet'. He is humane and fundamentally good, and is often equated with 'the ordinary man' or with Blake himself. Los is a whole, many-sided personality, then. One element in Los is reason, or analytical thought. Reason is an important faculty, bringing understanding; but it must not dominate. If reason dominates, imagination and vision will be imprisoned. Blake's story begins at this point, and is as follows.

Los's reason fell into error: it began to believe in duality instead of unity, and made the basic error of dividing the body and soul. Reason also began to believe it was the only truth, and tried to destroy or imprison all other truths including vision and imagination, so that reason could rule supreme. Los then created (or, in a sense, gave birth to) Urizen, which stands for the arrogant error of reason, when it sets itself above all else. He then fastened Urizen within time and the material world, cutting him off from Eternity and the infinite.

This, as we know, is really a statement of the obvious: all the 'Urizenic' characters we have met, from the 'jealous father' of 'Earth's Answer' to the cloudy tyrant of *Europe*, are materialists who cannot see the infinite, and are confined within the narrow 'chinks' of their five merely physical senses. This is how Urizen came into being – as an aspect of Los that he had to bring under control.

The story of Orc begins in a similar way – with a broader, more inclusive figure named Luvah. Luvah stands for love, and in many places in the Prophetic Books he is associated with Jesus. We will not go into Luvah's parentage and the early part of the story here; but eventually, Luvah is suppressed by Urizen, who melts him until he becomes a cloud, a shadow of suppressed desire. This sounds complicated, but makes clear psychological sense, and reminds us of what we have learned from the *Songs*. Love and desire are suppressed by Urizenic power in Earth's 'free Love with bondage bound', and in 'The Garden of Love' where priests are 'binding with briars, my joys and desires'; so it is natural that love and desire become vague, shadowy, unconscious. However, Luvah is also, really, a part of the universal character Los. The story tells that after his suppression, Luvah is re-born as a child of Los, as Orc. Orc is furious with rebellious hate, on the clear principle that love suppressed turns to its contrary, hate. This, then, is how Orc came into being: as a new incarnation of Luvah (love) after its suppression by Urizen.

The last three paragraphs have dipped into the mythological stories of the Prophetic Books. These are sometimes complicated, and there is a great deal more you can discover if you go on to study Blake's three longest works, *Vala: or, The Four Zoas*, *Milton* and *Jerusalem*, and if you read more widely among the reference-works and critics. The important point for us to appreciate is how each part of the myth acts to convey an insight into life. This is what will keep Blake's prophecies alive and meaningful for us.

If we look at the conflict between Urizen and Orc, then, we can re-phrase it in plainer language. Notice the ironic, yet perceptive truths that are expressed by the myth. For example, Blake shows that tyranny creates revolution: the more tyrannical Urizen becomes, the more angry the people are, the more they hate the tyrant and burn to destroy the authority which is their enemy and gaoler. This encapsulates a political truth, that a cruel regime breeds insurrection. Notice, also, how effectively the story of Orc's birth conveys a psychological process: violent hatred of authority, and murderous feelings towards a father, may become part of a person's character, but this depends on how that person's natural love is treated. If your desires are balked, frustrated and punished until they can only retreat into secrecy, and if they are ruthlessly suppressed into the unconscious, then their energy will be transformed into something else. A perverted and destructive energy will be the only outlet for them, since their natural outlet is blocked up by repression. In this way, Blake tells us, the violent burning hatred he calls 'Orc' is born – both in a society, and within an individual.

These are human truths, not mythological abstractions: 'birth' and the metamorphosis of figures into one another are metaphors for the dynamic processes in society and within people. As long as we remember to notice how expressive the mythology is, and remember to relate it to life, comparing it with our experience of the world around us, we will continue to read Blake with excitement and appreciation.

We began studying this extract from *Europe* by working out an understanding of the narrative and themes; and this has led us into meeting one of the major components in Blake's mythology, the cycle often called the 'Orc cycle'. Now we can turn back to the extract itself, and look at the poetry in a more literary way.

It is immediately clear that this is a different kind of poetry from the *Songs of Innocence and Experience*. There is no metre or rhyme, and there are no stanzas. The lines are grouped together in longer or shorter 'paragraphs', according to the movement of the story, changes of viewpoint or changes of subject. Lines are not equal in length, either. What kind of poetry is this, and what are its effects?

Our extract from *Europe* is lengthy and filled with image and symbol, and we do not have the space to study all of it in detail. We will only look at two passages, therefore: lines 10–20, which tell of the 'creation' of restrictive, material senses and therefore a finite material world; and lines 61–7, which describe mankind's subjection by Urizen and Albion's Angel: in other words, Blake's view of the state of English society in 1793.

In lines 10–20 there is a bewildering procession of images. Here is a list:

1. The five senses compared to a 'deluge' or flood.
2. The stationary eyes compared to two 'orbs'.
3. The ways to the heavens compared to spirals.
4. Sensitivity / lack of sensitivity to smell compared to 'golden gates' of the nostrils, open or shut.
5. Shutting out the infinite compared to the 'gold' of the gates further barred and turned to stone.

6. What reason makes of the infinite, compared to a serpent.
7. Pity compared to a devouring flame.
8. Man's refuge in a finite world compared to 'forests of night'.
9. The gaps between separate refuges compared to space and then to a rushing ocean.
10. The body's skin compared to a wall resisting a flood.

Looking at this list, we can suggest that the images fall into three groups. First, there are wild forces of nature: deluge, flame, forests and the rushing ocean. Secondly, there are images of coils and spirals, beginning as 'spiral ascents' and turning into a serpent. Finally, the third group of images refers to hard and man-made things: orbs, gates (made from gold, then from stone), bars, and a wall.

The first group, of natural forces, conveys power and threat. These may remind us of 'The Tyger' or the dark forest in which the little boy is lost in *Innocence*. The swell-like diction of 'whelmed' and sibillance of 'ocean rushed' present a fearful natural attack that threatens annihilation; but our reading of the *Songs* should remind us that fear of nature is only one, limited perspective: the perspective of experience which is scared of infinity and energy. The third group, of hard manufactured objects like orb, gate and wall, is a response to the wildness of nature: a rigid attempt to shut out what cannot be faced or contained.

By means of this contrast in imagery, Blake manages to invest his abstract story with concrete qualities. Great natural forces provoke our fear of becoming nothing – we can sympathise with the need to build walls, lock up the gates, to keep the infinite flood from over-whelming us. At the same time, gold, stone and wall are hard and cold; and there is something wrong, something unnatural in the hard / soft, dead / living juxtaposition 'wall of flesh'. Blake confirms this implicit criticism by adding the word 'finite'. So, the imagery casts the reader's sympathy onto both sides in this conflict, and thus reminds us of the complexity 'The Tyger' and 'Earth's Answer' present. We must see beyond our fear, have the vision to overcome it. At the same time, the terror is real, and extraordinary courage is demanded if we are not to succumb to our fear of life.

In the common shape of spiral and coil, which links the ways up to the heavens, with the closed coil of a serpent of finite thought,

Blake has created an ambivalent shape capable of transforming into its opposite. This is a paradoxical image which seems to stand between the two other, contrasting groups.

The rhythms and style in Blake's Prophetic Books are difficult to define. We hear a voice which seems to declaim with heavy emphasis; on the other hand, it is hard to identify any consistent techniques. Much more seems to depend on effectively-paired words, and sonorous phrases. Notice, in these lines, the assonance of 'fluxile eyes'; the contrast between poly- and mono-syllables in 'concentrating all things', and the modulation of sounds combined with alliteration, in 'rolling circles of space'.

Many constructions are formed in an archaic order. See, for example, 'then turn'd the fluxile eyes / Into two stationary orbs', and 'that like an ocean rushed'. This lends the diction a kind of formality, and with the long phrases and sonorous tone, reminds us of Biblical poetry as rendered in the English Authorised Version. Another Biblical characteristic is parallelism, or repeated constructions with altered vocabulary. See, for example, 'Thought chang'd the infinite to a serpent, that which pitieth / To a devouring flame'. Notice also that parallelism is well-suited to Blake's ideas, where a single event or action often has multiple consequences, or is manifested in several different ways at once.

Our second passage from the extract shows these stylistic traits prominently, including a great deal of parallelism. This is a clear description of miserable oppression, and several elements remind us of *Songs of Experience*. However, the imagery again creates one of our strongest impressions. Here, Blake uses prison and metal images intensively: 'bound', 'wove . . . iron', 'bands of iron round their necks fasten'd into the walls', 'leaden gyves' create a grim concrete impression of bondage, heavy with dark and dull metals.

Despite the free form of Blake's poetry in the Prophetic Books, we should not forget the economy and mastery of style displayed in his short lyrics. Often, we can find the same instinct for effective placing of words, or fluctuations of rhythm and pace, in the Prophetic Books. In these lines, for instance, notice the phrasing of run-on lines which leads up to two sudden, heavy stresses at the start of a line: '. . . in leaden gyves the inhabitants of suburbs / **Walk** heavy . . .'. This rhythmically, and in its sense, emphasises the oppressed effort of the people by placing the verb and two stresses at the start of the line. Similarly, the three words 'Thou shalt not' carry three stresses here, as in 'The Garden of Love'; but in a parallel construction 'Over the doors "Thou shalt not", & over the chimneys "Fear" is written', the second parallel phrase climaxing on the long, open-ended stress 'Fear'. It is a mistake to read the Prophetic Books without attending to Blake's poetic skill, then. Despite the declamatory free-verse form, these works are rich in rhythms, changes of pace, sound-effects, and vivid concrete imagery.

The First Book of Urizen

Our next extract from a Prophetic Book describes the creation of Urizen out of Los. Remember that Los is an inclusive and universal human figure, sometimes known as 'poetry' or 'prophecy'. The story tells how Los's reason grew out of control and threatened to enslave all other faculties, such as vision and imagination. Los was therefore forced to give his arrogant reason a separate, limited form, called 'Urizen'. As we will see, the following extract from Chapter IV of *The First Book of Urizen* tells us a great deal more than the bare story of this myth:

> 1. Ages on ages roll'd over him.
> In stony sleep ages roll'd over him,
> Like a dark waste stretching, chang'able,
> By earthquakes riv'n, belching with sullen fires:
> On ages roll'd ages in ghastly   5
> Sick torment, around him in whirlwinds
> Of darkness. The eternal prophet howl'd,
> Beating still on his rivets of iron,
> Pouring soder of iron; dividing
> The horrible night into watches.   10
>
> 2. And Urizen (so his eternal name)
> His prolific delight obscur'd more & more
> In dark secrecy, hiding in surging
> Sulphureous fluid his phantasies.

The eternal prophet heav'd the dark bellows,   15
And turn'd restless the tongs, and the hammer
Incessant beat, forging chains new & new,
Numb'ring with links hours, days & years.

3. The eternal mind, bounded, began to roll
Eddies of wrath ceaseless round & round,   20
And the sulphureous foam surging thick,
Settled, a lake, bright and shining clear,
White as the snow on the mountains cold.

4. Forgetfulness, dumbness, necessity,
In chains of the mind locked up,   25
Like fetters of ice shrinking together,
Disorganiz'd, rent from Eternity,
Los beat on his fetters of iron,
And heated his furnaces & pour'd
Iron soder and soder of brass.   30
                                                        (K 227–8)

The story, of reason out of control and Los therefore deciding to
give his reason a separate being, sounds calm and abstract; but the
extract, even on a cursory first reading, gives no such impression.
There is wild and violent movement, effort and power and extremes.
The materials mentioned in this extract, such as iron, solder, brass,
ice, sulphur and so on, are concrete; and the poetry seems densely
physical.

It is easy to confirm this impression. The verbs, section-by-
section, are: [1] *rolled, rolled, stretching, riven, belching, rolled,
howled, beating, pouring, dividing.* [2] *hiding, heaved, turned, beat,
forging, numbering.* [3] *bounded, rolld, surging, settled, shining.* [4]
locked, shrinking, rent, beat, heated, poured. These are predominantly
verbs of violent force and movement, briefly interrupted by some
abstraction or stillness at the ends of the first three sections, with
dividing, numbering and *settled, shining,* respectively. The verbs seem
to be arranged in waves of great physical force leading to stasis in
each of the first three sections.

Here is a more general selection of descriptive words: *stony, dark,*

changeable, sullen, ghastly, sick, horrible, prolific, dark, surgeing, sul-
phureous, dark, restless, incessant, ceaseless, sulphureous, thick, bright,
clear, white, cold, disorganized, iron. Blake's Biblical diction also uses
adjectival phrases 'of darkness', 'of wrath' and so on; but the above
list is both densely dramatic, and contains extremes of temperature
(sulphureous / cold), consistency (changeable or surgeing / iron) and
light (dark / bright).

We know that the subject of this passage is a mythic change, in a
myth which signifies abstract concepts. The intense physicalisation
of the extract is further underlined, then, when we select and list
nouns, which are the grammatical subjects of the language: *ages,*
sleep, waste, earthquakes, fires, torment, whirlwinds, prophet, rivets,
soder (solder), night are all in the first section. We do not need to
continue: obviously, Blake's ideas – however abstract – are conveyed
in an intensely concrete or physical language.

Having confirmed the physical impact of the poetry, we need to
look more closely at what is happening here: how does Los 'create' a
separate being from a part of himself? How do these mythic figures
divide?

The 'eternal prophet' is Los, and in this extract he figures as a
blacksmith who forges metals, pours solder, and hammers iron and
brass ceaselessly, struggling to imprison and restrict the newly separate being, Urizen. Los's actions are described in lines 7–10, 15–18,
and 28–30. The remainder of the extract describes what happens to
Urizen as Los's chains and fetters are constantly forged around him.
Urizen is characterised by 'surgeing', 'whirlwinds', 'eddies' and
'surgeing' (again); and the imagery surrounding Urizen's picture is of
volcanic activity ('belching . . . fires', 'sulphureous fluid' etc.) within
a 'waste' and 'darkness' ('dark', 'darkness' or 'night' occur four times).
The energies in Urizen, then, seem wild and liquid, in contrast to
the hardness of Los's hammer, iron and brass. However, as the
struggle continues and Los prevails, the imagery depicting Urizen
cools and finally freezes ('as the snow on the mountains cold' and
'Like fetters of ice shrinking together'), and his 'surgeing' liquid fires
become a limited stretch of water, a still 'lake' which merely reflects
('shining clear').

Urizen is also endowed with a powerful psychological story. He begins in 'stony sleep' and 'torment'. His 'delight' and 'phantasies' are more and more hidden away and confined, until they spend their energy in a vivid image for repression, 'The eternal mind, bounded, began to roll / Eddies of wrath ceaseless round & round'. Eventually his mind is imprisoned in 'Forgetfulness, dumbness, necessity', 'chains of the mind'. Blake emphasises that he is now finite, 'rent from Eternity' and uses the term 'Disorganiz'd' to describe his state. This story leaves Urizen in the state we are familiar with from our earlier meetings with him – repressed, chained in a finite universe and cut off from 'the infinite'; unaware of himself and full of destructive secrets. He has also acquired his characteristic associations of whiteness and coldness (we remember him associated with stars, white hair and impotence, ideas of 'white' purity, stones and mountains, etc., in the *Songs* and in *Europe*). We can therefore see that the twisted, dishonest despot who rules the dark forests of *Experience* is being formed in this extract.

However, if we remain sensitive to the effect of Blake's writing, we are surprised and can become confused. We are used to meeting Urizen as a villain, the oppressive tyrant of the material world. He rules an unjust society with gross hypocrisy and cruel laws. Suddenly, in this extract, he is a victim, violently chained and fettered by Los. Who has created the terrible Urizenic state of mind we are familiar with? Los, the 'eternal prophet', is clearly responsible here. On the other hand, we appreciate that this was necessary: images of what Los struggles to restrain, a 'dark waste . . . belching with sullen fires . . . in ghastly / Sick torment' are threatening and destructive.

You will come up against many apparent conundrums of this kind when studying the Prophetic Books; the solution is to step back and remind yourself of the larger story. Remember that this is only one event in the cycle, and remind yourself of the whole. First, we remember that Los creates both Urizen and Orc, his contrary, the rebellious energy that eventually overthrows Urizen. Los creates both contraries, and sets going the cycle of their repeated conflicts. Clearly, Urizen is only one part of what Los creates. Secondly, remember that the whole cycle describes a dynamic process taking place *within Los himself.* Despite the vivid concrete language, Urizen is one force within a whole society, or within a whole individual. This point is underlined by the story of Orc. If we look at the story of oppression and division which gives birth to Orc, we are never sure whose child he is: he is produced by both Urizen and Los; and although he is Los's son, his eventual rebellion is against Urizen.

There is no need to become even more confusing. Remembering the wider myth has reminded us of what is important, because it resolves our confusion: the event in our extract is only part of a whole, and it is part of a process: Blake's aim is to describe the dynamic processes within a *whole* society or a *whole* person, and this extract describes one of them.

We return, then, to the strongest, most immediate impression this extract created: violence, wildness, conflict – intense and vivid. It is important to learn from this: Blake's Prophetic Books tell a story of conflicts and struggles which continuously lead into further conflicts, in an apparently endless series of contraries which seem both to oppose and create each other. Each state runs through cycle after cycle: birth, rebellion, destruction, re-birth; or division, transformation, re-surgence.

What does this tell us about society? First, Blake describes a process we can call **dialectical**. This means that the process is one of struggle between opposed forces, and progress is the outcome of this struggle. The revolutionary content in *Europe, A Prophecy* foresees – as we have seen – that there will be a conflict between the oppressors and the oppressed, which will be violently destructive (Orc's 'burning fires' are raging across Europe) but, at the same time, will be liberating: a smashing down of tyranny and oppression which will lead to a new situation.

We have no space to go into the revolutionary books more fully, but we know enough of the myth to guess that, gradually, new 'contraries' will form, oppose each other and struggle for dominance; their conflict will lead to a further violent liberation; and so on. The dynamic, dialectical analysis of society we have described in this paragraph and the last, is strongly reminiscent of Marxism, that most influential theory formulated almost a century later.

It may be argued that we cannot compare Blake, a visionary idealist, with Marx, an avowed materialist – that they are fundamentally opposed to each other for that reason. As we shall find in the next chapter, there is truth in this objection: Blake's idealism leads him in directions where Marx the materialist would never follow. On the other hand, the central social myth we have been investigating in this chapter, commonly called the 'Orc cycle', applies to what Blake called a 'fallen' or 'material' world. Blake may not have objected to being bracketed with Marx in his analysis of society: their insights into the ills around them, and into capitalist economic and power structures, are startlingly alike.

Concluding Discussion

In this concluding discussion our central aim is to draw together the social issues we have found explored in the *Songs of Innocence and Experience*, and the vision we have begun to investigate in the Prophetic Books. During our discussion we will refer to the 'Proverbs of Hell' from time to time. This is a collection of pithy aphorisms that makes up most of plates 7–10 of *The Marriage of Heaven and Hell*. They appear on pp. 150–152 of Keynes, and are compulsory reading for all studying Blake's Prophetic Books.

1. The *Songs* we have looked at have highlighted specific instances of injustice, suffering and hypocrisy in society. These range from the child-slavery of chimney sweepers and the oppressive charity seen in the 'Holy Thursday' poems, to the more broadly-aimed outrage of 'London' and 'The Garden of Love'. In the context of the *Songs* we have seen that these social ills are connected to Blake's analysis of families (see 'The Little Girl Lost' and 'The Little Girl Found') and individuals (see 'Earth's Answer' and 'The Angel'). Wider study of the *Songs* would confirm the integration of Blake's social and political thought with his insights into family, friendship and relationships. Studying 'A Little Boy Lost', 'A Little Girl Lost', 'The Poison Tree' and 'The Human Abstract' would further emphasise the unity of thought behind these varied themes.

2. Blake moves our focus on from the specific injustice which stim-

ulates initial outrage. Each poem either implies or expresses an underlying cause, something more universal than – for example – the plight of some children who are sold to sweeps. The establishment's invented heaven; Church law in the form of bans ('Thou shalt not') policed by black-gowned priests; economic power and slavery in London's 'charter'd' streets; and that personal fear and limitation Blake calls the 'mind-forg'd manacles', are the culprits of a corrupt world. Here is an attempt to summarise what we have learned:

[1] Fear – born from both a failure of vision, and the distortion of establishment propaganda, leads to cruelty. The insight that fear rules the powerful is well-expressed in the Proverb of Hell: 'The weak in courage is strong in cunning'.

[2] Law – whether Church or state law, is fixed and therefore oppressive. In connection with this view, we can consider the Proverbs of Hell 'Expect poison from the standing water'; and 'Prisons are built with stones of Law, brothels with bricks of Religion'.

[3] Charity – Blake views charity as a crime that supports the unequal status quo. We have remarked that his analysis of charity seeks its cause. Charity can only exist where there is injustice in the first place, and it is therefore unnatural.

[4] Religion, Patriotism, Commerce and War – these are all hypocritical excuses for the status quo which exploit the weak. We have studied the direct imputation of blame in 'The Chimney Sweeper' and 'London' (both from *Experience*). In addition, look at the following Proverbs of Hell: 'As the caterpillar chooses the fairest leaves to lay her eggs on, so the priest lays his curse on the fairest joys'; 'Shame is Pride's cloak'; 'A dead body revenges not injuries'; 'Prudence is a rich ugly old maid courted by incapacity'.

The evils we have enumerated here, however, can be called **symptoms**, and we have found that a further underlying **cause** occupies Blake's thoughts. This ultimate 'cause' is, however, a concept that defies a single label: it is an idea that includes the dominance of reason over imagination and energy, materialism and the finite over the spirit and the infinite; lack of 'vision' and restriction within the five physical senses. Above all, Blake highlights the artificial division of body from soul.

How does the division of body and soul come about? Blake shows that a Urizenic God is the **cause**. This original punishing deity is 'cruel, jealous, selfish' and uses oppressive law and fear to impose his own fear of natural and sexual energy onto mankind. It is clear that our analysis is coming back to its starting-point: **cause** and **symptom** are interchangeable, both part of a 'circle' of ills that is self-reinforcing, and self-caused.

3. Each of the individual poems issues a challenge to the reader, and in several the challenge comes in a complex form, so that the problem leaves no 'easy' moral way out. In 'The Chimney Sweeper' of *Innocence*, for example, we are challenged to disabuse Tom Dacre and cause him misery, or leave him happily deluded. In 'Holy Thursday' of *Experience* we are challenged to reject palliative charity and embrace total revolution. In other poems we are invited to share outrage against the Church, marriage, the King – all the supposed pillars of morality. We have recognised that the social commentary in the *Songs* makes them strong campaigning literature; and they imply the need for a fundamental upheaval.

4. The general insights we have discussed above are still particular criticisms of Blake's targets: British society and its state and religious authority; British capitalism and its exploitations. However, the circular analysis of society where symptoms and causes perpetuate each other leads us on to investigate the integration of Blake's ideas into a unified philosophy. Blake saw – and presents – a vision of dynamic, dialectical process in society and history which he sees as an essential truth about the material world. Both the fall into oppression and division, the violent cycles of revolution, and the ever-present means of redeeming this cycle and reopening life to eternity are thus shown to be universal dynamics in humanity in both individual and social contexts. Different energies, forces and 'desires', and different stages in the process are given names, characteristics and stories, in a 'prophetic' vision of society. We have met some of these symbolic figures: particularly Urizen, Orc and Los. The characteristics of these major

figures can be traced back to the *Songs*. For example, the selfish 'father of men' from 'Introduction' and 'Earth's Answer' in *Experience*, and the beadles from 'Holy Thursday' in *Innocence*, show the characteristics of Urizen; while the outraged speaker of 'The Garden of Love' and the child in 'Infant Sorrow', a poem we have not studied, show signs of becoming Orc later in the cycle of their lives: the first has rebellious anger, and the second patiently gathers strength, waiting for his time to come.

5. So, the complex and symbolically-presented 'prophetic vision' of human life in Blake's Prophetic Books is his expression of eternal truths that lie behind the injustices of his own time, many of which are represented at first hand in the *Songs*.

6. Blake is a revolutionary. One Proverb of Hell reads: 'The tigers of wrath are wiser than the horses of instruction'. We have briefly mentioned the relation between Blake's time and our own. It is likely Blake would still be a revolutionary now.

Methods of Analysis

1. In this chapter we have approached the lyrics from *Songs of Innocence and Experience* using the same broad range of techniques as in the first two chapters. We have begun to use these techniques more flexibly, as and where each approach seems appropriate, so that our analysis gains more unity and continuity.

2. **The Prophetic Books**. We have studied an extended extract from one of the Prophetic Books (*Europe, A Prophecy*) and a shorter extract from another (*The First Book of Urizen*). We have developed certain important principles, which are helpful when approaching the Prophetic Books:

   [a] First, read without worrying about what you do not understand, until you find a passage where imagery and events are strong and evocative. You can recognise a passage of the right kind, even if you have only a very uncertain grasp of the subject-matter and story. The passage you select in this way is your focus for closer study.

   [b] Obtain a general idea of the subject and story of the

Prophetic Book you are studying. At this early stage, it is important to avoid detailed commentaries and critical works, which will introduce too many new names and concepts and confuse your approach. Instead, read the head-note at the start of the work you are studying, in your edition. When we were studying *Europe, A Prophecy* in this chapter, I gave some general information about the story (see pp. 136–7). This information, and more, is readily available from the head-note in Erdman and Stevenson, pp. 223–4.

[c] Return to your selected passage and read carefully. Your aim is to understand the story and events, and to select the symbolic figures who play a prominent part in your selected extract. Describe their relationships, and the parts they play, in brief notes, but as accurately as you can.

[d] Using a Blake reference-work (for example, S. Foster Damon's *A Blake Dictionary*, Providence, Rhode Island, Brown University Press, 1965) look up the figures who play a prominent part in your extract. Remember that your aim is to look up **as few of them as possible**. You should be ready to ignore both minor figures who are mentioned in your extract and other names referred to in the reference-book. Concentrate on grasping the significance of the few **main actors** you need to understand.

At this stage you will have a firm grasp of the story and events in one particular part of Blake's myth, and you will understand who the main actors are. You will find that you have a growing understanding of **why** these figures act in the way they do, and **what** the story is about. It can be helpful to summarise what you have found. For example, when we reached this stage in analysing our extract from *Europe, A Prophecy*, I could have summarised as follows:

'Albion's Angel is the British government. The extract is about a government which has just been defeated by a liberation movement (the American war of Independence). The government reacts by increasing oppression and using religion both to justify its hard-line actions and as a propaganda tool. In the poem, Albion's Angel (the government) invokes Urizen (tyranny of reason and religious law) to fight against Orc (rebellion, energy, the desire for liberty). The conflict is undecided at the end of the extract.'

When you have a summary like this, which is a 'framework of understanding', you are ready to return to the selected passage again. You can now pursue three further inquiries:

[a] Think about your summary, looking for connections to the poems you know from *Songs of Innocence and Experience*. In our study of *Europe*, we recognised attributes of Urizen and related these to white-haired, old authority figures from the *Songs*, such as the 'father of men' from 'Earth's Answer'; and we recognised the picture of oppression near the end of the extract, relating this to the poems 'London' and 'The Garden of Love'. This helped us to enrich our understanding of 'mind-forg'd manacles' and oppressive religious law, in Blake's thought.

[b] Study the poetry and imagery in your selected extract. It is important not to allow the business of interpretation to mask the power of natural effects achieved by the writing. Remember that Blake wrote about real conditions and problems, and he conveys them to us in vivid concrete terms.

[c] Now, finally, you can take your investigation further. Select other suitable passages from the work you are studying, or re-read and study the whole work. Look up more of the names and figures involved in your reference-work. At this stage, when you yourself have a clear grasp or 'framework of understanding', you can read the different interpretations of the professional critics.

Blake's Prophetic Books are esoteric and allusive, and they are intricate allegories. The method of approach explained here will help you to understand them, and will make use of the more accessible lyrics in the *Songs*, showing that Blake's thought is a consistent, integrated system of ideas. The most important single piece of advice is: **don't worry about the minor details; grasp the broad outlines and main figures first**. There will always be time to go into the details later in your studies.

Suggested Work

1. Analyse two further poems from the *Songs*. I suggest you study 'The Divine Image' from *Songs of Innocence* (K2, 18) and 'The Human Abstract' from *Songs of Experience* (K2, 47).

2. Study plate 11 of *The Marriage of Heaven and Hell* (K 153). This is an explanatory plate, similar in kind to plate 14, which we studied in Chapter 2. Compare the story of the origins of priesthood told in this plate with your conclusions from studying 'The Divine Image' and 'The Human Abstract'. It should be possible to trace clear insights from the *Songs* to *The Marriage of Heaven and Hell*, and back again. You will notice ways in which each text – lyric poem and Prophetic Book – enlarges on and enriches your understanding of the other.

3. Building on our analysis from plate 10 of *The First Book of Urizen* in this chapter, study the further 'changes of Urizen' which are told in the remainder of plates 10, 11 and 12 of *The First Book of Urizen* (K 227–9). The struggle between Los and Urizen, and the prison of the senses, continues from where we left our extract in powerful concrete imagery and continuing impressive style. Use the method of approach demonstrated in this chapter and explained in Methods of Analysis above. Our study of plate 10 will give you a head start.

4. One further task is a useful exercise which will increase your familiarity with the principles underlying Blake's works. Look at the Proverbs of Hell in *The Marriage of Heaven and Hell*, plates 7–10 (K 150–152). Consider each 'proverb' in turn, asking yourself whether you can relate it to a specific poem or part of a poem from the *Songs of Innocence and Experience*. You are likely to find the 'proverb' exemplified, enacted or partly demonstrated by something in the shorter poems. See how many of the proverbs you can relate to the lyrics in this way.

4

Sexuality, the Selfhood and Self-Annihilation

We have referred to the 'integration' of Blake's ideas several times, pointing out that his insights are simultaneously applicable to a whole society and to an individual. In the chapter on Society, we began to understand the mythic process called the 'Orc cycle', and commented that the struggles and other dynamic processes this myth describes can be seen in operation both in society and in the individual. In this chapter, we will explore Blake's presentation of individual consciousness in his works.

'The Blossom' and 'The Sick Rose'

The first two poems for study in this chapter are a 'pair' – 'The Blossom' from *Innocence* and 'The Sick Rose' from *Experience* – and we will look at them together:

'The Blossom'

Merry Merry Sparrow
Under leaves so green
A happy Blossom
Sees you swift as arrow
Seek your cradle narrow
Near my Bosom.

Pretty Pretty Robin
Under leaves so green
A happy Blossom
Hears you sobbing sobbing
Pretty Pretty Robin
Near my Bosom.

'The Sick Rose'

O Rose thou art sick.
The invisible worm,
That flies in the night
In the howling storm:

Has found out thy bed
Of crimson joy:
And his dark secret love
Does thy life destroy.

(K2, 11 and 39 respectively)

'The Blossom' is a beautiful pattern of words and sound. There is much repetition, as is characteristic of the *Songs of Innocence*. We are aware that this is a simple song playing on a very limited range of language: there are only twenty-five different words in this forty-two-word poem. The metre is mostly trochaic, and all rhyme-words except 'green' (lines 2 and 8) have the falling or 'feminine' ending. 'Green' consequently carries an echo which emphasises the colour of youth and innocence.

'The Sick Rose' has a lumpier rhythm. There are elements of anapaestic and iambic metre, and Blake passes easily from one to the other. For example, the line 'That **flies** in the **night**' is an iamb followed by an anapaest; the following line 'In the **howl**ing **storm**' scans the other way around. The opening line is disturbing because it is difficult to find or decide a rhythm: arguably, all five words can be stressed, or we can read it with stress on four of them, thus: '**O Rose** thou **art sick**'. In this poem we find the characteristic doubled stresses of *Experience*, also. For example, see '**found out**' in line 5, and '**dark secret**' in line 7.

A sparrow, a robin and a blossom; a rose and a worm in a storm: what are these poems about? There are broad clues in the sparrow's likeness to an 'arrow' seeking a cradle 'narrow' near the speaker's bosom and similarly in 'The Sick Rose', the traditional phallic symbol of a snake or 'worm' has 'dark secret love'; while the rose herself is on a 'bed of crimson joy': both of these poems are about sexual intercourse. Some critics have made much of the speaker's ambiguity as neither bird nor blossom, and have attempted to build unlikely allegorical meanings about souls, bodies, earth and birth.[1] However, the story of the poem is so clear that this seems a diversion. It is quite natural for the blossom to speak of herself in the third person as 'A happy Blossom', particularly as this, in such a concise poem, avoids the clumsy construction '*I am* a happy blossom *who . . .*'. Another problem is sometimes seen because the 'merry' sparrow seems to become a 'sobbing' robin. Again, we should keep in mind both the effect of the whole poem – which is clearly positive – and what we have learned about Blake's ideas.

'The Blossom' is an account of joyous and natural sex. 'Blossom' and 'under leaves so green' set it firmly in the benevolent pastoral mode of *Innocence*, and setting and form are reminiscent of 'The Lamb'. If we worry about the apparent paradox of 'merry' and 'sobbing', we should remember the extremities of fear and joy yoked together at the creation of 'The Tyger', and the wondering reaction a combination of extreme emotions evokes: 'Did he who made the Lamb make thee?'. One of the 'Proverbs of Hell' succinctly reminds us that Blake saw extremes of emotional experience as combining together. The combination of two extremes produces a heightened state of wonder and ecstasy: 'Excess of sorrow laughs. Excess of joy weeps' (*The Marriage of Heaven and Hell*, plate 8). Therefore, there is no difficulty in understanding that the robin in 'The Blossom' is 'sobbing' with joy.

The sexual act is more explicit, in more conventional symbols, in 'The Sick Rose'. There is a strong contrast between these two poems. We have noticed how much more violent and disturbed the rhythm

---

[1] See, for example, E. D. Hirsch, Jr., *Innocence and Experience: An Introduction to Blake*, New Haven and London, Yale University Press, 1964, pp. 181–4.

of 'The Sick Rose' is, and this contrast is apparent in every aspect of the poems. The phallic bird, the 'sparrow' compared to an arrow, is transformed into something foul and sinister: the 'worm' of the *Experience* poem is 'invisible' and flies in darkness. It seeks satisfaction against the will of the woman who unsuccessfully attempts to hide from it (implied by the phrase 'found out'). The woman in this poem is a hypocrite: it is her 'bed of crimson joy' that she hides, suggesting that she hides her own desires. Many critics are more specific than this, pointing out that the rose is a traditional emblem of female genitalia so her 'bed of crimson joy' refers to masturbation.[2] Whether the rose's sexuality is hidden, or masturbatory, or both, does not matter: either way, she denies and refuses her natural desires, and her pleasure is self-enclosed, exclusive.

The 'howling storm' through which the worm flies stands for the materialistic world of experience; and dishonesty is emphasised again in his 'dark secret' love. 'The Sick Rose', then, is densely packed with sinister, disgusting and dishonest sexuality. It gives an account of selfish male aggression and unwilling female hypocrisy. The final words of the poem seem to sum up the effect of such sex: this kind of lovemaking 'does thy life destroy'.

It is easy to place these two experiences in the context of other *Songs*. We have frequently met the idea of natural, uninhibited sexual development, both as a possibility in the world of *Innocence*, and as prevented by adult interference. For example, in the design for the second plate of 'The Ecchoing Green', boys are handing down bunches of grapes to girls, but 'old John with white hair' leads some reluctant children away from their games. We remember that Lyca, despite her parents' fears, is not frightened of the lion's masculine mane or ashamed of her nakedness in 'The Little Girl Lost'. Blake's outrage at puritan attitudes to sex has been repeatedly and powerfully expressed. We have met Earth's complaint about 'That free Love with bondage bound' and the deadening effect of 'Thou shalt not' in 'The Garden of Love' where the speaker used to 'play on the green'. There, too, prudish attitudes are 'binding . . . joys and

---

[2] See, for example, Camille Paglia, *Sexual Personae: Art and Decadence from Nefertiti to Emily Dickinson*, Yale, 1990 (Penguin, 1992, p. 277).

desires'. In 'A Little Girl Lost' (*Experience*), the opening stanza acts as a kind of 'sentence' or moral, and expresses Blake's outrage at the denial and perversion of natural sexuality in a clear campaigning call:

> *Children of the future Age,*
> *Reading this indignant page;*
> *Know that in a former time,*
> *Love! sweet Love! was thought a crime.*
>
> (K2, 51)

There is a clear message about personal relationships, then, to be taken from 'The Blossom' and 'The Sick Rose'. Natural sexuality, free from interference by adult prudery, materialism and hypocrisy and unfettered by oppressive laws, is possible positive and fruitful, and is an intense form of ecstasy ('sobbing sobbing . . . near my Bosom'). It is not sex itself, but darkness, secrecy and hypocrisy that lead to destruction and sinister, negative forms of 'love'. The *Songs* reveal a world where religious and social laws imprisoned natural desire, and express Blake's indignation at this state of affairs. The social conse-quences of driving sex into secrecy are spelled out in 'London':

> But most thro' midnight streets I hear
> How the youthful Harlots curse
> Blasts the new-born Infants tear
> And blights with plagues the Marriage hearse.
>
> (K2, 46)

The personal consequences of dishonesty in relationships and with one's self are spelled out in the final lines of 'The Angel', with their evocation of a wasted life:

> For the time of youth was fled
> And grey hairs were on my head
>
> (K2, 41)

The two small poems we have studied, then, define Blake's under-standing of sex very clearly. It is important to divest ourselves of 'conditioned' attitudes in reading them, however. Blake is clearly in favour of what Earth calls 'free Love'; but we must not allow our modern paradigms to equate this with promiscuity. We have found that Blake repeatedly emphasises one contrast. On the one hand, there is natural, open and honest love. On the other hand, there is 'dark secret', perverted sex which is pornographic (see the 'Harlot' in 'London'), dishonest (see the 'maiden Queen' who hides her 'heart's delight' and is then 'armd . . . with ten thousand shields and spears' in 'The Angel'), and wastes our 'winter and night' in 'disguise' ('NURSES Song', K2, 38).

'A Poison Tree'

Honesty in personal relationships is the focus of the next poem we take for analysis, 'A Poison Tree' from *Experience*:

> I was angry with my friend:
> I told my wrath, my wrath did end.
> I was angry with my foe:
> I told it not, my wrath did grow.
>
> And I waterd it in fears,
> Night & morning with my tears:
> And I sunned it with smiles,
> And with soft deceitful wiles.
>
> And it grew both day and night,
> Till it bore an apple bright.
> And my foe beheld it shine,
> And he knew that it was mine.
>
> And into my garden stole,
> When the night had veild the pole;
> In the morning glad I see,
> My foe outstretchd beneath the tree.

(K2, 49)

The story of this poem is a straightforward recommendation of honesty in personal relationships. Whatever our feelings towards others, they should be expressed. Poison and destruction are bred by hidden feelings and dishonest behaviour. The poem is metrically simple and largely regular, the only noticeable interruptions of easy iambs and trochees being the missing syllable which adds a hanging effect to the hissing sound of 'sunned' and 'smiles' in line 7, and the doubled stress of 'outstretchd' which weighs down the final line, emphasising the murderous outcome.

The imagery is typical of Blake, in that abstracts perform concrete actions. So, 'tears' water the tree and 'smiles' sun it, while the tree itself is a concrete manifestation of hidden, growing 'wrath'. We need not examine the clear sense and form of this poem at greater length, then. However, it is again important to place this poem in context by tracing the images found here to analogous imagery in other *Songs*, and by relating the story told by 'A Poison Tree' to some other stories we have met, which provide parallel narratives. Adding this simple poem to a wider context will enrich our understanding, and again shows how the *Songs* act together to express a complex, and fully integrated analysis of human behaviour.

We know that this is a poem about hidden hostility and disguised murder. However, it is also a poem in which a tempting apple and a special tree, in a garden, prove lethal to the speaker's 'foe'. We should not miss the obvious reference to Eden and the Fall, and we have already studied two analogues in particular: first, the opening two poems of *Experience*, 'Introduction' and 'Earth's Answer'; secondly, plate 14 of *The Marriage of Heaven and Hell*, which we looked at in Chapter 2.

We commented (see p. 23) that the figure variously described as the 'Holy Word' walking in the Garden of Eden and the 'Selfish father of men' is used by Blake to propose a subversive and radical re-interpretation of the Bible. This figure is the type of Urizen. He is hypocritically sad ('Weeping in the evening dew') and overwhelmed by 'Cruel jealous selfish fear'. As a result, this Old Testament God oppresses man and woman with vicious punishments and imprisons them in chains of fear. He is the author of 'Thou shalt not', those rigid and unnatural laws which bind 'free Love' and 'joys and desires', and responsible for 'every ban' which forges the 'mind-forg'd manacles' of tyranny. Who plays the role of 'God' in 'A Poison Tree'?

The answer is illuminating, and takes Blake's analysis of tyranny much further again. The speaker of the poem owns both garden and apple; and the victim is both tempted by the fruit ('my foe beheld it shine') and knows whose possession it is ('he knew that it was mine'). The poem's speaker is also responsible for punishing the thief, having poisoned the apple himself, just as God was responsible for the curses heaped upon Adam and Eve, and binding Earth in 'this heavy chain / That does freeze my bones around', in 'Earth's Answer'.

'A Poison Tree' adds two further shocking implications to Blake's analysis. First, it suggests that God's hypocritically hidden hostility to man carries the blame for the entire story of the Fall. Who set the first ban and demanded the first obedience to a law? God. Who placed the forbidden apple in the garden? God. Who, then, tempted mankind? God. Why did he do this? In order to work out a hostility he felt but denied all along. Even further: the image of a 'Poison Tree' implies that God knew what the outcome would be: he poisoned the tree in advance. In short, Blake suggests that the jealous, Urizenic God of the Old Testament set a deceptive trap for mankind, and anticipated the satisfaction of issuing punishment and feeling self-righteous. Furthermore, God always wanted to use eternal human guilt as a lever to manipulate future generations.

Secondly, this poem fills out the psychological story. The villain of the piece is unspoken emotion, unacted feeling. Blake clearly states a dynamic truism of modern psychology – that suppressed emotion does not go away: instead it grows and, the more it is prevented from expressing itself, the more it grows and seeks another outlet. The apple image conveys another truism of modern psychology. It is a commonplace of analysis that repressed urges, when they do show themselves, often come out in deceptive clothes, pretending to be something different – often the opposite – from what they actually are. Blake is categoric in this statement: the negative 'wrath' is transformed in appearance into a tempting, 'bright' apple containing the hidden poison of hostility. These psychological truths about repressed emotion are condensed into the rhyme-words of the first stanza in 'A Poison Tree': 'friend' and 'end' encapsulates the honesty with which we should treat each other; 'foe' and 'grow' allows wrath to fester and infect.

In *The Marriage of Heaven and Hell*, we heard Blake call for the 'cherub with his flaming sword to leave his guard at the tree of life'. This will lead to an 'improvement of sensual enjoyment' and will melt 'apparent surfaces away'. Here again Blake attacks jealousy, possessiveness and hypocrisy. In 'A Poison Tree' the pride of possession is conveyed by the long, ringing rhymes 'shine' and 'mine' (lines 11 and 12). The passage from the *Marriage* also reminds us of what should be, in place of the poison of selfish hypocrisy. A friendship could, and should, be 'infinite and holy', not 'finite and corrupt'. Finally, the evil of repression is again emphasised, for 'man has closed himself up, till he sees all things thro' narrow chinks of his cavern'.

We know that Blake blamed the idea of separate body and soul for much of the oppression he saw around him, and for the psychological prisons people fashion around themselves. In 'A Poison Tree', another sort of internal division is in operation: repression divides us internally, preventing our natural emotions from finding an outlet. The speaker's natural wrath in 'A Poison Tree', and other natural urges and desires are called 'Energy' in *The Marriage of Heaven and Hell*, while the agent of repression is called 'Reason'. In typically inverted irony, Blake tells us in the *Marriage* that 'Good is the passive that obeys Reason. Evil is the active springing from Energy' (K 149). Here are two further 'Proverbs of Hell' which reinforce the importance Blake attaches to emotional honesty, and the danger he sees in its opposite:

He who desires but acts not, breeds pestilence (plate 7).
Sooner murder an infant in its cradle than nurse unacted desires (plate 10).

(K 151 and K 152 respectively)

Before we move on to look at further poems dealing with kinds of love and problems in personal relationships, we should pause to consider the progress of the speaker's character in 'A Poison Tree'. The bright and poisonous apple which is the final outcome of a character-process in the speaker has a variety of qualities. It is lethally destructive, tempting, attractive and selfishly 'mine'. In this poem Blake uses the apple as a concrete symbol of what the character's original dishonesty has made. The process which grew the tree and its apple is also clearly given. It is watered with 'fears' and sunned by 'soft deceitful wiles', following the original descent into dishonesty which divided the speaker from himself – hardening a part of him against the natural flow of self-expression.

We have already found other examples of figures who gradually form a hardened shell, erecting barriers around themselves and closing themselves off from vision or nature. For example, see our analysis of 'the Changes of Urizen' from *The Book of Urizen* in the last chapter, or consider 'Earth's Answer' and 'The Angel'. The process by which a person manufactures a hard and selfish object from within themselves, will be discussed and further pursued later in the current chapter.

'My Pretty Rose Tree'

We now turn to 'My Pretty Rose Tree', from *Experience*:

> A flower was offerd to me:
> Such a flower as May never bore.
> But I said I've a Pretty Rose-tree,
> And I passed the sweet flower o'er.
>
> Then I went to my Pretty Rose-tree:
> To tend her by day and by night.
> But my Rose turnd away with jealousy:
> And her thorns were my only delight.

(K2, 43)

The story Blake tells in this poem is self-evident. Many critics take it to be autobiographical, telling us of a rocky patch in Blake's own marriage; but it does not matter whether the poet was writing from his own experience or not. The first stanza tells of an offer of extramarital love ('flower'), an offer the speaker found attractive but turned down due to loyalty to his wife ('my Pretty Rose-tree'). The second stanza tells us the outcome of this episode. If it were Blake himself, we can imagine him honestly telling his wife that he was in love with another woman, but had turned down the chance of having an affair. Again, however, it hardly matters whether the poem is autobiographical or not, or whether the speaker told his wife about the other woman. The point is that his 'Pretty Rose-tree' senses his feelings anyway, and reacts with anger and jealousy, punishing him for the unfaithfulness of his desires whether he acted on them or not.

There is enough in the poem to tell us how this might have happened, without having to suppose the husband's confession. The speaker went home to his wife 'To tend her by day and by night'. Such duteous and conscientious attention, clearly not the result of spontaneous love, would have been enough to alert her jealousy even without a confession. The 'Rose-tree' belongs within the confines of a garden he controls and cultivates – representing the constraints of marriage. By contrast, the flower is wild: indeed, it is even suggested that the flower exists on a superlative plane somewhere above or beyond the natural world: 'Such a flower as May never bore'.

There is a lilting rhythm to this little poem which Blake exploits with extraordinary subtlety. The pattern is anapaestic, and is established in the opening two lines:

> A **flow**er was **off**erd to **me**:
> Such a **flow**er as **May** never **bore**.

There are two irregularities, each creating a clear, purposeful effect. First, the speaker's regret and longing after he has lost the 'flower' is conveyed by a slowing doubled stress in line 4: 'And I **passed** the **sweet flow**er o'**er**' so that the reader dwells on the long vowel – and the melancholy loss – of 'sweet'. Secondly, the lumpy rhythm and unexpected extra stress in line 7 ('But my **Rose** turnd **away** with **jeal**ousy') seem to break down or obstruct the flow of the poem, just as jealous conflict obstructs the couple's life together.

Otherwise, the anapaestic lilt is maintained throughout. It is not quite the same kind of lilt in the two stanzas, however. The first stanza is full of long, soft and open sounds such as 'flower', 'May', 'bore', culminating in a clutch of fs and ws in 'sweet flower o'er'. The only noticeable speed and hardness of language comes in the reference to his 'Pretty Rose-tree'. The second stanza contrasts with this, with an increased number of short vowels and closed words (particularly the clipped rhymes 'night' and 'delight'). The effect is that the rhythm becomes a little faster and less flexible. By this subtle manipulation Blake manages to indicate a change of tone. The first stanza uses anapaests to express a wave-like and pleasing lilt. In the second stanza the anapaestic rhythm is faster and more restricted, giving an effect that can almost be described as relentless.

This is, then, a subtly crafted poem. However, the problem it presents us with is not resolved. We have read enough Blake already to know that he believed in freedom, movement and spontaneity; and it is easy to apply the principles we are already familiar with to the situation described here. For example, the Proverb of Hell 'He who desires but acts not, breeds pestilence', applies to the speaker of 'My Pretty Rose Tree' who suffers the 'thorns' of his wife's anger and jealousy after denying his own impulses. On this evidence, we might conclude that he should have followed his desires and had the affair. Additionally, we know that Blake repudiated all binding contracts and legal or religious restrictions – he believed them to be an unnatural prison. In this poem, the speaker deliberately chooses the possessive prison of marriage over the freedom to love where nature leads. The outcome is, therefore, predictably unhappy. Again, we might say, he should have followed his natural feelings.

On the other hand, the poem highlights a problem that would cause suffering and sadness whatever the speaker did. Clearly, the speaker's and 'flower's' desires coincide; but the world is not arranged so that the Rose-tree's desires are in harmony. The question is whether the wife's behaviour records her failure to rise above convention, allowing herself and her husband the freedom to follow natural impulse; or whether her jealousy records her natural reaction to a natural situation: she still loves, but her husband now loves another woman. The 'thorns' of jealousy, and the angry 'turnd away', paint a picture of the wife's possessiveness which favours the former interpretation. However, there is no doubt that she would have suffered – quite naturally – even had there been no statute of marriage in question.

What should the speaker do? The only firm conclusion we can draw from the poem is that nature contains suffering as well as joy. Even in a life of freedom and energy (which, we remember, is 'Eternal Delight') there is a rich, complex and often paradoxical combination of emotions. This insight – the fundamental 'love-triangle' – is placed in the context of a social prison: a marriage, with all the obligation and artificial restriction that entails. The forced behaviour of the speaker who tends his wife 'by day and by night', and the possessive demands of her punishing jealousy, emphasise what Blake saw as the evils of emotional dishonesty, unacted desires, selfishness and religious morality. When we finally attempt to balance the unresolved experiences this poem communicates, we may decide that the 'mind-forg'd manacle' of marriage has fuelled and exacerbated suffering in both partners, in a situation where some natural suffering was inevitable.

'The Clod & the Pebble'

Our next poem also focuses on different forms of love. It is 'The Clod & the Pebble', the third poem in *Songs of Experience*:

> Love seeketh not Itself to please,
> Nor for itself hath any care;
> But for another gives its ease,
> And builds a Heaven in Hells despair.
>
> So sang a little Clod of Clay,
> Trodden with the cattles feet;
> But a pebble of the brook,
> Warbled out these metres meet.
>
> Love seeketh only Self to please,
> To bind another to Its delight:

Joys in another's loss of ease,
And builds a Hell in Heavens despite.

(K2, 32)

The symmetrical form of this poem impresses itself on us immediately. There are six lines devoted to each of Clod and Pebble. Each of the first six lines has its contrary in the last six, so that each of the two viewpoints is equally weighted and forms a mirror-image of the other. As we have come to expect from Blake, the metre is beautifully managed, using a predominantly iambic beat, but with an easy, natural flexibility allowing the omission of the unstressed first syllable in some lines (see for example lines 7 and 8) and the occasional extra syllable between stresses (as in 'To **bind** another *to* **Its** de**light**' [my italics]). The whole poem conveys a calm tone of voice: this is a statement and description of contrary forms of love, and there are no violent disturbances, sweet melodies, or angry indignation. Indeed, when we look more closely at the two extreme forms of love presented, the poet's style seems understated.

What are these two forms of love? Clearly, the Clod puts forward a 'love' consisting of submission and self-sacrifice. The contrary, selfish and aggressive form of 'love' is espoused by the Pebble. The only difficulty we have in following the poem's plain account is in the two lines about Hell and Heaven, lines 4 and 12. These two enigmatic lines are best unravelled by referring to the context of other *Songs* we have studied.

First, the Clod 'builds a Heaven in Hells despair'. The sense of this is quite clear. Hell is the actual situation of the Clod's life, and the poem furnishes evidence that in truth that life is one of oppression and misery. The Clod 'gives its ease' for others, and is 'Trodden with the cattles feet'. However, the Clod uses the idea of self-sacrifice and names it 'love', so that it 'builds a Heaven'. In other words, 'Heaven' is a false pretence that hides the true misery of a life where the individual has no pleasure but is only oppressed. We can relate this to Tom Dacre, the deluded Chimney Sweeper of *Innocence*, who endures misery over losing his fair hair, and submits to the cruel conditions of his life because he believes the imaginary 'heaven' given to him by an angel in a dream. The Chimney Sweeper of

Experience explicitly blames the establishment for their own and
Tom Dacre's illusions: his neglectful parents have 'gone to praise
God & his Priest & King / Who make up a heaven of our misery'.
The similarity between the Clod's and the Chimney Sweeper's final
lines points out the close relation between the two. In the realm of
love, the Clod covers its misery with a false delusion of 'Heaven'.

The Pebble is said to build 'a Hell in Heavens despite'. This form
of love creates a 'Hell' in the sense that it has a pernicious effect on
others (whom it 'binds' with the coercion of its possessive self-will),
and because its only pleasure is a sadistic perversion: it 'Joys in
another's loss of ease', and can take no natural pleasure. So, the
Pebble is just as much a slave to its victims as they are to it. The
words 'in Heavens despite' remind us that the world is 'infinite &
Holy'. It is only when we close ourselves off from vision that it
appears 'finite & corrupt'. So, the Pebble is 'closed' and can only see
'thro' narrow chinks of [his] cavern', *despite the fact* that a heaven
exists all around it.

Neither form of love is successful. Both are deluded and dishonest, suitable to the world of *Experience* which is the context for
this poem. We should notice also, that both are fundamentally
selfish and that they symmetrically demand and so perpetuate each
other. So, a submissive, self-sacrificing person (a 'Clod') *demands* a
controlling and domineering partner; while the selfish Pebble *needs* a
submissive Clod to lord it over. Both live deluded, also: the Clod
creates an imaginary heaven and denies its real suffering, and the
Pebble is prisoner of its narrow senses, and its unnatural needs,
unable to see infinity and freedom around itself.

'The Clod & the Pebble' acts as a kind of summary which elucidates the two forms of love we find in the world of *Experience*. The
Clod and the Pebble's statements are extreme, exact and symmetrically opposed. In many other poems from *Experience* we can recognise elements of their approaches to love, more or less strongly
delineated. So, for example, the 'maiden Queen' in 'The Angel'
denies her own pleasure and presents a clod-like weakness to her
lover, weeping 'both night and day' so that the attentive angel 'wip'd
my tears away'. In later life she is 'armd with ten thousand shields and
spears' and selfishly repulses her lover's advances. In 'My Pretty Rose

Tree' the Clod and Pebble forms of love are potential behaviours for the married partners. The husband begins by sacrificing his own 'ease' for his wife, and her response is to draw satisfaction from his pain, his 'loss of ease'. In this way, the seeds of a false relationship between Pebble and Clod, selfish and selfless, taker and martyr, are sown. The term may seem too strong for the situations Blake presents in his *Songs*, but the pattern of such a relationship is sado-masochistic.

Following our analysis of 'A Poison Tree', we remarked that the speaker of that poem had manufactured a bright, tempting concrete object from within himself: he had turned part of himself into something hard and lethal, despite its attractive appearance. The process of manufacturing a hardened, inflexible self occurs within some of the other figures we have now met. So, we can think of the Clod building a false self, rigidly denying its pain and dedicated to a false appearance of happiness in self-sacrifice. This is not the Clod's true or natural self, but a fixed and artificial self which closes the Clod away from seeing the truth. The Pebble equally manufactures a false self and a false, narrow perspective: its selfish pleasures are like a rigid doctrine, and they keep the Pebble blind to the potential infinity a more natural self might perceive. The husband in 'My Pretty Rose Tree' apparently did not dare to break away from the marriage-convention, or was intimidated by the thought of his wife's suffering. So he manufactured an artificial attentive self, tending his wife 'by day and by night' and submitting to the 'thorns' of her jealousy. She also forms a hardened self, aggressive and defensive to hide her pain, and the fear of losing her husband; and as a possessive assertion of power over him.

The process of building false 'selves', and attempting to fix a 'self' beyond the reach of natural change is seen at work throughout the *Songs*, then. It seems to spring from a variety of different causes, but we notice that in each case it can be seen to originate in fear. We have discussed various examples in the last paragraph, but one of the clearest is that of Lyca's parents in 'The Little Girl Lost' and 'The Little Girl Found'. Fear of their daughter growing up and desire to keep her dependent and as a child turns them into tyrants, blind to natural truth, until their moment of vision. Fear of nature, fear of energy (see 'The Tyger'), fear of change, fear of freedom (see 'Earth's

Answer'): these all develop fixed delusions which close the person-ality away from infinity, vision and truth. In the second half of this chapter, we will explore this idea in the Prophetic Books, where we meet concepts called 'Selfhood' and 'Self-Annihilation'.

At this stage, we can sum up one conclusion. We have found a repeated emphasis on natural impulse, honesty and freedom in love in all the poems we have studied. One small quatrain from Blake's notebook of 1791–2 seems to express the evil of any coercion in love most powerfully:

> He who binds to himself a joy
> Does the winged life destroy;
> But he who kisses the joy as it flies
> Lives in eternity's sunrise.

> (K 179)

Selfhood and Self-Annihilation in the Prophetic Books

We have become familiar with a great variety of human behaviours which originate in fear, and we have begun to develop an inclusive concept of how the various 'deadly terrors' Blake's figures encounter coalesce into a unified concept. We have met fear of energy, fear of sex, fear of change, selfish fear of others, fear of death. There is an obvious logic which brings all these together: since energy, sex, change, others and death are all unavoidable aspects of our existence, the 'terrors' Blake characterises are all – really – a fear of life.

In the *Songs*, Blake has already taught us that these fears are every-where and in everyone: the poet conveys deep sympathy with the fearful feelings of his figures (Blake's unwillingness to summarily judge the fearful is one of the reasons for the ambiguous complexity of 'The Tyger', for example); but he castigates them for failing to confront and overcome the intimidating appearance of things, for giving in to their fear and allowing it to rule their lives. The Bard who introduces *Experience* expresses this clearly, and with a measure of irritation, in his call to Earth: 'Turn away no more: / Why wilt thou turn away'.

The Book of Thel

The Book of Thel, an early and beautiful Prophetic poem written between *Innocence* and *Experience*, is a study in fear of life. The speaker, Thel, is an unborn soul overwhelmed by thoughts of her own future death, and the mutability of all things. To place her in a familiar context, Thel lives in an undeveloped world of *Innocence*, the kind of ironically limited paradise we have glimpsed in 'The Lamb', 'The Ecchoing Green' or 'The Shepherd'. She fears experience and is unwilling to leave. Thel's lament is a triumph of affecting verse which balances sensitivity to her sentiment, with ironic satire of her refusal to accept experience:

> "O life of this our spring! Why fades the lotus of the water,
> "Why fade these children of the spring, born but to smile & fall?
> "Ah, Thel is like a wat'ry bow, and like a parting cloud;
> "Like a reflection in a glass; like shadows in the water;
> "Like dreams of infants, like a smile upon an infant's face;   5
> "Like the dove's voice; like transient day; like music in the air.
> "Ah! gentle may I lay me down, and gentle rest my head,
> "And gentle sleep the sleep of death, and gentle hear the voice
> "Of him that walketh in the garden in the evening time."

> (K 127)

The poetic rhythms of this passage are much more regular than in *Europe, A Prophecy*, where Biblical characteristics are yoked within a more volatile form. Here, Blake seems to have developed lines from Spenser and the poetic books of the King James Bible, providing lines and phrasing of even length and numbered stresses. There is much parallelism, from the reiterated rhetorical questions 'why fades the lotus of the water? / Why fade these children . . .', to the soft cadences and sugary assonance in which she imagines her refusal of life: 'gentle may I lay me down, and gentle rest my head'. The overall effect is of a plaintive, heavily sentimental but nonetheless beautiful voice. Blake has managed to make Thel, at the same time, appealingly sympathetic, and slightly nauseating.

The irony lies in the passage's hints at Thel's underlying obstinacy. We can take one example from the rich plethora of images she proposes for herself: 'Thel is like . . . a smile upon an infant's face' (lines 3 and 5). Taken out of the context of her emotion, the image is self-evidently revealing. The happiness Thel feels, and refuses to part with, is infantile, and so is her pointless complaint which only rejects life without making any attempt to understand. The range of images she chooses for herself – rainbow, cloud, reflection, shadows, dreams and so on – is also significantly restrictive. They are all vague, evanescent and soft. So, just as we noticed the exclusion of 'urban' from the 'rural' world of *Innocence* at the beginning of our study (see p. 14), here we notice an absence of solidity: of rocks, mountains, beasts: even of solid earth itself.

Blake's touch is very delicate. We may be going too far to detect a hint of Caliban, the 'natural savage' of Shakespeare's *The Tempest* in the echo 'music in the air'; but there can be no doubt of the irony intended by Thel's final wish to join 'the voice / Of him that walketh in the garden in the evening time'. He is, of course, the God of Genesis we have met before in *Experience*. The reference tells us a great deal. First, Thel will refuse to eat the apple, thus rejecting experience. She therefore dreams (in schoolchild terms) of keeping on God's good side and avoiding the punishment of mortality. Thel wishes to hear his voice 'gentle', not his wrath. However, Blake also suggests by this reference that Thel's state has vicious potential. She allies herself with the God of the fall and expulsion. He becomes the Urizenic, intemperate tyrant of *Experience*. By association, the potential cruelty of Thel's unnaturally prolonged innocence is suggested. We can imagine an older Thel as the 'maiden Queen' hiding her pleasures and refusing experience until she has wasted her life, in 'The Angel'.

The second passage we will examine from *Thel* comes from near the end of the poem. In the interval, Thel has consulted a lily, a cloud, a worm and a clod of clay; and all of them have advised her. Each of their accounts of life is limited, but they have faith and accept their lot, and all suggest that their lives are not separate but part of the lives of others and of nature itself: 'we live not for ourselves,' says the clod of clay. Although gentle, Blake's satire again highlights the hard core of selfishness and isolation in his weeping character.

At the end of the poem, Thel is allowed to visit the physical world into which she refuses to be born. Here is the description of what she sees:

> Thel enter'd in & saw the secrets of the land unknown.
> She saw the couches of the dead, & where the fibrous roots
> Of every heart on earth infixes deep its restless twists:
> A land of sorrows & of tears where never smile was seen.
>
> She wander'd in the land of clouds thro' valleys dark, list'ning
> Dolours & lamentations; waiting oft beside a dewy grave
> She stood in silence, list'ning to the voices of the ground,
> Till to her own grave plot she came, & there she sat down . . .
>
> (K 130)

The picture painted in the first four lines contains more concrete elements and harder language; 'fibrous roots' which every heart 'infixes deep', and their 'restless twists' are more substantial than anything Thel has encountered before. Thel also sees, clearly, the 'couches of the dead'. However, the second part of our extract introduces a subtle change, with the return of insubstantial imagery ('land of clouds', 'dewy') and a reminder that she cannot see clearly, in 'valleys dark'. Ironically, it seems as if what Thel sees and hears in the real world is only a reflection of her own lamentation: a shadowed reiteration of her own insubstantial complaint.

At the end of the poem, Thel is further terrified by the natural senses which are open to energy and life – and its terrors ('Why a nostril wide inhaling terror, trembling and affright?'). With increasingly intense irony, the poem reiterates her rejecting question 'why?' before she runs back to her infantile state 'with a shriek'.

The Book of Thel is a sensitive portrayal of fear of life, then. Blake maintains a complex attitude to the terrified maiden he has created: the delicate beauties of cloud, lilly and child are feelingly evoked in beautiful poetry; and Thel's lament is often strongly moving. Ignorant acceptance of mystery and death, and the simple faith of the three other speakers – lilly, cloud and clod of clay – is defined without mockery. On the other hand, *Thel* is profoundly revealing because it explores the origins of Urizenic tyranny and personal hypocrisy. There are three conclusions to draw from *Thel*, which we can take with us as we approach two later Prophetic Books, *Urizen* and *Milton*.

1. Fear of life goes right back to the beginning of consciousness. This moment can be put philosophically. At the same moment when the individual consciousness becomes aware of itself, it is faced with an intolerable contradiction: it knows both 'I am' and 'I shall not be'. It is both frightening and illogical to conceive of one's own non-existence. Indeed, the very word 'I' pre-supposes existence and consciousness. Death is 'not I', an absurd idea. As Thel looks around her she realises that all the beauties she sees are in the same case – doomed to non-existence – and this reinforces her first impulse, to reject.

2. Rejection is a fundamentally selfish act. It asserts the supreme importance of preserving 'I', and to do so it attempts to isolate 'I' and insulate 'I' from all change or attack. Notice that, for the fixed self which is unwilling to develop because it wants to protect its dream of permanence, it is only a small step from running away, to fighting back. In *Thel*, the fixed self only runs; but her alliance with the God of Genesis reveals the vicious potential that lies in such a fixed self. Urizen is a fixed self, fighting to survive unchanged. He tyrannically imposes his own dream of permanence upon the world around him.

3. Blake here characterises fear of life as an infantile state. In the *Songs* Blake portrays childhood and innocence as positive and natural states; and there is much in his poetry to suggest that he viewed childhood as a time of vision and love, a bright and imaginative period before the oppression of experience. In this, Blake appears to share a theme with the other 'romantic' poets, and in particular Wordsworth.[3] However, Blake also shows children naturally seeking experience, only restrained by the fears of adults. In *Thel*, a further psychological insight is apparent. The poem

---

[3] See, for example, Wordsworth's 'Ode: Intimations of Immortality from Recollections of Early Childhood', where the child is said to come into the world with a memory and vision of heaven ('heaven lies about him in his infancy') but 'shades of the prison house' surround the child as he approaches adulthood, and his early 'imagination' is dimmed.

reveals an infantile attitude – of fear and rejection – which unnaturally survives childhood. In Blake's picture of personal development, the driving motive behind adult cruelty and error is this self-preserving fear – an impulse of rejection which can begin at the beginning of life. This analysis has much in common with psychoanalytical theory: the imbalance and destructiveness of an adult personality is caused by a failure to cope in infancy.

Thel, then, tells us a story about the early genesis, in infancy, of the hardened self-protective delusion Blake came to call the 'Selfhood'. The poem narrates an early phase in its development, when the heroine fails to overcome her fears, and chooses to run away.

The First Book of Urizen

In *The First Book of Urizen*, the Selfhood is portrayed in a more violent phase, creating itself in hostility and striking out against life. We will sample one passage from *Urizen*, which focuses on the formation and rise of the Selfhood, Urizen, and his first promulgation of the terrible 'One law'. The passage is quite long, and we will not analyse it in exhaustive detail, only drawing enough conclusions to proceed in our quest. However, it is worth reading in its entirety for its power and its use of imagery. We begin with the emerging Urizen's first words:

> 4. "From the depths of dark solitude, From
> "The eternal abode in my holiness,
> "Hidden, set apart, in my stern counsels,
> "Reserv'd for the days of futurity,
> "I have sought for a joy without pain,   5
> "For a solid without fluctuation.
> "Why will you die, O Eternals?
> "Why live in unquenchable burnings?
>
> 5. "First I fought with the fire, consum'd
> "Inwards into a deep world within: 10
> "A void immense, wild, dark & deep,
> "Where nothing was: Nature's wide womb;

"And self balanc'd, stretch'd o'er the void,
"I alone, even I! The winds merciless
"Bound; but condensing, in torrents   15
"They fall & fall; strong I repell'd
"The vast waves, & arose on the waters
"A wide world of solid obstruction.

6. "Here alone I, in books form'd of metals,
"Have written the secrets of wisdom,   20
"The secrets of dark contemplation,
"By fightings and conflicts dire
"With terrible monsters Sin-bred
"Which the bosoms of all inhabit,
"Seven deadly Sins of the soul.   25

7. "Lo! I unfold my darkness and on
"This rock place with strong hand the Book
"Of eternal brass, written in my solitude:

8. "Laws of peace, of love, of unity,
"Of pity, compassion, forgiveness;   30
"Let each choose one habitation,
"His ancient infinite mansion,
"One command, one joy, one desire,
"One curse, one weight, one measure,
"One King, one God, one Law."   35

(K 224)

Elements of the opening section (lines 1–8) give us a clear indication of Urizen's state of mind: 'dark solitude' and 'set apart' reveal Urizen's self-centred separation from life. 'Hidden' supplies the corollary of such isolation, implying that for all his boastfulness about 'stern' counsels, he hides from fear and failure, while 'holiness' gives a foretaste of the vicious self-righteousness to come, which Urizen is forming, in a sinister promise, 'for the days of futurity'. Meanwhile, the tyrant's delusion is as facile and self-evidently wrong as that of Thel. He searches for 'a joy without pain' and 'a solid without fluctuation', both of which are false dreams in a world where we know that progress comes through a dialectical struggle of contraries, and where movement and change are the principles governing life. Finally, Urizen intones the same pathetic, plaintive questions as Thel, in a bitter parody of her self-pity: 'Why will you die, O Eternals?'. This section, then, reveals that Urizen's error is the same as the infantile Thel's.

The second section is equally revealing. We may be bemused by the impression of a titanic struggle at first: words like 'consum'd', 'immense', 'wild, dark & deep', 'stretch'd', 'torrents' and 'repell'd' may throw us around in the hurly-burly of Urizen's struggles, as we read. However, a clear summary of the story will help us to define the further error Urizen leads himself into. Here is a brief account of lines 9–18: *Urizen fights fire, and achieves a partial victory over water.*

The truth is that Urizen's first adversary, fire, has disappeared in the course of the account, and been replaced by water. His eventual success in raising 'a wide world of solid obstruction' is 'on the waters': fire, a symbol of energy and life, has never been vanquished at all. The brilliance of this is in the psychological story it tells. Urizen has not noticed his own unconscious mental action. The 'winds' had 'Bound' him, but the word 'condensing' transforms his foe into water which, after a further struggle, he is able to surmount. Urizen's self-deception is made clear by our summary, and under-lined by the ambiguous, satirical effect of 'obstruction' – a negative, bathetic term for his supposedly great creation.

Following the creation of 'solid obstruction', Urizen's concrete imagery becomes harder. His books are 'form'd of metals' and he places his 'Book / Of eternal brass' on 'this rock' with 'strong hand'. Blake's mischievous command of bathos satirises the deluded tyrant again, in the phrase 'eternal brass' – a terrible let-down that Urizen again fails to notice, and we are reminded of the original fear which cut him off from life, for his book has been 'written in my solitude'.

Finally Urizen promulgates his law. We are familiar enough with Blake to recognise that the apparently Christian virtues he enumer-ates in lines 29 and 30 (peace, love, unity, pity, compassion, forgive-ness) are invalidated by their context. These qualities are natural and impulsive, and can neither be produced nor contained by 'Laws'. Urizen's promise of these virtues is hypocritical, then; and the final two lines of our extract reveal the true nature of his tyranny: 'One curse, one weight, one measure' hints at the tyrant's mistake. Remember, from plate 14 of the *Marriage*, that everything is 'infinite', and therefore cannot be weighed or measured as Urizen's ruling idea of reason and 'natural science' attempts to do. The last line, 'One King, one God, one Law' may remind us of *Experience*'s Chimney Sweeper whose parents praise the deluded authorities 'God & his Priest & King'. Urizen's 'one Law' takes no account of the variety – the infinity – of life. It is wrong and cruel to impose this finite singleness on infinity. A motto at the bottom of plate 24 in the *Marriage* puts this succinctly: 'One Law for the Lion & Ox is Oppression' (K 158).

The passage we have commentated clearly presents the birth of tyranny, and we recognise the Urizenic character easily. This is the oppressor who supports Albion's Angel in *Europe, A Prophecy*; the establishment that excuses child slavery in 'The Chimney Sweeper' and forges 'mind-forg'd manacles' in 'London'; the religious authority that martyrs the child with 'Priestly care' in 'A Little Boy Lost', and binds the speaker's 'joys and desires' in 'The Garden of Love'; and so on. What we have discovered, however, is that Urizen should not be dismissed as a mere hate-figure. He is characterised with subtle psychological depth. He is also closely related to the sympathetic appeal of Thel. Finally, his cruelties are firmly rooted in fear and error, and Blake's satire acknowledges that we can identify with these. If we are honest, we can find Urizen within ourselves.

We pointed out in Chapter 3 that Urizen is only one aspect of the universal man, Los. Reason is a necessary faculty within Los, and becomes Urizen when it attempts to dominate, to usurp authority and oppress imagination and vision. Remember that Blake's mythological figures are emblems, not people. They are born to represent states of mind and are constantly being transformed into each other in a process. Their subtle characterisation, powerful voices and the density of concrete imagery surrounding them may deceive us into picturing them as 'characters' in the conventional sense, but this is an illusion.

In Chapter 3 we studied the struggle in which Los chains Urizen. After imprisoning the tyrant, Los suffers a revulsion of pity which divides him and forms a female within him. In a complex development of the psychological story of Los, the deceptive weeping female formed from his pity becomes the object of his desire, and he mates with her. Their child – that is, the child of Los's mistaken love of pity for Urizen – is Orc, the wild rebellious anger which will eventually destroy Urizen and, even later still, assume his tyrannical place. This story is told at length in plates 16–21 of *The First Book of Urizen*. We do not have the space to give a detailed commentary here, but the shape of Blake's myth has been briefly introduced in the last chapter, and the genesis of the 'Orc cycle' is what matters to our understanding of the 'Selfhood'.

The significant point is that Blake's mythical figures turn into each other, from their creation – narrated in *Urizen* – onwards. Urizen and Orc are contraries: tyranny and rebellion, oppression and revolution, alternate in history, as our last chapter suggested. However, these contraries are ultimately fruitless. On the one side stands Urizen, a violent, destructive tyrant; on the other side Orc, a violent, destructive rebel. By the inevitable laws of nature and change, Orc is eventually strong enough to break free from oppression and overthrow the tyrant. However, also by the inevitable laws of nature, Orc himself grows an authoritarian selfhood and is gradually transformed into Urizen, taking the tyrant's place. And so the cycle continues.

So, the story of the 'Selfhood' is of continual formation, manufacture and growth. Blake's myth shows that the hardening shell of selfishness is constantly creating and re-creating itself: even a revolutionary liberation will, eventually, grow rigid and hard, manufacturing its own fixed self over time. The 'Orc cycle', then, although it periodically acts to liberate and renew the self and the world is ultimately fruitless and repetitive. What does Blake propose to redeem mankind? Is there some means to escape the turning wheels of a limited history, and bring to an end the hard, Urizenic 'Selfhood' once and for all?

Our studies have already provided us with the seeds of an answer to this question. We have encountered various terms such as 'vision', 'imagination', 'infinite & holy', and that resonant idea from *The Marriage of Heaven and Hell*, 'If the doors of perception were cleansed': all of these suggest an escape from restrictions, limitation and time into the realm of 'eternity'. Significantly, moments of vision we have met seem to lead to an absence of fear, also; and we know that fear is the generative power behind the 'Selfhood'. In 'The Little Girl Found', for example, Lyca's parents arrive at a fearless state: 'Nor fear the wolvish howl, / Nor the lions growl'; and the wonder of creation in 'The Tyger' suggests a similar victory over fear in the question 'Did he smile his work to see?'.

Milton, A Poem

Our final focus in this chapter develops the answer already implicit in Blake's ideas of 'vision' and 'imagination'. In one of the three longer Prophetic Books, *Milton, A Poem* (circa. 1800–1803) Blake sees the seventeenth-century poet of *Paradise Lost* returning to earth to correct his errors and renew his inspiration. When he descends to earth into Blake's cottage garden in Felpham, Milton still carries his own errors within himself. We know the futile battles of Orc and Urizen, and the constant re-creation of a negative, hard shell called the 'Selfhood'. We also know that Blake blamed much on organised religion, the Church of his time and the conventional doctrines espoused by Milton in *Paradise Lost*. As he descends to earth, Milton still carries all these negative struggles and errors with him in the form of a figure that represents his Selfhood, which is here called his Spectre, or Satan:

> Descending down into my Garden, a Human Wonder of God
> Reaching from heaven to earth, a Cloud & Human Form,
> I beheld Milton with astonishment & in him beheld
> The Monstrous Churches of Beulah, the Gods of Ulro dark,
> Twelve monstrous dishumaniz'd terrors, Synagogues of Satan,
> A Double Twelve & Thrice Nine: such their divisions.
>
> (K 528)

Remember the method we developed for approaching complex passages in the Prophetic Books. Here, we will ignore the names 'Beulah' and 'Ulro'. The repeated 'monstrous', 'churches' and 'gods', and the term 'dishumanized' convey as much as we need to know about them for our present purpose: they are related to false religion. We can also ignore the number-symbolism in the final line. Then, focusing on the effect of the whole extract, we may be struck by the paradoxical impression it creates. The opening lines are positive, describing Milton as 'a human wonder of God / Reaching from heaven to earth'. The later lines are negative, describing the 'monstrous' false churches Blake beheld 'in him'.

Satan or Milton's Spectre is addressed by Milton. In this speech Milton describes the futile struggle between Orc and Urizen – the destruction of one 'Selfhood' by a new 'Selfhood'. This process, which we have touched on as the 'Orc cycle' is eternally pointless and brings no change. So, Milton describes it as a continuity: each apparent change is merely Satan under a new covering. He then proposes something different: a real change and a solution to the endless conflict, which he calls 'Self Annihilation':

> "Satan! my Spectre! I know my power thee to annihilate
> "And be a greater in thy place, & be thy Tabernacle,
> "A covering for thee to do thy will, till one greater comes
> "And smites me as I smote thee & becomes my covering.
> "Such are the Laws of thy false heav'ns; but Laws of Eternity   5
> "Are not such; know thou, I come to Self Annihilation.
> "Such are the Laws of Eternity, that each shall mutually
> "Annihilate himself for others' good, as I for thee.
> "Thy purpose & the purpose of thy Priests & of thy Churches
> "Is to impress on men the fear of death, to teach   10
> "Trembling & fear, terror, constriction, abject selfishness.
> "Mine is to teach Men to despise death, & to go on
> "In fearless majesty annihilating Self, laughing to scorn
> "Thy Laws & terrors . . . "
>
>   (K 529–30)

Milton proposes 'Self Annihilation' and so passes beyond the laws of Urizen / Satan's 'false heav'ns'. We recognise much of the description of futile struggles which change nothing but perpetuate 'Satan' from our earlier studies. The 'fear of death' motivated both Thel and Urizen, whom we looked at earlier in this chapter; and the teaching of 'Trembling & fear, terror, constriction, abject selfishness' is widely apparent in Blake's attacks on the Church in the *Songs*. Self-annihilation, on the other hand, is new to us. In this passage, it seems to consist of sheer courage: it is to 'despise death' in 'fearless' majesty; and 'laughing to scorn' all the 'Laws & terrors' of Urizen. We may remember noticing some puzzling early stirring of this attitude in *Experience*'s chimney sweeper, who was fully aware of the injustice of his life. He understood the 'Laws & terrors' of 'God & his Priest & King'; yet he remained inexplicably happy: '. . . I am happy, & dance & sing'.

We have arrived at the end of our quest. We have discussed the origin, growth and anatomy of what Blake called the 'Selfhood', and identified this as essentially the same hardening process within a society, or within the personality, that can be variously called 'Urizen', 'Spectre' and 'Satan'. We have explored the negative cycle set up by the chaining of Urizen and the subsequent birth of his opposite, Orc. Now Milton's speech reveals the task each individual must undertake: to destroy self in a moment of inspired courage. We will finish by quoting from Milton's great speech of self-annihilation, which by this time needs no commentary. There are four points to clarify, in the form of conclusions, before we do so.

1. Inspiration, 'imagination' and 'vision' occur outside the restrictions of time. So, Blake developed the concept of a 'moment' in which vision occurs and truth is revealed; and he contrasted this with the limiting structure of time itself. In an inspired 'moment', 'all' can be seen in a flash; within time, on the other hand, only little parts of the whole can be seen, each in turn. The following lines from *Milton* beautifully express this concept:

> Every Time less than a pulsation of the artery
> Is equal in its period & value to Six Thousand Years,
> For in this Period the Poet's Work is Done, and all the Great
> Events of Time start forth & are conceiv'd in such a Period,
> Within a Moment, a Pulsation of the Artery.

> (K 516)

2. Blake distinguishes between two different kinds of conflict. On the one hand, there is a battle between 'opposites' which are

essentially the same, and which are transformable into each other. This kind of conflict brings no renewal or change, and is merely a futile repetition of victories and defeats. In the passage we are about to read, Milton refers to this kind of opposite as a 'Negation' rather than a contrary; and his speech clearly distinguishes futile conflict or 'Negation', from the creative conflict of 'Contraries' which brings progression. We remember that *Innocence* and *Experience* are contraries: between them, they produce progress.

3. In the speech quoted above, Milton describes his purpose as 'to go on / In fearless majesty annihilating Self'. In our final extract from *Milton*, he talks of the selfhood 'which must be put off & annihilated alway' and a process where he will 'cleanse the Face of my Spirit by Self-examination'. The point is that self-annihilation cannot be a once-only event. The selfhood re-builds and re-creates itself forever, so constant 'Self-examination' and self-annihilation is needed 'alway'. The individual must continually destroy and re-destroy the hardening self by seeking moments of vision and inspiration.

4. In Chapter 3, we compared Blake's social and political analysis with that of Marx; and at the time we remarked that this is perhaps an invalid comparison, since Marx was a materialist, and Blake a 'romantic'. As we reach the end of this study, we begin to appreciate their differences more fully. Blake calls for a renewal within each individual, and suggests a solution to obstructions, blindnesses and divisions within the personality. His analysis of society may be closely analogous to that of Marx, but his philosophy as a whole applies to the individual consciousness, and urges a renewal on psychological, spiritual and imaginative levels. The passage we are about to read makes this abundantly clear: it is a grand affirmation of the power of imagination over the material world. It is a ringing assertion of idealism.

This final extract is also an extended rant, where we recognise many of the targets we have studied before, as well as Blake's virulent hatred of both injustice and suffering, and the inferior materialist with his unimaginative works:

        . . . Milton
Replied: "Obey thou the Words of the Inspired Man.
"All that can be annihilated must be annihilated,
"That the Children of Jerusalem may be saved from slavery.
"There is a Negation, & there is a Contrary: 5
"The Negation must be destroy'd to redeem the Contraries.
"The Negation is the Spectre, the Reasoning Power in Man:
"This is a false Body, an Incrustation over my Immortal
"Spirit, a Selfhood which must be put off & annihilated alway.
"To cleanse the Face of my Spirit by Self-examination,   10
"To bathe in the Waters of Life; to wash off the Not Human,
"I come in Self-annihilation & the grandeur of Inspiration,
"To cast off Rational Demonstration by Faith in the Saviour,
"To cast off the rotten rags of Memory by Inspiration,
"To cast off Bacon, Locke & Newton from Albion's covering,   15
"To take off his filthy garments & clothe him with Imagination,
"To cast aside from Poetry all that is not Inspiration,
"That it no longer shall dare to mock with the aspersion of Madness
"Cast on the Inspired by the tame high finisher of paltry Blots
"Indefinite, or paltry Rhymes, or paltry Harmonies,   20
"Who creeps into State Government like a caterpillar to destroy;
"To cast off the idiot Questioner who is always questioning
"But never capable of answering, who sits with a sly grin
"Silent plotting when to question, like a thief in a cave,
"Who publishes doubt & calls it knowledge; whose Science is Despair, 25
"Whose pretence to knowledge is envy, whose whole Science is
"To destroy the wisdom of ages to gratify ravenous Envy
"That rages round him like a Wolf day & night without rest:
"He smiles with condescension; he talks of Benevolence & Virtue,
"And those who act with Benevolence & Virtue they murder time on time. 30
"These are the destroyers of Jerusalem, these are the murderers
"Of Jesus, who deny the Faith & mock at Eternal Life,
"Who pretend to Poetry, that they may destroy Imagination
"By imitation of Nature's Images drawn from Remembrance.
"These are the Sexual Garments, the Abomination of Desolation, 35
"Hiding the Human Lineaments as with an Ark & Curtains
"Which Jesus rent & now shall wholly purge away with Fire
"Till Generation is swallow'd up in Regeneration."
                                              (K 532–3)

Suggested Work

At the end of Part 1 of this book, we have studied a large number of the *Songs of Innocence and Experience*, and we have carried our conclusions forward towards the Prophetic Books. It would be sensible, at this stage in studying Blake, to consolidate the grasp of the shorter Prophetic Books we have built up in Part 1 by studying further extracts from them, and suggestions are given below. This final section mentions some further extension study in other works by Blake.

1. We have referred to *The Marriage of Heaven and Hell* (K 148–158) several times, quoted the 'Proverbs of Hell' frequently, and studied two extracts. Now is the time to read the *Marriage* in its entirety. Use the method we have demonstrated for approaching a Prophetic Book: *The Marriage of Heaven and Hell* is made up of 'The Argument', 'The Voice of the Devil', 'Proverbs of Hell' and five 'Memorable Fancies'. Select one of these at a time for study, using our method to 'contact' the main subject-matter and narrative of each passage, before looking to the professional critics for further enlightenment and debate.

2. Use the same method to complete your study of *The First Book of Urizen* (K 222–237). The overall narrative of *Urizen* is already familiar from our work in the preceding chapter and this one: you can choose further passages in the way we have done, and study them in isolation first, or you may decide to read the whole work, building on the framework of understanding we have already gained. This, in turn, may lead you to read and study *The Song of Los* (K 245–8) and *The Book of Los* (K 255–260).

3. An important poem we have not touched on, which will reward study by confirming and encapsulating much that we have found about processes and cycles, is *The Mental Traveller* (K 424–7). This poem begins by telling of a baby boy given to an old woman, who nails him to a rock and lives off his 'shrieks'. Cycles, ages and gender-dominances shift and change throughout the narrative, until the cycles re-start in the final stanza: 'And all is done as I have told'. *The Mental Traveller* gives a plainer account than those filled with symbolic figures in other Prophetic Books.

It should therefore be required reading for the student intent on tackling the three longer works, *Vala, or The Four Zoas*; *Milton*, and *Jerusalem*.

4. The avowed aim of this book is to study *Innocence* and *Experience*, and provide a foundation, or a bridge, for approaching the Prophetic Books. Where your studies take you from here is partly a matter of choice and depends on your particular interests. If you are interested in Blake's social and political poetry, for example, one of the next tasks to undertake will be to complete the study of *Europe, A Prophecy* begun in Chapter 3, and then go on to read *America, A Prophecy* (K 195–203). If, on the other hand, your interest is in personal and sexual relationships, one of the next texts to study will be *Visions of the Daughters of Albion* (K 189–195).

PART 2

THE CONTEXT
AND THE CRITICS

5

Blake's Life and Works

Blake's Life

This is a brief account of Blake's life. The main story is quickly told, but the intricacies of his friendships and quarrels, slights received and given, commissions, hopes and failures in his art, admirers and detractors, and so on, are very complicated and would take more space than this chapter affords. Full-length biographies make fascinating reading, and three of these are mentioned in *Further Reading* at the end of this book.

The outline facts of William Blake's life are indicative. He was born on 28 November 1757 in his family's house, 28 Broad Street, Golden Square, in what is now the Soho area of London. His father, James Blake, was a tradesman with a hosiery shop which occupied the ground floor of the house. William Blake lived almost seventy years, and died on 12 August 1827 at his lodgings on the first floor of 3 Fountain Court, just off the Strand.

At the age of ten, Blake went to a drawing school, and at fourteen he was apprenticed to James Basire, master engraver. He began to earn a living as an engraver as his apprenticeship ended, at the age of twenty-two; at the same time he became a student at the Royal Academy. Blake earned an insecure and often penurious living at engraving throughout his life, and was working on the day of his death. He married Catherine Boucher on 18 August 1782, when he was twenty-four. They had no children, and she was by his bedside as he died forty-five years later. Apart from three years in a cottage in the Sussex village of Felpham, between 1800 and 1803, Blake lived in London all his life.

This cursory framework of Blake's life – the 'limits' of birth and death, trade and marriage – tells us that he was a Londoner all his life; that he lived a life of unremitting labour for a small return, and that he and his wife lived alone together, with no children, for nearly half a century. However, we would be wrong to draw the conclusion that he lived an 'ordinary' life: as soon as we begin to look more closely, we are struck by how extraordinary Blake's character was even in his childhood, and how extraordinary his views and behaviour remained.

First, let us deal with the poet's family. William had an elder brother, James, born in 1753, who inherited and ran the family hosiery business. He apparently tended to give advice to his wayward brother, and William had little to do with him in adulthood. However, James did let William use the hosiery shop in Broad Street for an exhibition of his pictures in 1809. There were also three younger siblings: John lived to be a man but was apparently dissipated. He enlisted as a soldier and died young. Catherine was the youngest. She lived with James for most of her life, but also lived with William for a period. It is reported that Blake's wife did not like her, and the arrangement was short-lived, so she returned to James's house. Robert, ten years younger than William, was the only one with whom the poet remained close. Robert also saw visions, had ambitions as an artist, and lived with Blake and his wife. However, he was consumptive. Blake nursed him through his last illness to his death in 1787, and for the remainder of his life Blake said that he often conversed 'in the Spirit' with this much-loved brother who died aged nineteen.

It is difficult to assess whether Blake felt deeply about either of his parents. He hated any kind of restraint or authority, yet they seem to have been more flexible and understanding than might have been expected in the way they brought him up; and his father gave considerable financial support to Blake's ambitions as an artist. His parents, however, disapproved of his marriage (Catherine was born into a lower, 'servant' class) and Blake seems to have been little involved with the main family from then onwards. His father died in

1784 and his mother in 1792. Many commentators who suggest that Blake's childhood was full of conflict base their theory on the poet's lifelong aversion to patriarchal authority-figures, and his equally vivid aversion to possessive, consuming maternal 'love', as demonstrated in his poetry.

Blake apparently began seeing visions in early childhood: it is recorded that God 'put his head to the window' and he screamed, at the age of four; and that he saw angels walking among haymakers in the fields around London at a similar age. His father seems to have realised that this strange and wilful child should not be sent to school, so he was taught to read and write at home. His passion for drawing led to him being placed in Pars's drawing school when he was ten. From fourteen to twenty-one he was an apprentice engraver, and from twenty-one to twenty-seven he studied at the Royal Academy. Blake, then, was taught the visual arts; but he educated himself in all other matters.

Blake's 'visions', which he continued to see throughout his life, have been the subject of voluminous speculation, interpretation and explanation from biographers and critics. Almost every attitude towards them has been adopted and argued, almost every variety of credulity and incredulity expressed. Some commentators argue that the 'visions' were Blake's way of explaining a new idea or insight, and they argue that the 'visionary heads' Blake drew for Varley (more of whom later) during supposed trances are evidence of the artist teasing the astrologer. Others have gone to clinical psychology for explanations, such as the 'eidetic imagery' suggested by Peter Ackroyd.[1]

The fact is that Blake asserted the reality of these visions consistently, both in credulous and sceptical company; at the same time, it is noticeable that the 'visions' Blake reported were perceptive and intelligent revelations, even when seen from a rational perspective. Our discussion of 'vision' in Chapter 2 also points out that a different way of seeing played an important role in Blake's ideas, which we can understand irrespective of whether we accept or reject stories about angels on staircases, and other such apparitions, in which the

---

[1] Ackroyd, Peter, *Blake*, London 1995, p. 35.

poet's reported life abounds. In that discussion we also point out that he claims continuous awareness of his surroundings, of 'literal' or sensory reality, during visionary moments.

It is also important to adjust our own perspectives. In the present secular age, seeing visions is taken as evidence of mental illness. In Blake's time, on the contrary, 'visionaries' of one kind or another were common. London was seething with dissenting sects and groups of enthusiasts both religious and political. When you read the reactions of Blake's contemporaries, it is noticeable that few of them object to the fact that he 'saw visions'. Those who thought that he was mad did so because they rejected *what he saw* as madness, not *that he saw it*. In other words, they took exception to his opinions, not his hallucinations.

Blake was never a 'joiner': he was too individual and ironical to join in with religious and political organisations wholeheartedly or for long. He read the works of Swedenborg, a Swedish spiritual philosopher, and between 1789 and 1790 he and his wife attended the Swedenborgian New Jerusalem Church in Great East Cheap; but as the new church began to take on the trappings of organised religion, ordaining priests and dressing them in robes and authority, Blake denounced Swedenborg. Swedenborg appears in *The Marriage of Heaven and Hell* as 'the angel sitting at the tomb; his writings are the linen clothes folded up' (K 149), a plain statement that Blake has left him behind. Apart from this short period as a Swedenborgian, Blake did not otherwise espouse any recognised church: his religion was his own, and unique.

There are many stories of Blake's outrage at injustice and cruelty: he could not bear to witness it, and often interfered, denouncing and threatening oppressors in the street, taking the side of the oppressed. In the 1790s Blake worked as an engraver and illustrator for a well-known republican bookseller, Joseph Johnson, who also published Mary Wollstonecraft and Tom Paine, along with other explicitly anti-monarchy and pro-revolutionary writers. Blake met both Wollstonecraft and Paine and other radicals, and tried to have Johnson publish his own revolutionary poems. But he was never a natural member of this radical group, and was never persuaded about working for social and political reforms in a political way. It appears that he was present, and may have participated in, the Gordon Riots in 1780, when Newgate Prison was sacked, but the majority of his forays into social action were independent of any organisation and limited to when he saw a woman or a child being beaten, and hotly intervened to defend them. Blake's political views, on the other hand, were more radical and far-seeing than most of his contemporaries' (see the discussion in Chapter 3).

The poet's friendships (and quarrels) during his life were many, and largely connected to his artistic activities and ambitions. A brief account of Blake's main associations can be given here, beginning with an account of the groups or coteries with which he was associated at one time or another.

The Reverend and Mrs Mathew were patrons of poets and artists, and their drawing-room was a meeting-place for performance and conversation. Blake was part of this well-off circle for a short time. He sang his lyrics to his own tunes in their drawing-room, and they took him up with some enthusiasm, and partly funded the printing of the *Poetical Sketches*. In about 1787 there was a rupture between the poet and the Mathews circle, however, and Blake satirises them savagely in a private manuscript now called *An Island in the Moon*.

We have already mentioned Blake's association with the republican writer Tom Paine, the radical bookseller Joseph Johnson, Mary Wollstonecraft, and other republican activists. However, Blake was not politically active himself and his revolutionary 'prophecies' of this period, *The French Revolution, Europe* and *America*, as well as *The Marriage of Heaven and Hell*, were never publicly published and sold; so, when Johnson and some others were arrested and imprisoned late in the nineties, Blake was not affected. He clearly feared that he might be attacked by the authorities for his association with this group, however. Even in 1803, when defending himself against a charge of sedition (see below), Blake speculated that he had been 'framed' by the authorities because he was a known radical.

In 1818, at the age of sixty, Blake was introduced to a successful painter in his mid-twenties, John Linnell, and through the friendship with him which lasted throughout the final decade of Blake's life, he also met and befriended John Varley, and the group of eager, unconventional young artists who called themselves 'The Ancients'.

Varley was a well-known painter of watercolours and a teacher, some twenty years younger than Blake. He was a large and effusively extravagant man, enthusiastic about doubtful sciences such as palmistry, astrology and spiritualism. Blake and Linnell would attend séances with Varley, where Blake – supposedly entering a 'visionary' state – would draw portraits of the spirits of the dead. This is how the series of drawings known as 'visionary heads' came into being. Blake's understanding of 'vision' as a constant inner eye of the imagination was undoubtedly very different from Varley's beliefs which centred on séances, trances and other spiritualist and astrological paraphernalia, yet they seem to have collaborated happily. The biographers are divided on whether Blake really drew what he saw, or whether he enjoyed the ironic fun of teasing and bamboozling his more credulous friend.

'The Ancients', who met monthly in London and often roamed the country to hold all-night vigils together for the promotion of poetry, painting, imagination and vision, were enthusiastic believers in Blake's genius and visions: they adopted him as a sort of master, or even 'prophet', and frequently visited him, asking questions and urging him to join them in their meetings and expeditions. Blake must have felt appreciative of the recognition he was receiving at last. He also appears to have been patient and kind, even when the young men visited in Fountain Court so frequently as to hinder his work. 'The Ancients' were far from being a set of hare-brained enthusiasts, either: they were a talented group. We now recognise Blake himself as the greatest genius out of anybody he knew in his lifetime (possibly excepting Coleridge, who he met). Of 'The Ancients', perhaps the only one whose name is still well known is Samuel Palmer; but there were also Edward Calvert, George Richmond, Francis Oliver Finch, Henry Walter and Frederick Tatham, all of whom, though largely ignored today, became prominent in the artistic world of the nineteenth century.

Aside from these circles of friends who were temporarily around Blake at very different times in his life, there were a few longer-lasting friendships. The most significant of these were with Thomas Stothard, John Flaxman, Henry Fuseli, the first two Blake's contemporaries and Fuseli somewhat older, all artists; Thomas Butts and

William Hayley, who were both significant patrons supporting Blake in times of hardship; and John Linnell, the younger artist already mentioned in connection with Varley and 'The Ancients'.

Stothard, Flaxman and Fuseli were close friends and admirers of Blake's genius from his twenties, and remained more-or-less friends and supporters for most of his life. There were quarrels, and a definite breach occurred with Stothard in 1807, when he appears to have stolen the idea and a design for 'The Canterbury Pilgrims' from Blake (at least, Blake believed that this was plagiarism, and accused him of it). In youth, Flaxman and Fuseli had given considerable help to Blake, with introductions to patrons and commissions for work. After his return from Felpham in 1803, however, they seem to have cooled in their friendships, tending towards patronising him with apologies to others for his wildness and possible madness. There were also some quarrels and resentments, but not the absolute breach which occurred between Blake and Stothard. The final comment to make on all of these friends is that they were commercially much more successful than Blake himself: they all made a good living, and achieved recognition from the contemporary public.

Thomas Butts was a rich civil servant. He was introduced to Blake in or about 1799, and a firm friendship was formed not only between the two men but also involving their families, who often visited each other and dined together. Thomas Butts seems to have been a discerning, humorous man, who chose to commission and collect as many of Blake's works as possible, filling his house with them. It is no exaggeration to say that for twenty years, Butts's commissions and purchases from Blake, and his additional payments 'on account' to the needy artist, singlehandedly kept the greatest poet and designer of the age out of the workhouse. We owe a vast debt to him.

William Hayley was also a patron who gave considerable financial support to Blake. He was a successful poet, now regarded as sentimental and rather worse than mediocre. The story indicates that he was also a conceited man who enjoyed the role of patron with dependents who were obliged to him. He does seem to have liked Blake, and admired his artistic skill; but relations between the poet and this patron soured after a time.

Flaxman introduced Hayley and Blake in 1800, arranging a commission for some engraving work. In September of the same year, the Blakes moved to a cottage in the village of Felpham where Hayley had his home, so that the artist could be near to his employer. Much enthusiasm and idealism went into this move into the country, and Hayley and Blake spent a great deal of time together in the former's study, working on various commissions, discussing art and poetry, and Hayley taught Blake to read Greek. However, during the Blakes' stay Hayley imposed increasing pressure for Blake to work on commercial engraving and designing, and to moderate his style to make it more conventional, as well as to sideline his own writing – which Hayley seems to have thought pointless. Hayley clearly wanted to help Blake into a better commercial situation, but his advice, patronising attitudes, and undervaluing of Blake's genius, gradually built up a powerful resentment, which eventually exploded in accusations. During 1802 the Blakes were forming the resolve to escape from an obligation and patronage which had become insufferable, and in the late Summer of 1803 they returned to London.

John Linnell remained a close friend of the Blakes from 1818 until the poet's death in 1827. He provided commissions and introductions, which helped Blake financially; and he made regular 'payments on account' which were thinly-veiled financial help simply to keep Blake from real hardship. Blake visited the Linnells regularly on Sundays, and continued to do so when they moved out of their house in Cirencester Place to North End in Hampstead. Blake would walk out to Hampstead and spend the day, apparently in happy harmony with the Linnells. He was gentle and entertaining to the children, who loved his visits. As already mentioned, Linnell introduced Blake to 'The Ancients', to some other patrons as well, and to John Varley.

Blake's life was a long and intricate struggle to find patrons, commissions and public recognition: our 'outline' of his friends and associates is necessarily very selective, and necessarily – due to the pressures of space – omits numerous stories of his hopes or arguments with booksellers, printers and many others who offered him commissions. As his struggle to achieve recognition continued, Blake clearly harboured the feeling that others conspired against him; yet at the same time he had joy in his own vision and a naïve optimism, something like that of a child. There were times of both despair, and unreasoning hope. Despite his insecure circumstances, childless marriage, and the artistic and poetic isolation in which he worked; and despite his volatile temper, reports from those who met him of his gentleness, charm and humour are recorded throughout his life.

One external incident needs to be mentioned. In 1803, a soldier called Scofield who was a friend of Blake's gardener was lounging in the cottage garden at Felpham. Blake asked him to leave, an altercation began, and this ended with Blake forcibly ejecting Scofield from the garden, and marching him down the road to the inn, gripping him firmly the while. According to Scofield, Blake also shouted throughout their argument and all the way down the road, damning King and country, and the uniform of the King's soldiers, saying that the French should invade and it would be a good thing, and they would win, and so on. We must remember that this was at a time when England feared a French invasion, at the height of the war against Napoleon. Scofield accused Blake of sedition and assault, and the charge – with its attendant threat of execution – hung over Blake for a long time, until his trial in Chichester, in January 1805.

Soon after the accusation, Blake imagined that Hayley had set the soldier on to 'frame' him; but he later regretted this suspicion when Hayley supported him materially and kindly at the trial. Blake also vaguely suspected the authorities of 'framing' him because he was known to have associated with Tom Paine's republican set in the seventeen-nineties. However, it seems to have been a simpler case of a rowdy soldier trying to take advantage of the fearful patriotism which was the prevailing atmosphere of those years.

Blake was acquitted: Scofield and another soldier differed in their evidence, and Blake's witnesses, mostly solid and reliable villagers from Felpham, supported his good character. We can amuse ourselves by wondering whether Blake really did shout out all those treasonable opinions in his fury: they are quite in tune with his beliefs as we know them. Was the trial a victory for justice and truth, or a miscarriage where the wrong evidence was believed? More seriously, we must consider the real fear this trivial incident brought into the lives of Mr and Mrs Blake, and the real relief they must have felt when he was acquitted and the threat was lifted from their lives.

Blake's Works

Blake created hundreds of paintings, engravings, drawings, sketches, prints and so on during his nearly fifty years as artist and engraver. We cannot give any detailed account of these works, and will concentrate on his writings. The reader interested in looking at Blake's works of visual art will find them in many of the major galleries: in England at the Tate and the British Museum, in London, and the Fitzwilliam Museum in Cambridge, for example; in the US, copies of *Innocence and Experience* are held in many libraries and galleries including the Library of Congress, the Metropolitan Museum of Art, New York, and in collections at Princeton and Harvard.

Blake also wrote a great deal. He kept notebooks, and annotated the books he read; he wrote letters, and a few prose works such as the 'Descriptive Catalogue' for his exhibition of paintings in 1809, and the 'Public Address', which was to advertise his engraving of the Canterbury Pilgrims (1810). The account we give here concentrates on his poetic works, and is necessarily selective even among these. We will mention the places where the poet lived, during our account.

Blake lived at the family home in Broad Street, Golden Square, or at James Basire's while he was an apprentice, until his marriage in 1782. Some of the poems he had written during his teenage years and early twenties were collected and printed with the support of Mrs Mathews and her circle, in 1783, under the title *Poetical Sketches*. These – some written when the poet was only about fourteen years old – already show the plain, strong style married to vigorous rhythm we associate with the later *Songs of Innocence and Experience*, many of which we have studied in this book. In particular, the well-known lyric 'How sweet I roam'd from field to field', and the 'Mad Song', gave promise of what was to come.

Following their marriage, Blake and Catherine lodged at Green

Street, Leicester Fields until 1784, when his father died. In that year Blake and his wife moved to 27 Broad Street, next door to his father's (now his brother's) business, where Blake set up a print shop in partnership with an ex-fellow apprentice named Parker. The next year the Blakes moved around the corner to a house in Poland Street, where they lived until 1790. The death of Blake's brother Robert occurred there in 1787, and Blake continued to use Robert's notebook for sketches, epigrams and poems, filling the book in both directions over a period of many years.

It was during the late eighties that Blake developed his technique of 'relief etching', which allowed him to combine text and images and thus marry his two great gifts. The desire to work with both words and pictures, as well as the beginnings of the Blakean myth and 'prophetic' voice were evident in the first Prophetic Book, *Tiriel*, written in about 1789 and accompanied by twelve pen-and-wash illustrations. Simultaneously Blake was trying out the new technique of 'relief etching' in two small works, *There is No Natural Religion* and *All Religions Are One*, where each design is accompanied by a short statement carrying the argument of the series forward. These would seem to have been experiments which helped the craftsman to develop his new technique. In the same year Blake wrote, engraved and coloured the first of the Prophetic Books to reach its final form, *The Book of Thel*, and this was quickly followed (both were printed and issued in 1789) by the *Songs of Innocence*.

In 1790 the Blakes moved to a house in Lambeth, at 13 Hercules Buildings. Here they had a large garden. It is difficult for a present-day Londoner to imagine that Lambeth was a semi-rural area, but the Blakes moved into a new development adjoining a marsh and largely surrounded by fields. During the ten years they spent there, Lambeth was extensively developed, and it had taken on some of the characteristics of an urban slum before they left at the turn of the century. Between 1790 and 1793 *The Marriage of Heaven and Hell* was written, engraved and printed, as were the *Songs of Experience*. Also during the ten Lambeth years Blake wrote the series of prophecies known as the 'Lambeth prophecies', which many believe carry out his promise from *The Marriage of Heaven and Hell*:

I have also The Bible of Hell, which the world shall have whether
they will or no.

(K 158)

These were *The First Book of Urizen* (1794), *The Song of Los* (1795),
The Book of Ahania (1795) and *The Book of Los* (1795). Together,
they advanced Blake's myth of Los, Urizen and Orc, introducing
further symbolic figures or, as Blake called them, 'states', and telling
a creation story which makes an alternative to the Bible's Book of
Genesis. Political prophecies were written at the same time: *The
French Revolution* (1791) was followed by *America, a Prophecy*
(1793) and *Europe, a Prophecy* (1794).

Visions of the Daughters of Albion, dated 1793, is more difficult to
classify: it concerns Blake's characteristic mythic figures and has
some political elements in the narrative, similar to *America* or
Europe, yet the central interest is in love and sexuality. In its form,
written sonorously in Blake's seven-beat 'septennary' line and
making much use of parallelism, it is close to the Prophetic Books of
Los or *Urizen*. Perhaps it is a development from *Thel*, that tale of a
fearful innocent maid who flees from experience and life (see our
discussion in Chapter 4).

In 1795 Blake began to write a much longer and more ambitious
Prophetic Book, conceived as a large and complex 'dream in nine
nights'. He continued to work on this for the next nine years,
making countless changes and revisions, cancelling and re-writing;
and the form in which it has been left to us is clearly still not final.
This, *Vala, or the Four Zoas*, was the first of the three vast 'prophecies' which stand as Blake's final mythic and poetic creation. The
poet continued working on this epic task during the move to
Felpham and afterwards. Passages from this large unfinished work
were later transplanted into the other two prophecies, *Milton* and
Jerusalem.

When the Blakes left their cottage at Felpham and the patronage
of William Hayley, they took two rooms on the first floor of 17
South Molton Street, just off Oxford Street, and there, in 1804,
Blake conceived and began both of the great poetic 'books' that were
to occupy him for the next sixteen years: *Milton, a Poem in 2 Books*

was written and engraved between 1804 and 1808; and *Jerusalem* between 1804 and 1820. In the same year as the great vision *Jerusalem* was completed, the Blakes undertook their final move from South Molton Street to 3 Fountain Court, just off the Strand, where they lived until Blake's death.

The summary of 'works' given here is selective: browsing in Sir Geoffrey Keynes's Oxford edition *Blake: Complete Writings*, or in Erdman and Stevenson's Longman edition of *The Poems of William Blake*, you will meet numerous other poems, written within letters to Thomas Butts and other patrons and friends, other verses from the notebooks that were never engraved, as well as occasional stanzas and epigrams, other prose writings, and so on.

Blake in English Literature

William Blake was certainly idiosyncratic, and was largely ignored by the public of his own time. Despite the enthusiasm of Samuel Palmer and 'The Ancients', recognition of his genius only began to spread significantly after the publication of Alexander Gilchrist's *Life* in 1863, and gained momentum slowly with the help of some unconventional later Victorians who became supporters of his cause, such as D. G. Rossetti (1828–1882) and A. C. Swinburne (1837–1909). Although his name became more familiar in literary circles from the 1860s onwards, Blake's poetry itself remained relatively unknown until editions began to appear. E. J. Ellis and W. B. Yeats edited his poetry in 1895, and Dr John Sampson's and Sir Geoffrey Keynes's editions (1905 and 1925 respectively) established a standard of scholarly accuracy that had been lacking in previous versions. However, the longer Prophetic Books were not included in Sampson's edition, and waited until the 1920s to be printed in full, a century after the poet's death.

The work of Keynes, Joseph Wicksteed, David V. Erdman, Northrop Frye and S. Foster Damon[2] has fuelled an ever-growing

---

[2] The influential critical works by these twentieth-century interpreters of Blake are briefly discussed in the next chapter, and bibliographical details of them can be found in *Further Reading*.

appreciation of and interest in Blake's poetry and his ideas, so that by the beginning of the twenty-first century his place as one of England's greatest poets is firmly established.

It is notoriously difficult to pursue comparative discussion of Blake's works. The similarities we discuss below, between him and other 'romantics', are something of a coincidence, but it is a distortion to regard Blake as part of any movement for the simple reason that the world did not meet his work until long after his death. When considering influences, we must remember that Blake was a self-taught and obscure writer, working largely in isolation; and that many of his ideas were far in advance of his time. The major influences on him are not his immediate contemporaries or predecessors, but distant texts such as Dante's *Divine Comedy*, Milton's *Paradise Lost*, the Bible, and Shakespeare. His own ideas reach forward into a far distant future, provoking comparison with figures all widely different, both from each other and Blake, such as Marx, Freud, Lawrence, Yeats and Shaw. For these reasons, the present chapter cannot undertake or even initiate any meaningful assessment within a wider context, but is limited to the following brief discussion of Blake and the 'romantics'.

Blake as a 'Romantic' Poet

In this section I have the limited aim of introducing a discussion of Blake's 'romantic' credentials, by suggesting some points of comparison between his poetry and the works of Wordsworth and Coleridge only. 'English Romantic Poetry' is an enormous field for the interested reader to explore. It is far too wide and contentious a subject to treat in full within the present volume, and I therefore only refer to two of Blake's 'romantic' contemporaries.

William Wordsworth and Samuel Taylor Coleridge published their *Lyrical Ballads* in 1798, and a second edition together with the famous Preface appeared in 1800. Both of them saw and commented on copies of the *Songs of Innocence and Experience*, and Coleridge met Blake. Coleridge was critical of the copy of the *Songs* he read, although he was more averse to the designs, and marked several of the poems with approval. However, there was never any sense in which any of these 'romantic poets' considered Blake to belong in the same movement, sharing their aims.

On the other hand, we can use hindsight and identify several themes and concerns about poetry that they held in common. In particular, they were all interested in ideas of 'vision' and 'imagination'; they all used childhood and innocence as a prominent theme; they all developed new and radical ideas about nature; and they shared a belief that poetry would be revived by using a more colloquial and vigorous language. We will enlarge on each of these topics briefly.

We discussed Blake's ideas about different levels of perception, and 'vision', in Part 1. Remember that Lyca's parents could only remove the blinkers of their oppressive fear in a moment of vision when the lion appeared as 'a spirit arm'd in gold'; that the *Experience* Chimney Sweeper's happiness was incomprehensible to his parents; that Blake called for 'the doors of perception' to be 'cleansed' in *The Marriage of Heaven and Hell*, so that everything would appear 'infinite' rather than 'finite & corrupt'; and that Blake insisted:

> For double the vision my Eyes do see,
> And a double vision is always with me.
>
> (K 817)

Blake's idea of 'vision' is clearly fundamental to his beliefs, then: it is the faculty which enables people to escape from their mental prisons, their 'mind-forg'd manacles'; to defeat and annihilate their hard-shelled egos or 'selfhoods'; to renew themselves and open themselves to the infinite by means of 'God, the Human Imagination' (K 623).

A different and imaginative way of seeing was also fundamental to the beliefs of Wordsworth and Coleridge. In *The Prelude* (subtitled 'The Growth of a Poet's Mind') Wordsworth records the importance of visionary moments in his own development. From his childhood, he remembers when 'The sky seemed not a sky of earth', and when:

> No familiar shapes
> Remained, no pleasant images of trees,

Of sea or sky, no colours of green fields;
But huge and mighty forms, that do not live
Like living men, moved slowly through the mind . . .
                              (*The Prelude*, Book I, lines 395–399)

Wordsworth argues that this faculty of vision nurtured his mind and
soul, and the account of a moment of vision he experienced as a
young man crossing the Alps underlines the crucial place 'imagination' and vision occupy in his beliefs:

Imagination – here the Power so called
Through sad incompetence of human speech,
That awful Power rose from the mind's abyss
Like an unfathered vapour that enwraps,
At once, some lonely traveller. I was lost;
Halted without an effort to break through;
But to my conscious soul I now can say –
'I recognise thy glory:' in such strength
Of usurpation, when the light of sense
Goes out, but with a flash that has revealed
The invisible world, doth greatness make abode . . .
                              (*The Prelude*, Book VI, lines 592–602)

We recognise several features of Blake's concept of 'vision' here.
Wordsworth agrees that vision is different and separate from normal,
physical sight. He saw 'No familiar shapes' when 'the light of sense /
Goes out'. He clearly identifies vision with a great 'Power' and with
his 'soul'; and the faculty of imagination helps him to 'recognise [his
soul's] glory'. Finally, Wordsworth agrees with Blake that these
moments of vision are the great creative moments of humanity. So
Wordsworth insists that with the 'Imagination' '. . . doth greatness
make abode', just as Blake ascribed infinite power and influence to
his 'moment':

For in this period the poet's work is done, & all the great
Events of time start forth & are conceived in such a period,
Within a moment . . .

                                                          (K 516)

There is no doubt that Coleridge also ascribed great power and importance to vision and imagination. The extraordinary poem 'Kubla Khan' begins with the memory of a visionary dream, a fragment which Coleridge tells us is all that remains of a longer poem dictated to him in his sleep. The second section of 'Kubla Khan' seems to reflect on the magic associated with that vision. Coleridge longs to revive his vision because it would fill him with 'such a deep delight' that he would then have the imaginative power:

> . . . with music loud and long,
> I would build that dome in air,
> That sunny dome! those caves of ice!

The imaginative power Coleridge conjures in 'Kubla Khan' turns the poet into a figure of magic and fear to others, a figure reminiscent of the wild seer or prophet, shocking and frightening conventional society, sometimes called 'Rintrah' in Blake's writings. Coleridge describes popular reaction to such a poet:

> And all should cry, Beware! Beware!
> His flashing eyes, his floating hair!
> Weave a circle round him thrice,
> And close your eyes with holy dread,
> For he on honey-dew hath fed,
> And drunk the milk of Paradise.
>> (all quotations are from 'Kubla Khan', *S. T. Coleridge: Poems*, ed.
>> John Beer, London and New York, 1963, pp. 167–8).

In Part 1 we noticed that the conjunction of opposite extremes, or heightened states of emotion, is significant in Blake, and is closely related to 'vision'. We remember the extreme terror which leads to vision for Lyca's parents in 'The Little Girl Found'; the shock the poet expresses in 'The Tyger', 'Did he who made the Lamb make thee?'; and the Proverb of Hell: 'Excess of sorrow laughs. Excess of joy weeps'. Coleridge's juxtaposition of 'sunny dome!' and 'caves of ice!', and his combination of fear ('Beware!') with 'the milk of Paradise' suggest that both poets were investigating similar, paradoxical states of emotion in their efforts to express the potency of a moment of vision. All three poets seem to agree that imaginative experiences break through the limits of language and rationality, and expose what Wordsworth calls the 'sad incompetence of human speech'.

We are familiar with the importance of Blake's ideas about childhood and innocence. We have looked at 'The Lamb' and 'The Garden of Love', for instance, which clearly suggest that childhood is a blessed state; and a fundamental theme of *Innocence* and *Experience* is the process of growing up, which cuts us off from vision and delight, sadly imprisoning our minds within the 'manacles' of materialism and convention. The following lines from Wordsworth's 'Ode: Intimations of Immortality from Recollections of Early Childhood', are self-explanatory, and clearly enunciate a comparable theme and belief:

> Not in entire forgetfulness,
> And not in utter nakedness,
> But trailing clouds of glory do we come
> From God, who is our home:
> Heaven lies about us in our infancy!
> Shades of the prison-house begin to close
> Upon the growing Boy
> But He beholds the light, and whence it flows,
> He sees it in his joy;
> The Youth, who daily farther from the east
> Must travel, still is Nature's Priest,
> And by the vision splendid
> Is on his way attended;
> At length the Man perceives it die away,
> And fade into the light of common day.
>
> ('Ode: Intimations of Immortality etc.', *Wordsworth: Poetical Works*, ed. Thomas Hutchinson, London, 1950, p. 460)

This is a clear statement of belief in the power and divinity of childhood imagination and tells a story of decline into *Experience* that can be closely related to Blake's ideas, even to the detail of 'prison-house' imagery. We have already noted that Wordsworth ascribed the 'growth' of his 'poet's mind' to a series of visions from his early childhood, in *The Prelude*.

It has been easy to find close comparisons between Blake and the two poets of *Lyrical Ballads,* to show how similarly they exploited themes of childhood, innocence and imagination. The theme of nature is a more complicated matter, and we do not have sufficient space to investigate the three poets' differing developments of the theme here. It will be enough for our purpose to point out that nature is a fundamental theme in all three poets' works; and to cast a critical eye over the common misapprehension that Wordsworth, the 'poet of nature', spent his time looking at mountains, rivers and waterfalls, woods, valleys and so forth.

Wordsworth did indeed spend a great deal of time in wild places; as the tourist industry constantly reminds us, he settled in the English Lake District. However, careful reading of *The Prelude* and the *Lyrical Ballads* will remind us time and again that Wordsworth only used his contemplation of nature for a further purpose – to nurture and trigger his moments of vision. The concept of 'Nature', with a capital 'N', that we meet in Wordsworth's poetry has little to do with physical senses or the material beauties of a landscape: it is a spiritual and moral force. He repeatedly focuses on moments when his senses are blinded: there are 'no familiar shapes' and 'the light of sense goes out'. Then, he perceives in a different, spiritual manner, 'the invisible world' filled with 'huge and mighty forms, that do not live like living men'. Wordsworth, then, does not so much look *at* nature, but look *through* it towards a spiritual entity he calls 'Nature'.

There is one further aspect of the Nature theme where we can discern common ground between Blake and his two 'romantic' contemporaries. All three seem to develop a concept of nature in reaction against the ideas of harmony and proportion that had come to dominate conventional taste. In contrast to the conventional emphasis on moderation and gentleness, and the transformation of nature within harmonious limits in – for example – the eighteenth-century art of landscape gardening, all three of the poets we are discussing emphasised elemental power, wildness and natural extravagance.

We have discussed the 'rural' landscape of *Innocence* in Chapter 2, pointing out that the rural settings of 'Introduction', 'The Shepherd' and 'The Lamb' are deliberately partial expositions of nature. Together with the naïve 'heavens' dreamed in *Innocence* (by, for example, Tom Dacre in 'The Chimney Sweeper' and the speaker in 'Night'), the *Innocence* landscape becomes almost a parody of conventional taste – a limited, tamed nature that excludes the power and fear explored in 'The Tyger'. Blake clearly identifies the *Innocence* landscape with a limited and falsified vision of 'heaven'.

Wordsworth also focuses on wild and extravagant elemental forces, and his autobiographical *Prelude* repeatedly tells how he sought out the dangers and perils of his mountainous home. So, when stealing from nests:

> Oh! when I have hung
> Above the raven's nest, by knots of grass
> And half-inch fissures in the slippery rock
> But ill sustained, and almost (so it seemed)
> Suspended by the blast that blew amain,
> Shouldering the naked crag, oh, at that time
> While on the perilous ridge I hung alone . . .
>
> (*The Prelude*, Book I, lines 330–336)

The mere prettiness or harmony of nature was only a partial view to Wordsworth, as to Blake; and Wordsworth further highlights the importance of terror as a force that formed and bore 'a part, and that a needful part' in the growth and instruction of his soul. He states that he grew up 'Fostered alike by beauty and by fear' and refers to 'such discipline, both pain and fear' which formed his creative vision.[3]

Similarly, Blake, Wordsworth and Coleridge all wrote in reaction against precious and ornamental poetic style. They rejected the idea that the language of poetry should be ornamental, and sought a more ordinary 'voice'. In his preface to the *Lyrical Ballads*, Wordsworth sets out this aim as if it were a reforming manifesto, to revive the vigorous and common roots of poetic language. He asserts that he chose to write about 'Low and rustic life' because in these sit-

---

[3] All quotations are from *The Prelude*, Book I.

uations the 'essential passions . . . speak a plainer and more emphatic language', while the common people, being free from 'social vanity . . . convey their feelings and notions in simple and unelaborated expressions'. Wordsworth goes on to profess his faith in a simplified poetic diction, distinguishing between plainness and what was conventionally expected of a poet in his day:

> . . . such a language arising out of repeated experience and regular feelings is a more permanent and a far more philosophical language than that which is frequently substituted for it by Poets, who think that they are conferring honour upon themselves and their art in proportion as they separate themselves from the sympathies of men, and indulge in arbitrary and capricious habits of expression in order to furnish food for fickle tastes and fickle appetites of their own creation.
>
> (Wordsworth and Coleridge, *Lyrical Ballads*, ed. R. L. Brett and A. R. Jones, second edition, London and New York, 1991, pp. 245–6)

That Blake shared his 'romantic' contemporaries' contempt for vacuous and ornamental poetic diction is obvious from the plain vigour of his own style in the *Songs*. However, when we turn to Blake's writings for his opinions, we find them also expressed in a more direct and forthright style than the rather apologetic convolutions of Wordsworth's manifesto:

> The Enquiry in England is not whether a Man has Talents & Genius, But whether he is Passive & Polite & a Virtuous Ass & obedient to Noblemen's Opinions in Art & Science. If he is, he is a Good Man. If Not, he must be Starved.
>
> (*Blake: Complete Writings*, ed. Sir Geoffrey Keynes, Oxford, 1966, pp. 452–3)

Or:

> . . . the tame high finisher of paltry Blots
> Indefinite, or paltry Rhymes, or paltry Harmonies,
> Who creeps into State Government like a catterpiller to destroy;
>
> (K 533)

Much of what Wordsworth produced in *Lyrical Ballads*, which was meant to be a radical departure from conventional Augustan style, seems mannered and literary to a present-day reader. Many would argue that Blake achieved far more than Wordsworth in reviving the common language. Look at the naturalism of voice in 'The Chimney Sweeper':

> Theres little Tom Dacre, who cried when his head
> That curl'd like a lambs back, was shav'd, so I said,
> Hush Tom never mind it, for when your head's bare,
> You know that the soot cannot spoil your white hair.

(K2, 12)

And the direct expression of outrage in 'Holy Thursday':

> Is this a holy thing to see,
> In a rich and fruitful land,
> Babes reduced to misery,
> Fed with cold and usurous hand?
>
> Is that trembling cry a song?
> Can it be a song of joy?
> And so many children poor?
> It is a land of poverty!

(K2, 33)

We cannot imagine Wordsworth having the courage to break a stanza into four separate, sharp expressions of incredulous outrage, as Blake does in the second stanza here. It is possible to argue that Wordsworth's comparative failure in finding a less 'literary' diction is due to the fact that he was not one of the 'Low and rustic' types he aspired to represent; and he could no more help writing like a Cambridge graduate than Blake could help saying, forcefully and directly, what he felt!

So far we have confined ourselves to noticing some common areas of interest and belief shared between Blake and two of his contemporary 'romantic' poets. However, the term 'romantic' has been subjected to continuous argument and discussion in literary-critical debate. Hundreds of attempted definitions of the phrase 'romantic poet' exist, each one completely or slightly differing from the one before. A number of these definitions seek to connect the poetic movement with the division between 'romantic' and 'materialist' philosophies. In this context there is only one thing to say about Blake: he is emphatically a 'romantic', and an enemy of materialism. He repeatedly asserts his perception of forces, forms, beings and existences beyond the bounds of the material world; and he emphatically rejects the limits of sense. Sense-perception is described as seeing 'thro' narrow chinks of [man's] cavern' in *The Marriage of Heaven and Hell*, and Blake urges us to transcend these limits, saying:

> . . . May God us keep
> From single vision and Newton's sleep!
>
> (K 818)

Our discussion of 'vision' and 'imagination' above demonstrates beyond contradiction that Wordsworth and Coleridge were both also 'romantic' in this sense.

This brief discussion has shown that it is possible to consider Blake as a 'romantic' poet, and that some similarities of theme and emotion between him and other 'romantics' are quite striking. However, we may be equally struck by the startling differences between Blake and his contemporaries. For example, there is nothing in Wordsworth or Coleridge as trenchant and radical as Blake's political insights (see Chapter 3); and there is little in common between the roles of Bard and Prophet expounded in Blake's works, and Wordsworth's concept of the poet as 'Nature's Priest'. The gulf between them is expressed by Blake's own note, written in a copy of Wordsworth's 'Poems':

> There is no such Thing as Natural Piety Because The Natural Man is at Enmity with God.
>
> (K 782)

6

A Sample of Critical Views

General Remarks

William Blake gained gradual critical recognition during the final decades of the nineteenth century, in large part thanks to his biographer Alexander Gilchrist and his editors Ellis and Yeats; while the first major contribution to Blake criticism was the long essay published by Algernon Charles Swinburne in 1868.[1] Blake's fame continued to grow throughout the first half of the twentieth century, and he attracted an increasing amount of critical attention. However, the most significant contributions to Blake scholarship, in the early part of the century, came from the editorial work of Dr. John Sampson (1905), Sir Geoffrey Keynes (1925), and Sloss and Wallis (1926); the boost to interpretation of the designs given by Joseph Wicksteed's commentary on *Blake's Vision of the Book of Job* (1910); and the biography by Mona Wilson (*The Life of William Blake*, 1927) which remained the standard account of his life for a long time.

S. Foster Damon's *William Blake: His Philosophy and Symbols* (1924) was one of the most ambitious earlier contributions to a full critical understanding. Then, in the middle of the twentieth century and accelerating up to the present day, the business of Blake criticism began in earnest. Important contributions to a growing debate

[1] See *Further Reading* for titles and bibliographical details of the works mentioned.

came from Northrop Frye, David V. Erdman, S. Foster Damon, Jacob Bronowski, Harold Bloom, and many others. In recent years, Blake has continued to be intensively studied: the Marxists, Cultural Materialists, Structuralists and Poststructuralists, Deconstructionists, Psychoanalysts and Feminists have all mined his work. It is characteristic of Blake studies that there has been little agreement, and lively continuing debate, throughout its history.

This chapter makes no pretence of surveying the criticism. We have a different purpose, which is simply to start some debates which you can follow up for yourself in a good library, by using the suggestions in *Further Reading*. Always be independent when approaching the critics' ideas: you are not under an obligation to agree with them. Your mind can be stimulated by discussing the text with your teachers and lecturers, or in a class. Treat the critics in the same way: it is stimulating to debate Blake by reading the critics' books and articles, challenging your ideas and theirs. We summarise three critical views, chosen for no other reason than that they are different from each other, so they challenge each other.

Northrop Frye and David V. Erdman

Before looking at three views in greater detail, we will glance at two influential critics from the middle of the last century. *Fearful Symmetry: A Study of William Blake*, by Northrop Frye (Princeton, 1947),[2] ranges widely through mythic, religious and symbolic analogues in a vast and eclectic work of interpretation. Frye acknowledges that writing *Fearful Symmetry* led him to become absorbed 'in the larger critical theory implicit in Blake's view of art'; and he begins to construct a Blakean aesthetic in his opening chapter. 'The artist', he says, is 'the man who struggles to develop his perception into creation, his sight into vision'; and art itself is a 'technique of realizing . . . a higher reality'. Frye confronts what we have called 'vision' in these terms:

---

[2] Page-references are to the Beacon Paperback edition of 1962.

It is no use saying to Blake that the company of angels he sees surrounding the sun are not 'there'. Not where? Not in a gaseous blast
furnace across ninety million miles of nothing, perhaps . . . To prove
that he sees them Blake will not point to the sky but to, say, the four-
teenth plate of the Job series illustrating the text: 'When the morning
stars sang together, and all the sons of God shouted for joy.' *That* is
where the angels appear, in a world formed and created by Blake's
imagination and entered into by everyone who looks at the picture.

Frye thus deduces three worlds, of 'vision', 'sight' and 'memory', and
pursues his argument by pointing out that the world of 'vision' is a
world in which we see 'fulfilled desire and unbounded freedom'. In
childhood, we feel that if we imagine a thing is so, it 'is so' or 'can be
made to become so'. The visionary never deserts the principle that
what he imagines 'ought to be so', and never accepts the advice of
sensible, practical people who counsel him to moderate his expectations. Frye leads his reasoning to the assertion that 'imagination
creates reality, and as desire is a part of imagination, the world we
desire is more real than the world we passively accept' (all the above
quotations are from Frye, *op. cit.*, pp. 26–7).

As in Blake's poetry, the idea that 'vision' is more 'real' than the
dull or oppressed world we perceive with our everyday senses, is
attractive. The argument Frye constructs does not add reasoned
support to the assertion of higher 'reality' (inevitably, all such assertions beg the question of 'reality') but it does confirm that his
absorbing interest in Blake focuses on aesthetic issues: the themes of
'vision' and 'imagination', the interpretation of Blake's symbols as an
exposition of creative and prophetic process and purpose.

By the end of his study, Frye has drawn analogies between Blake's
self-created 'system' and a wide range of texts, traditions, myths and
periods; and has steadily expounded Blake's concept of an original
imagination and language, derived by the 'Poetic Genius' directly
from God, the 'Human Imagination': 'All had originally one language, and one religion' (K 579). Blake's symbols are, in fact, 'archetypal', in the sense that they are distilled from a tradition of
emblems and myths which are profoundly expressive throughout
our history, and which speak to us deeply. It is this quality which
makes Blake's symbolic system continuously relevant and fasci-

nating. Frye's interest in the 'archetypal' and therefore timeless quality of imaginative vision is clear:

> Every poet, including Blake, must first be studied in connection with his own age, but there comes a point at which the value of this study becomes exhausted and the conception of 'anachronism' is rendered meaningless. What makes the poet worth studying at all is his ability to communicate beyond his context in time and space: we therefore are the present custodians of his meaning, and the profundity of his appeal is relative to our own outlook.
>
> (Frye, *op. cit.*, p. 420)

From the study of Blake, Frye deduces that there is such a thing as an 'imaginative iconography' and that Blake's apparent difficulty as a text is because he forces us, much more than other writers, to 'learn so much of its grammar in reading him'. Frye suggests, then, that there is something constant underlying the varieties of different texts, something all have in common irrespective of time and place; and that Blake's mythic system presents this underlying 'imaginative iconography' in an unusually explicit and dense form.

David V. Erdman's *Blake: Prophet Against Empire* (Princeton, 1954)[3] can almost be taken as a complementary volume to Frye. He does not so much contradict Frye's literary-mythic scholarship as show no interest in that enquiry at all, while he pursues another, equally detailed and scholarly enquiry of his own. Erdman's book is informed by detailed research into the political, social and historical conditions and events of Blake's lifetime, and his interpretation of Blake's works looks, first and foremost, for a connection between the text and the politics of its time. This is exemplified in Erdman's comment on the engraving commonly known as 'Glad Day':

> Gilchrist saw a personification of sunrise, Wright the exhilaration of youth aglow – making nothing of the lines Blake engraved under the picture some time in 1800 or later:
> Albion rose from where he labourd at the Mill with Slaves.

---

[3] Page-references are to the Anchor Books paperback edition of 1969.

> Giving himself for the Nations he danc'd the dance of Eternal Death.
> The symbolism of this inscription derives from Blake's paraphrase of the Declaration of Independence in *America*, though it is a later symbolism than that of *America*, for Albion is here more than a place name: he is 'Albion the ancient Man' of *The Four Zoas*, that is, the eternal Englishman or, more broadly, the people. Blake is saying that in 1780 the people of England rose up in a demonstration of independence, dancing the dance of insurrection (apocalyptic self-sacrifice) to save the Nations (Blake's term in *America* for the colonies).
>
> (Erdman, *op. cit.*, p. 10)

Erdman proceeds to describe the Gordon Riots, explaining how near England was to a revolution during the crisis years 1780–2, and providing background information documenting the depth of opposition to the American war that existed in the country.

Throughout his book Erdman adopts the same pattern of argument: as his commentary confronts interpretation, he looks to the immediate political environment at the time of Blake's writing. So, for example, he explains the curious appearance of 'Erin' as a harbinger of liberty, near the end of *Jerusalem*, by pointing out how many reformers and radicals were looking to the new Irish Movement of Daniel O'Connell, with the hope that it would succeed in liberating Ireland, at the time when Blake was finishing his great poem (see Erdman, *op. cit.*, pp. 481–4); and, in commentating 'the voice of Bath' in *Jerusalem*, plate 39, he points out that Richard Warner, minister of St James's parish in Bath, published sermons against war in 1804 and 1808, and was a noted campaigner for peace and reform throughout the period (see Erdman, *op. cit.*, pp. 475–8).

In short, Erdman's book is a great achievement combining literary and historical scholarship. His interest complements Frye: the latter explores Blake's aesthetics and the story of imagination, while Erdman pursues the social and political Blake.

We noted in Part 1 that Blake's symbols have the quality of application to several simultaneous contexts: that the 'Orc cycle', for example, can tell a personal story of emotions and psyche; or a historical story of social evolution. It should be no surprise, therefore, that Blake criticism is so various, and that the differences reveal the critic's approach rather than textual problems. Blake's works are thus a particularly metamorphic body of texts: they yield up their fruits, generously, in response to the specific bent of each critic.

The three critics whose views we move on to now are therefore to be considered as widely different views of Blake, but each equally valid. We can think of the text itself as something that throws its light in many different directions. We have chosen one early, traditional critic; one deconstructive view; and a neo-feminist approach, as three of the directions in which light shines.

John Middleton Murry

Our first critic is John Middleton Murry. His *William Blake* appeared in 1933, with the professed aim 'solely to discover and, as far as may be, expound the *doctrine* of William Blake: 'The Everlasting Gospel', as he finally called it'[4] and we will look in some detail at both the beginning and end of his interpretation.

The first chapter of Murry's study is called 'Spiritual Sensation'. He points out that Blake broke out into one of the loveliest songs of *Innocence* in the middle of his disillusioned, satirical manuscript now called *An Island in the Moon*. Murry deduces that there was a moment of 'vision' or revelation, and his first chapter dissects and discusses this experience, which he regards as supremely important because: 'Such was the beginning of the *Songs of Innocence*, from such a poised and silent vortex of spiritual sensation they took birth' (Murry, p. 13). He then quotes the first proposition of *There is No Natural Religion*: 'Man's perceptions are not bounded by organs of perception: he perceives more than sense (tho' ever so acute) can discover' (K 97). Murry says that 'The recognition of this sense beyond sense is fundamental to Blake, and to an understanding of Blake'; and he begins his discussion by pointing out that spiritual experience is twofold in character because it reveals both the 'world

---

[4] Murry, *op. cit.*, p. 7. Page-references are to the Life and Letters Series edition, Oxford and London, Jonathan Cape, 1936, and will appear in brackets thus: (Murry, p. *).

without' – the world we see with our physical senses every day is suddenly 'clarified' – and the 'world within', because, 'Subjectively, we are also clarified. The world and we, alike, are cleansed. Both pass into a new medium: the medium of the Imagination, as Blake called it' (Murry, pp. 14–15).

We have to see the physical things around us to carry on with our everyday lives, but we must not see that world only. Therefore, seeing imaginatively involves surrendering our normal way of seeing: 'To see the thing as it is demands and compels a subjugation of the self' (Murry, p. 15). To do this we have to become passive, utterly open and receptive. However, our outward passivity allows a supreme activity of 'an other within us', and Blake explains this state as: 'Therefore God becomes as we are, that we may be as he is' (K 98). This spiritual happening was a historical event for the orthodox Christian: it happened once, through Christ. Blake, on the other hand, tells us that the visionary or spiritual moment must be a recurrent experience, constantly cleansing and renewing us. Murry explains:

> . . . [God] constantly takes possession of us, dispossesses us of ourselves, and we become God. Not we, in our selves; for of our selves are we dispossessed. We, in our selves, are never God; our selves are but the barrier and obstacle to God, which he puts aside to enter into that which is his own.'
>
> (Murry, p. 17)

When we return to the normal way of seeing, after this experience, we are different: the experience has changed us. However, no visionary moment is final, and Blake urges us to go on seeking what Murry calls 'Spiritual Sensation': 'that God can and will dispossess us of our selves entirely, and the injunction that we should suffer Him to do so' (Murry, p. 17).

In his second and third chapters, Murry turns to the two short doctrinal texts *There is No Natural Religion* and *All Religions are One* (both from about 1788) and examines their propositions because he sees these texts as Blake's attempt to give an account of his visionary experience to the world. Murry points out that Blake went beyond asserting the 'truth' of vision, by saying that the man who only sees in the ordinary, physical way is not able to perceive beyond himself ('He who sees the Ratio only, sees himself only.'). This is because such a man remains in a world in which he sees everything through his own senses and in relation to himself, and he therefore has no experience of an other. By contrast, 'when the eternal individuality of things is recognized, the Self is in abeyance. The 'infinite' in things is at one with the 'infinite' in man' (Murry, p. 23). From this Insight, Murry is able to develop two related ideas: first, that the crucial element in imaginative seeing is becoming aware of the individuality of all things, which he equates with Blake's phrase 'the Poetic Genius'; secondly, that Blake was developing and elaborating a doctrine of 'two selves'. There is a something in us which is prior to the 'will', and:

> . . . more profound than the self, from which the will proceeds. What Blake is trying to express . . . is that there exists in all men a profounder Man, who is negated in act by will, in thought and word by mind. This will and mind derive from or compose the unregenerate self, which is a negation. Man's real potentiality lies in this positive and profounder self, which Blake has previously called 'The Poetic Genius or true Man'.
>
> (all from Murry, p. 32)

Murry has thus begun his book by focusing on a revelation, a moment of 'imaginative seeing' which transformed Blake; and has analysed and discussed the meaning of 'imagination' as far as this is further expounded in Blake's works of the late 1780s. Murry then states that this is the fundamental essence of Blake – that all the further writings, complications of vision, setbacks and experiences recorded in the Blake canon are directly and logically connected to the understanding Blake broke through to at this early stage of his life. The remainder of Murry's book is therefore elaboration rather than further insight, because everything else about Blake's doctrine follows *necessarily* from the revelation of 'imaginative seeing':

> In reality he has no more to tell us. His work, in essence, will be to repeat this same vision over and over again; but since this vision

involves a dedication, since this vision, being Life, has to be lived, has
therefore to be failed, but never forgotten . . . the destruction and re-
creation of this vision ends only with Blake's death.

(Murry, pp. 35–6)

Murry does indeed follow up his analysis of 'imagination' and all it
entails, through the remainder of Blake's works. In doing so, he pays
particular attention to *The Marriage of Heaven and Hell*, *The
Everlasting Gospel*, and *Milton*. It is an instructive and lucid account
of the coherence of Blake's thought, emphasising the way that each
of the poet's particular insights seems to be 'necessarily' part of his
large vision, so that when his poetry is at its best we can follow his
ideas easily. Murry highlights how the doctrine of 'two selves'
develops into the mythic states explored in the late Prophetic Books
– *Milton* in particular – called 'Selfhood', 'Spectre' or 'my Satan';
and he examines the doctrine of 'Self-annihilation' which grows
from what he described as being 'dispossessed of our selves' in the
original experience. 'Self-annihilation' absorbs other concepts also,
such as the significance of an 'eternal' moment in time, which is
'equal in its period & value to Six Thousand Years' (K516); and the
concept of forgiveness, to which Murry devotes a chapter.

Murry's central thesis, then, is twofold. First, that the fundamental truths in Blake's poetry concern vision and imagination,
because all of Blake's other various symbols and doctrines grow from
this. Secondly, that the final form of Blake's doctrine is a compelling
'Everlasting Gospel' based on visionary insight.

Murry's book is 'traditional' in comparison to the eclectic scholarship of Northrop Frye, in that he focuses on Blake's writings themselves and concentrates his efforts on explaining the text to his
reader, relying very much on the internal evidence of Blake's words
and not indulging in journeys through analogies from literary-myth-
ical history. Murry is a persuasive and lucid writer, and outstand-
ingly successful in making the area of Blake's thought he is interested
in clear and accessible. His book therefore remains valuable, particularly in contrast to the gratuitously esoteric, so plentifully found in
Blake criticism.

Nelson Hilton

Our second critic takes a very different approach from that of Middleton Murry. Nelson Hilton's essay 'Blake in the Chains of Being'[5] was first published in 1980, and uses a close concentration on words as signifiers of meaning, as well as text subverting or undercutting meaning, to explore images of 'chains' and other related iron-work in some of Blake's poems. We will give Hilton's commentary on 'London' in some detail, partly because this poem is already familiar from our own analysis in Part 1[6] and partly because Hilton's concentrated approach to the text, a critical mode often called 'deconstruction', demands full exposition of the analysis. Hilton declares his thesis at the start of his essay:

> For the poet who hears 'mind-forg'ed manacles' and who describes our planet Earth pleading for someone to break her heavy chain, such devices assume more than material reference; they present themselves as key links in the linear, univocal speech and lockstep thought process that Blake strives to replace by the four folds of his vision. A 'chain' is not simply a chain, but also an instance of what it refers to and (as a word) itself participates in: an image of order variously epitomised as the 'great chain of being' and its double the 'chain of discourse', with its verbal 'links'.
>
> (Hilton, p. 71)

Hilton gives a brief discussion of the 'great chain of being', quoting Pope and saying that he 'sets the tone for the century's sense of the image'; and a longer discussion of Hume, Bacon and Locke on language. He points out that Locke's *Essay Concerning Human Understanding* acknowledged the arbitrary nature of the connection between signifier (word) and referent (thing) but concluded that language gives a 'constant connexion' between the two which is 'precise,

---

[5] From *The Eighteenth Century*, 21 (1980), pp. 212–35. Page-references given in this chapter are to the essay as reprinted in *William Blake: Contemporary Critical Essays*, ed. David Punter, in the Macmillan New Casebooks series, Basingstoke and London, 1996. Page-references are given in brackets thus: (Hilton, p. *).
[6] See the analysis of 'London' in Chapter 3.

determined', and that 'This is very necessary'. Hilton therefore con-
cludes that the 'links in the chains of association and language are
thus the instruments of an arbitrary, dictatorial power' (all from
Hilton p. 74) and relates this 'psycholinguistic' power to eighteenth-
century politics and philosophy: anathema to Blake.

Having highlighted the connection between 'chain' imagery and
language, Hilton suggests that Blake's use of poetry to subvert
Locke's 'chain' posed problematic questions: how does the critic of
'chains' know that he is not himself 'chained'; and what is the nature
of 'chains' that 'fasten in the mind'? (Hilton, p. 75).

Turning to 'London', Hilton shows how this poem creates these
questions in its language. He highlights the repeated 'charter'd' of
the first stanza, seeing a charter as 'writing' which is an example of
tyranny's 'arbitrary imposition' on the weakened inhabitants, in
other words power wielded by language. Hilton analyses the
remainder of the poem as radically calling into question the relation
between word and thing, particularly because of the disjunction of
senses, and use of sound-associations, in the poem. His argument is
best given in full:

> [the final line of stanza 2, 'The mind-forg'd manacles I hear'] . . .
> moves beyond the hint of simple political oppression to question the
> structure of our experience and our response to it. 'I hear', implicitly
> asks, 'do you hear?' . . . What do we hear? 'Forg'd' or 'fraudulent'?
> Mine or mind? Man in manacles? Whatever it is, it is everywhere
> mined and forged in the hearth of what is heard and seen. In this
> dungeon of London, Blake's strategy for unlocking the reader is the
> multiplication of significance, breaking the vocal chain at its weakest
> link, the univocal sign. This deconstruction involves reorienting logic
> according to synaesthetic relations of eye and ear. Thus we are urged
> to hear here ('hear' is everywhere in this poem) the soldier's sigh
> running in blood, while the chimney-s/weeper's cry casts a pall over
> St Paul's:
>
> (Hilton, p. 76)

Hilton quotes the third stanza, emboldening the first letter of each
line to show 'H . . E . . A . . R', to show Blake's injunction to us to,
as it were, 'read with our ears'; then he turns to the final stanza:

What is heard is not the 'curse' ending the second line, but how it blasts the 'tear' ending the third line and rhyming back to 'hear'. These words, hear-curse-tear, bring to bear the contradictions of sight and sound as we hear/see them coalesce in the final word, 'hearse'. The oxymoronic image of the 'marriage hearse' points to the impossibility of imagining that sight and sound, signified and signifier can be eternally 'linkd in a marriage chain' (E & S 352), wedlocked.

(Hilton, pp. 76–7)

Hilton finds that similar insights into the linguistic character of 'London' have been expressed by other critics, notably Gavin Edwards and Harold Bloom[7] but he takes issue with Bloom's conclusion that the deconstruction of language in the poem evokes nostalgia for a past but lost prophetic voice, like that of the Old Testament. On the contrary, Hilton sees 'London' in a positive light, as:

'. . . an affirming and self-deconstructing text, one that implicitly urges the reader to allow his or her eye to wander through its chartered lines, marking its marks, and hearing its 'every voice'. These invitations are conveyed through the contradictions in logic mentioned above and by dint of repetition: we simply cannot encounter 'charter'd . . . charter'd', 'mark . . . Marks . . . marks', and 'every' six times in five lines without being driven to wonder what the words mean and *how* they mean. Our delight as these questions, and then their several 'answers', come to light at once proves and loosens 'the mind-forg'd manacles'. The poem's self-unchaining does not, of course, usher the delighting reader into any realm of absolute free-play . . . One could characterise the 'liberated' version of 'London' as merely proliferated chains of association, but such prolific 'chains' are no longer limiting, enslaving, 'devouring'.

(Hilton, pp. 77–8)

We have looked at Hilton's analysis of one poem, 'London', in detail: clearly, it is in the nature of this kind of close focus on language, that

---

[7] Edwards in his 'Mind-forg'd Manacles: A Contribution to the Discussion of Blake's "London"', *Literature and History*, 5 (1979); Bloom in his *Poetry and Repression: Revisionism from Blake to Stevens*, New Haven, Yale University Press, 1976.

it will not be intelligible unless all the steps in reading the text are followed. The conclusion that 'London' is a 'self-unchaining' (or 'self-deconstructing') poem, and Hilton's suggestion that therefore the poem is itself a positive action in the liberation of mind from an arbitrary tyranny of 'determined' language, leads on to further analysis of 'chains' in Blake. Hilton devotes some time to the 'changes' of Urizen (noticing the aural pun on 'cha*i*nges'), and his essay finally suggests that:

> By his chains, Blake gives us to understand that man serves as his own jailer, imprisoned by his vocabulary, culture, and perception; that the inexorability of a 'chain of events' derives from our labelling it so, the logic in a 'chain of reasoning' from our being bound to its premise . . . it is in an imaginative vision of the nature of those chains and fetters, the nature of present perception and its transmission, that we find the key to our release . . .
>
> (Hilton, p. 89)

Camille Paglia

Camille Paglia's book *Sexual Personae: Art and Decadence from Nefertiti to Emily Dickinson* was first published in 1990.[8] We will look at her tenth chapter, called 'Sex Bound and Unbound: Blake'; but it is useful to indicate the scope and aim of the whole book beforehand.

Paglia declares her aim in her opening and introductory chapter. She comments that 'feminism' has made a mistake in believing that gender-oppression will go away if we change our societies and attitudes. This is a 'Rousseauist' mistake: like Rousseau's *The Social Contract* of 1762, this feminist view is optimistic and based on romantic ideas of a benign human nature. Paglia traces the effect of such unfounded optimism as 'the dominant ethic of American human services, penal codes, and behaviorist therapies'. On the con-

---

[8] Yale University Press, 1990. Page-references are to the Penguin edition, London, 1992, and are given in brackets thus: (Paglia, p. *).

trary, understanding of our gender attitudes and sexuality will only come from clarifying our attitude toward nature.

'This book takes the point of view of Sade', Paglia says deliberately, and elaborates that this means accepting that mankind's nature is 'violence and lust', that rape is natural because 'Sex *is* power. Identity is power' and there are 'no nonexploitative relationships' in western culture (all quotes are from Paglia, pp. 1–2).

Paglia's argument develops by ranging widely and with startling generalisations through a description of the characteristics of what she calls 'western culture', with its roots in Egyptian, then Greek and Roman classical periods. In pursuing her views, she suggests that all western art is a form of 'framing' and 'projection', which is an expression of male sexual aggression and fear. Art creates and defines 'beauty' as the coveted female, and at the same time imposes 'beauty' and a limitation (the 'framing') on the feared mystery of female sex. Thus art expresses 'sexual personae' – more-or-less artificial dreams, attitudes, personalities and gestures; and these 'personae' are created by the male need to dominate and control the fear of chaotic, dark, mysterious nature: 'Art is form struggling to wake from the nightmare of nature' (Paglia, p. 39). Paglia clearly identifies 'nature' with the female, as is evident from her expressed gratitude to men for all the liberating achievements of western art and capitalism, and her remark that 'If civilization had been left in female hands, we would still be living in grass huts' (Paglia, p. 38).

When she comes to Blake, then, we can expect Paglia's analysis to focus on sex both as it features in his works, and as his sexuality is expressed in the making of his works. Additionally, we are in the company of a 'pessimistic' (or matter-of-fact?) analysis of sexuality – particularly male sexuality – as expressing aggression, power-lust, and their correlation, anxiety. In her chapter on Blake, Paglia's central contention is that:

> Blake's writing is split by a terrible contradiction: Blake wants to free sex from its social and religious constraints, but he also wants to escape the domination of the Great Mother of chthonian nature. Alas, with every turn toward sex, we run right back into mother nature's dark embrace. Blake's tireless productivity as poet and

draughtsman came from the intolerable entrapments male imagination finds itself in when reflecting on nature.

(Paglia, p. 270)

Blake was unique among the 'romantics' in rejecting androgyny as the
solution to this conflict between sex and nature. Although he mentions an ideal, regenerate state where man and woman are one, his hermaphrodites are monstrous, and the poetry itself carries on a war of
contraries where the central conflict is between male and female. In
the *Songs of Innocence* where 'sex war is not yet an issue', we already
meet the sadism and vampirism of male authority figures such as the
exploiters and manipulators of 'The Chimney Sweeper' and 'The
Little Black Boy'. Paglia points out the symbolism of the impotent
phallic 'wands as white as snow' with which beadles herd children into
St Paul's in 'Holy Thursday', and enlarges on the significance of white
as the desexing colour of *Innocence*, connecting this with the eighteenth-century habit of both men and women wearing powdered wigs.

Paglia pays particular attention to the poem 'Infant Joy'. Here, she
says, 'we have regressed to the infancy of consciousness. We see
Rousseau's saintly child as it crosses the border into being. What do
we find there? Tenderness and innocence threatened on all sides'
(Paglia, p. 272). She focuses on the attitude of the speaker in 'Infant
Joy', and the complicity the poem inspires in the reader who is
encouraged to be a voyeur watching the newborn. Paglia argues that
we are encouraged towards an unconsciously sadistic response by the
very innocence the poem forces us to contemplate. The simplicity
and bareness of the poem – and the pre-verbal silence of the child –
remove the 'buffering between persons and beings . . . The egoless
softness of the poem awakes in us Kessler's sensation of over-
whelming power, which we unconsciously check. Sharpening the
senses inflames them – and here comes sadism . . . In 'Infant Joy' a
devouring presence waits, a Blakean tiger: the reader'. Paglia sees this
poem subverting the values of nurturing and caring by hypnotically
enticing the reader into sadism, so that, just as with the oppressive
hypocrisy of authority in 'The Chimney Sweeper', 'Every gesture of
love is an assertion of power. There is no selflessness or self-sacrifice,
only refinements of domination' (Paglia, pp. 273–4).

The contrary poem Paglia chooses to analyse is 'The Sick Rose', and in common with other critics she regards the flower as a symbol of female genitalia, and her 'dark secret bed of crimson joy' as her exclusive, reclusive sexuality: masturbation. However, Paglia notes the ambiguity of the poem. The courtly pattern of male pursuit and female fleeing and hiding is clearly Blake's target in this poem; and he clearly rejects the female's refusal to participate in sex. Yet, when the worm's attack – the inevitable rape which ends the pursuit cycle – takes place, Blake suggests that this does 'thy life destroy'. On the contrary, Paglia comments, 'It is male, not female identity that is annihilated in the night-storm of nature', and so, each time Blake argues for the liberation of sexuality, he comes up against the 'cul-de-sac' of female sexuality. *The Book of Thel* is another, similar text in which Blake expresses his hostility to chastity, his belief that Thel's isolation 'is sick because it rejects the strife of contraries by which energy evolves' (Paglia, pp. 276–9).

Paglia moves on to consider *The Mental Traveller* (K 424–7), in which she sees both evidence that Blake has moved on from his simplistic faith in sex liberated from social constraint, and a recognition that nature presents an insuperable problem. The poem is 'a cycle of sexual cannibalism enacted by a male and a female figure, who attack and retreat in obsessive rhythms of victory and defeat' (Paglia, p. 281). The first cycle begins when a male baby is given to an old woman, and she nails him to a rock. Feeding on his shrieks and groans she becomes young, he breaks free, rapes her, and so the dynamics of power and oppression continue to alternate:

> *The Mental Traveller* proceeds by sexual peripeties. The first is a pietà, where the old witch becomes a virgin with her 'bleeding youth.' The Great Mother, mourning her son-lover, is wrestled down and bound in turn. Now male exults in woman's masochistic vulnerability. Service has switched on the Sadean tennis court. Gender flames and fades in *The Mental Traveller*. Dominance and submission, nature's law, compulsively structures the poem.
>
> (Paglia, p. 282)

Paglia sees no sign in *The Mental Traveller* that the cycle of cruelty and alternating dominance will end, and she is scornful of critics

who have over-philosophised the poem, sugggesting that it has a
didactic message. Blake finishes the poem with a return to the beginning, indicating an endless repetition. Paglia believes that *The
Mental Traveller* is really what she calls 'circle magic': Blake has
created the horrors of sex war and nature as an endless cycle so that
it can go on repeating itself in the poem, over and over, and eventually it will spin off into space and 'devour itself'. That is, she sees the
poem as an act in Blake's struggle to rid himself of the intolerable
problem of sexuality: his simultaneous desire to liberate sex, and fear
of the 'Great Mother', which Paglia mentioned at the start of her
chapter.

She pursues this theme, sugggesting that the 'circle magic' did not
work, and this may be a reason for the steadily increasing complexity
and length of Blake's prophetic works: 'His poems got longer and
longer, as if epic scale could finally fix the matter. The unfixable
theme is universal female power' (Paglia, p. 283). Having discussed
'The Crystal Cabinet' (K 429–30), Paglia states:

> . . . I value Blake not as a prophet of sexual liberation but as a magus
> who has studied the secrets of nature and seen the outrageous enslave-
> ments of our life in the body . . . There is no sex without yielding to
> nature. And nature is a female domain. Blake's dreadful fate was to
> see the abyss from which most men shrink: the infantilism in all male
> heterosexuality. Criticism's disregard of Blake's blatant sado-
> masochism has censored him.
>
> (Paglia, p. 287)

However, Paglia combines this apparent admiration for Blake's
openness and unflinching honesty with her continuing opinion that
he was riven by his contradictory purposes: to liberate sex, and to
flee the devouring 'Great Mother'.

Further demonstrations of the sexual struggles she has identified
in Blake's work abound in the remainder of Paglia's chapter, much of
which discusses the idea of 'sexual personae' in relation to the
figures, 'Spectres' and 'Emanations' which are developed in the
longer prophecies, and which tell – as we have remarked in Part 1 –
psychological stories with startlingly modern characteristics. The
horrors of Blake's hermaphrodites are also documented: Paglia

quotes Vala's denial that a separate male sex exists from *Jerusalem* ('Womans Shadow, a Vapor in the summers heat . . . O Woman-born / And Woman-nourishd & Woman-educated & Woman-scorn'd!' [K 698]), and asks why androgynes have come to be presented as such horrific and threatening figures in Blake.

Paglia suggests that Blake was reacting against the Miltonic idea of heaven, where 'angels change gender and have sex in perfect purity'; because he rejected the idea that the sexual body is gross and inferior, that any happiness could exist in a realm where the body had been jettisoned or discarded. What Blake abhors in the androgyne, and in Milton's dilating and changing angels, is the dissolution of outline:

> The central reference point of his poetry and drawings is 'the Human Form Divine,' specifically the male form, with which Blake identifies human imagination struggling to free itself from female nature.
>
> (Paglia, p. 292)

Blake disliked and disapproved of chiaroscuro, and his writings on art repeatedly emphasise the supreme importance of the 'bounding outline'. He had an aversion to paintings which mingle or mix forms, or show any indefiniteness because without the outline and the clear form it brings, 'all is chaos again'; and because there is a danger of being accused of plagiarism – that is, the distinct identity of the artist himself is at risk without 'outline'. Paglia explains that these views reveal Blake's obsessional anxiety. She calls the fear of being called a plagiarist 'anxiety of influence' and explains that Blake clings to firmness of line to defend himself against an 'overwhelming precursor': 'Who is the ultimate precursor? The Great Original, mother nature', Paglia says, and completes her picture of Blake's anxiety by suggesting that his underlying fear is of losing his identity separate from the 'mother': the two faces threatening to 'collapse into each other' in Blake's nightmare, 'are those of mother and son' (Paglia, p. 294).

Blake was often called 'mad' in the past, but this was clearly wrong. However, Paglia argues that the critics have ignored the latent content of Blake's poems, in their eagerness to interpret symbols and reduce all to an intelligible philosophy. On the contrary:

> . . . in the longer poems there is a hysteria or excess unacknowledged by criticism. Art is born of stress, not repose. Art is always a swerve from primary experience. Blake's long poems are full of knots, breaches, and strains . . . They are held together by force of will . . . His hopeless but heroic task, to redeem sex from nature, is a western epic saga.
>
> (Paglia, p. 295)

Therefore, Paglia regards Blake's doomed and contradictory sexual themes as being fundamental to the story of gender, art and 'western culture' that is the larger subject of her book. Blake's struggle is against the threat of woman's dominance, also seen in nature's chaos and cruelty. The reason why so many books have been written about women by men is that:

> . . . The flood of books was prompted not by woman's weakness but by her strength, her complexity and impenetrability, her dreadful omnipresence. No man has yet been born . . . who was not spun from a pitiful speck of plasma to a conscious being on the secret loom within a woman's body.
>
> (Paglia, p. 296)

Camille Paglia clearly approaches Blake with an agenda, some of which is derived from modern analysis of gender-issues and the psychoanalysis of sexuality, as well as drawing on feminist analyses of society and culture. Paglia also has an interest in pursuing her chosen theme of 'sexual personae' through a vastly ambitious history of western culture, as her subtitle indicates: *from Nefertiti to Emily Dickinson*. Therefore, the reader may feel that Blake's poems are distorted, or partially 'flexed', in order to make them fit into her wider theories. This happens more with some texts than others, in my own view – so, for example, I accept a great deal of Paglia's analysis, and I find her comments on 'Infant Joy' fascinating as an exploration of *possible* invisible worlds around the poem. However, I do not feel that the poem can be called an invitation to sadism.

What Camille Paglia does with great success is to remind us of the struggling, constantly half-formed and conflicting emotional turmoil of the later Prophetic Books: her castigation of merely interpretative critics, and the reminder that Blake's works seethe with what she (psychoanalytically) calls 'latent content', are valuable. Paglia's theory that Blake could not reconcile his two aims, for sex and female nature, is persuasive also, and she adduces considerable evidence in its support.

It is interesting to note how criticism itself changes, reflecting the age in which it is produced. So, for example, Middleton Murry, the friend and contemporary of D. H. Lawrence and Bertrand Russell, describes Blake's vision in terms of 'individuality'; and sees Blake's sexual problems in terms of the 'free love' which was a fashionable talking-point between the wars:

> Blake had loved someone not his wife, and had straightway told his wife of his love; and the result had been disaster. To the simpler soul of his wife, Blake's doctrine that Love, being the mutual recognition of two Identities, was its own complete justification, was wickedness.
>
> (Murry, pp. 45–6)

As Murry writes we can almost hear Paul Morel lecturing an adoring Miriam in Lawrence's *Sons and Lovers*. Murry identifies this as 'one of the great disillusions of Blake's life'. We can speculate that Camille Paglia's ideas about what sex looks like to an observer ('sexuality by its very nature is an abridgement of contour') or the ugliness of female genitals ('female genitalia are not beautiful by any aesthetic standard') will eventually date her firmly in the 1990s – but her work on Blake will remain valuable, as Murry's has.

Nelson Hilton's analysis of 'London' as a 'self-deconstructing' poem which subverts both social and grammatical tyrannies or 'chains' is enlightening in a different way: he focuses on the actual text, the 'chain' of language, and its effect. As with all criticism, we have to read Hilton with the confidence to see his value without necessarily accepting all. So, I go along with the analysis of punning and sensory disjunction in 'London', and much of his analysis re-states in deconstructive terms comments made in Chapter 3. I agree that the poem's linguistic features contribute to a 'subverting' or 'liberating' effect for the reader. I am attracted to the optimistic mood of the statement that 'man serves as his own jailer', and that, in the self-unchaining language of the poem, 'we find the key to our release'. On the other hand, I cannot forget the redoubled weight of 'charter'd', 'marks', 'woe' and 'infants' misery. I therefore return to a primary reading of an angry poem against social and economic oppression.

All three of the critics we have looked at are stimulating: all three of them highlight aspects of Blake and elements in the experience of reading Blake to which we can relate. They expound insights which make us think 'ah, yes, I recognise what she / he is talking about'. Yet there is little common ground between them, and their declared aims and methodologies are widely different. This chapter has hardly begun to indicate the sheer variety of views, perceptions and opinions about Blake that can be found, however. The next section, *Further Reading*, will provide a number of suggestions on how to pursue and broaden an interest in Blake criticism.

Further Reading

General Remarks

Your first job is to study the text. There is no substitute for the work of detailed analysis: that is how you gain the close familiarity with the text, and the fully-developed understanding of its content, which make the essays you write both personal and convincing. For this reason it is a good general rule not to read other books around or about the text you are studying until you have finished studying it for yourself.

You may have to break this rule with Blake's Prophetic Books, however. In Part 1 we suggested a way of approaching these longer symbolic works. This approach involves (1) finding an accessible, naturalistic passage as a starting-place; (2) carrying out a rudimentary study, looking at narrative, imagery, mood and your response; (3) picking out the most important symbolic figures, then looking at their characteristics and their part in the action; (4) looking up their significance, to gain a clear grasp of the meaning or significance of the passage.

This approach to the Prophetic Books will enable you to build your familiarity with Blake's symbolic 'system' gradually. It also preserves your opportunity to respond to the poetry yourself, in the first instance. You can easily lose this crucial first response if you go to the professional interpreters too quickly, or if you rely on them and look everything up in a commentary. Remember that the critics disagree with each other, also. So, even when you look something up, you or another critic may disagree about what it means.

So you can break the rule when approaching Blake's Prophetic Books: you can use a reference work or the critics while still studying the text. However, be careful and sparing in your critical reading until you feel confident that you have a good grasp, and your own grasp, of the Prophetic Book on which you are working. Reference-works to use in approaching the Prophetic Books may be S. Foster Damon's *A Blake Dictionary: The Ideas and Symbols of William Blake* (Brown University Press, Providence, 1965), or David V. Erdman's *A Concordance to the Writings of William Blake* (New York, Cornell University Press, 1967). Alternatively, the Stevenson and Erdman edition of the *Poems* has longer, explanatory notes, each rather like a short article, on some of the most important 'figures, subjects and terms' in Blake's poetry. There is a helpful index to these longer notes at the end of the book, on p. 876, after the index to titles and first lines.

Once you are familiar with the text, you may wish to read around and about it. This brief chapter is only intended to set you off: there are hundreds of relevant books and we can only mention a few; but most good editions, and critical works, have suggestions for further reading or a bibliography of their own. Once you have begun to read beyond your text, you can use these and a good library to follow up your particular interests. This section is divided into *Reading Around the Text*, which lists editions of Blake's works, and some by other writers; *Biography*; and *Criticism*, which contains a selection of suggested titles that will introduce you to the varieties of opinion among professional critics.

Reading Around the Text

Blake's Works

There are two editions of Blake's writings which are the foundation for studying his text. These two 'texts' differ mainly in their treatment of Blake's inconsistent and unreliable punctuation, and most of the selections and anthologies published as smaller volumes adopt one or the other of them.

Geoffrey Keynes's text first appeared in the 1920s, and was brought out as the Nonesuch Press edition of 1957, then in the Oxford Standard Authors edition of 1966. It is available in both hardback and paperback as *The Complete Writings of William Blake*, ed. Geoffrey Keynes, London, 1966. Keynes has supplied a considerable amount of punctuation where Blake did not use any, making the text less ambiguous and more accessibly readable. Generally, Keynes's decisions clarify an acceptable meaning and provide a reliable text. However, he has made decisions about punctuation and these sometimes curtail possible alternative interpretations.

David V. Erdman's text first appeared in 1965 as *The Poetry and Prose of William Blake*, ed. David V. Erdman and H. Bloom, Doubleday, New York, 1965, and this text has been re-issued with corrections several times under the sole editorship of Erdman. This text but without the prose writings is also used in *The Poems of William Blake*, ed. W. H. Stevenson, text by David V. Erdman, Longman, London, 1971. Erdman has made fewer changes to Blake's erratic punctuation. In some places, this preserves Blake's ambiguity, and opens out interpretations that are not available to the reader of Keynes. One or other of these texts is a must for the serious student of Blake.

Geoffrey Keynes lamented in the preface to his 1957 *Complete Writings* that the illustrated editions he produced in the 1920s failed to reach a wide public: 'their rather monumental character has to some extent defeated their purpose. The high cost and limitation of the size of the edition has prevented their reaching much of the public for whom they were intended' (K ix). This was the same problem Blake himself experienced when he printed and hand-coloured his own poetic and Prophetic Books: only a small coterie of friends and patrons ever saw them. The problem has been largely resolved now, however, and the present-day student can obtain good illustrated and facsimile editions of Blake's poetic and graphic work, using modern printing techniques, at very affordable prices.

The basic text analysed in Part 1 of this book is *Songs of Innocence and Experience*, with an Introduction and Commentary by Sir Geoffrey Keynes, London, 1967, which is now available as an Oxford Paperback produced in London and New York, in association with the Trianon Press, Paris. A companion edition of *The*

Marriage of Heaven and Hell, also with Introduction and Commentary by Sir Geoffrey Keynes, 1975, is also available.

Others of Blake's illustrated books are also available in facsimile form from the publishers Thames and Hudson. I have *The Book of Urizen* and *Milton, A Poem,* both edited with a commentary by Kay Parkhurst Easson and Roger R. Easson, London and New York, 1979. Thames and Hudson have brought out all of the illustrated poetic books in one volume: *William Blake: The Complete Illuminated Books,* with an Introduction by David Bindman (London, 2000). These illustrated facsimile editions are the culmination of years of work by the Blake Trust and the American Blake Foundation.

Alternatively, but in black-and-white only, there are *The Illuminated Blake: The Complete Illuminated Works of William Blake with an Introduction and plate by plate Commentary,* Annotated by David V. Erdman, OUP, London, 1975; and *The Complete Graphic Works of William Blake,* ed. David Bindman assisted by Deirdre Toomey, Thames and Hudson, London, 1978.

Blake's illustrations to the Book of Job appeared in an elaborately-commentated edition by the early Blake scholar Joseph Wicksteed, in 1910; this edition was revised and re-issued in 1924. However, a much more recent edition of the Job illustrations, with an excellent commentary, is *Blake's Job: A Commentary,* by Andrew Wright, Oxford (Clarendon Press), 1972.

With these various editions available, even if you do not splash out on an expensive 'complete' illustrated Blake, you should be able to have access to the text you are studying in its original illustrated form.

Looking at the original works is more difficult. There are collections of Blake's paintings and engravings in several major museums and libraries in Britain and the USA,[1] where some graphic and painted works are exhibited. However, you are likely to need an academic reference and research justification before you will be allowed to handle copies of the Prophetic Books held in library collections such as the Fitzwilliam Museum in Cambridge, England, or the Library of Congress in the USA.

---

[1] See p. 206 above.

Other Reading Around

It is worth while for the general reader of Blake to have some familiarity with his contemporary 'romantic' poets, so I would suggest looking at S. T. Coleridge's *The Ancient Mariner* and 'Kubla Khan'; and William Wordsworth's *The Prelude*, Books I and II and 'Ode: Intimations of Immortality . . etc.', often called 'The Immortality Ode'. It will also help to read something of the more conventional poetry of the time, such as Thomas Gray's 'Elegy in a Country Churchyard' and Chatterton's poems (which Blake admired). I would also suggest that readers who do not already know it will benefit from reading parts of the Bible. For example, reading the first five chapters of Genesis, the Prophetic Books of Ezekiel and Isaiah, and the Book of Job would be helpful in terms of both style and understanding, if you are approaching Blake's Prophetic Books.

You can also look at some of the texts that were most influential on Blake (whether he approved of them or hated them!). A selection of these might include Rousseau's *The Social Contract*, Milton's *Paradise Lost*, Mary Wollstonecraft's *A Vindication of the Rights of Woman*, and Tom Paine's *Rights of Man*. If you are interested in Blake's philosophical positions you should be aware of the philosophies he reacted against: try Locke's *Essay Concerning Human Understanding* and Berkeley's *Essay towards a New Theory of Vision*, as well as Swedenborg's *Wisdom of Angels concerning Divine Love and Divine Wisdom*, which you can dip into in conjunction with Blake's annotations (see K 89–96). Many of these will be voluminous or uncongenial reading; but it is enough to 'dip' into them for a flavour of the opinions they express, or (in the case of Milton) for a flavour of the poetry.

Biography

Blake's Life was first written by Alexander Gilchrist (London, 1863 and 1880), but I shall suggest two more recent full-length biographies. First, there is Mona Wilson's *The Life of William Blake* (London, 1927 and 1948, re-issued edited by Geoffrey Keynes,

London, Oxford University Press, 1971). This is a careful and thorough biography which discusses Blake's character and ideas with natural sympathy. The other biography I suggest provides a vivid and intimate picture of the London of Blake's time: *Blake*, by Peter Ackroyd (London, Sinclair-Stevenson, 1995) introduces us to the turbulent, independently radical and dissenting lives of London tradesmen, the social milieu into which Blake was born and among whom he lived. For further social background, rather than biography, E. P. Thompson's *The Making of the English Working Class* (London, Gollancz, 1963) is of interest.

Criticism

The critical works sampled in Chapter 6 are: Northrop Frye, *Fearful Symmetry: A Study of William Blake*, Princeton, Princeton University Press, 1947; David V. Erdman, *Blake: Prophet Against Empire*, Princeton, Princeton University Press, 1954; John Middleton Murry, *William Blake*, London & Toronto, Jonathan Cape, 1933; Chapter 4 of Nelson Hilton, *The Literal Imagination: Blake's Vision of Words*, Berkeley, CA, University of California Press, 1983; and Chapter 10 of Camille Paglia, *Sexual Personae: Art and Decadence from Nefertiti to Emily Dickinson*, Yale University Press, 1990. Camille Paglia's book is widely available, published by Penguin Books in 1992.

Anthologies of critical essays and articles are a good way to sample the critics. You can then go on to read the full-length books written by those critics whose ideas and approaches you find stimulating. The New Casebooks series (general editors John Peck and Martin Coyle) published by Macmillan, collects a variety of critical articles together, and provides an introduction which discusses the critical history of the text. The volume on *William Blake* (1996) is edited by David Punter and includes the essay by Nelson Hilton we sampled in Chapter 6. Other collections which contain important critical views include *Essential Articles for the Study of William Blake 1970–84*, ed. Nelson Hilton (Hamden, CT: Archon, 1986); *William Blake: Essays in Honour of Sir Geoffrey Keynes*, ed. Morton D. Paley and Michael Phillips (Oxford, Clarendon Press, 1973); and *Critical*

Paths: Blake and the Argument of Method, ed. Dan Miller, Mark Bracher and Donald Ault (Durham and London, Duke University Press, 1987).

The following critical works are some of the most significant contributions to Blake studies (but do not forget Murry, Frye and Erdman who have already been mentioned in this bibliography): A. C. Swinburne, *William Blake* (London, 1868); S. Foster Damon, *William Blake: His Philosophy and Symbols* (London, Constable, 1924); Harold Bloom, *Blake's Apocalypse: A Study in Poetic Argument* (New York, Doubleday, 1963); and Morton D. Paley, *Energy and the Imagination: A Study of the Development of Blake's Thought* (Oxford, Clarendon Press, 1970).

A clear account of Blake's politics can be found in *William Blake and the Age of Revolution*, by Jacob Bronowski (London, Routledge, 1972); *Blake, Hegel and Dialectic*, by David Punter (Amsterdam, Rodopi, 1982) provides a Marxist discussion; and *Blake's Composite Art: A Study of the Illuminated Poetry*, by W. J. T. Mitchell (Princeton, Princeton University Press, 1978) takes a contemporary approach to both text and designs. *Blake and Freud*, by Diana Hume George (New York, Cornell University Press, 1980) is a psychoanalytical approach; for readings concerning gender politics, there are essays by Laura Haigwood and Brenda Webster in David Punter's Macmillan New Casebook anthology; and Alicia Ostriker's 'Desire Gratified and Ungratified: William Blake and Sexuality' can be found in *Essential Articles for the Study of William Blake 1970–1984*, mentioned above.

These are only a few suggestions, intended to provide a first step towards the abundant variety of Blake criticism. Use the bibliographies and 'further reading' lists in the books mentioned here to lead you in pursuit of different views on the text you are studying, or in pursuit of your particular interest.

It is worth remembering that discussions of Blake are also found in works which are not solely concerned with him. So, for example, we sampled the chapter on Blake from Camille Paglia's book, *Sexual Personae*, an extremely wide-ranging work; equally, Harold Bloom's *Poetry and Repression: Revisionism from Blake to Stevens* (New Haven, Yale University Press, 1976) and Heather Glen's *Vision and*

Disenchantment: Blake's 'Songs' and Wordsworth's 'Lyrical Ballads'
(Cambridge, Cambridge University Press, 1983) contain significant
discussions of Blake. When you are in a library, use the catalogue
system resourcefully. There are numerous books which appear to be
on different subjects – Romantic Poetry, the Literature of
Revolution, and so on. A large number of these contain chapters or
essays about Blake which may bring an illuminating angle to bear
upon his writing.

Index

249

nature – *continued*
wild beasts 92
Blake's theme compared with that of Wordsworth and Coleridge 215–16
New Jerusalem Church, The 200

Orc 141, 143–6
'Orc cycle, the' 146, 161, 186, 224

Paglia, Camille, *Sexual Personae: Art and Decadence from Nefertiti to Emily Dickinson* 164n, 232–9
Paine, Tom 200, 201, 205
Palamabron 137–8, 141
Palmer, Samuel 202, 209
perception
different perceptions of truth 44–5, 50–1
conflicting perceptions of nature 72–4, 92
'the doors of perception' 99–100, 132
Piper, the 13, 20–1, 44–5, 56
Prophetic Books, the
how to approach 96–7, 104–5, 130–4, 137–49, 157–9, 241
reputation for difficulty 3, 9
style, poetic 146–9

reference-books, using 137–8
religion, criticisms of the Church 93–5, 98–100, 116, 129, 136, 155
revolution 120, 129, 130, 156
Richmond, George 202
Rintrah 142, 213
Rossetti, D. G. 209

Sampson, Dr John 209, 220
Scofield 205
self-annihilation 177–91
a continual necessity 190
and courage 189
and time 189
selfhood, the 176–7
formation of 170
called Spectre, or Satan 187
continually re-created 186, 188
in the Prophetic Books 177–91
senses, the 100, 101, 139
sexuality and natural emotions 92–3, 98–9, 101, 123–5, 128, 163–6
Shakespeare, William 210
The Tempest 179
Sloss and Wallis (editors and interpreters of Blake's works) 220
Society 107–60
Spenser, Edmund 178
State, the
attacked by Blake 129, 153
militarism of 127–8, 129, 136
Stothard, Thomas 202–3
Swedenborg, Emmanuel 200
Swinburne, A. C. 209
William Blake 220
symbolism 3

Tatham, Frederick 202
Trochaic metre 4–5

Urizen 140–1, 142–3, 151–3, 167–8, 185–6

Varley, John 199, 201–2
Verulam 138
vision
compared with Wordsworth's and Coleridge's ideas 211–14
moments of 74–9
in poems in letters to Thomas Butts 75–8, 211, 219
redeeming and liberating 98–100, 132
related to 'Self Annihilation' 186–9
transforming perceptions of nature 92, 97

Walter, Henry 202
Wicksteed, Joseph 209
Blake's Vision of the Book of Job 37n, 220
Wilson, Mona, *The Life of William Blake* 220
Wollstonecraft, Mary 200, 201